Conversations with Ursula K. Le Guin

Literary Conversations Series
Peggy Whitman Prenshaw
General Editor

Conversations with Ursula K. Le Guin

Edited by
Carl Freedman

University Press of Mississippi
Jackson

www.upress.state.ms.us

The University Press of Mississippi is a member of the Association of American University Presses.

Copyright © 2008 by University Press of Mississippi
All rights reserved
Manufactured in the United States of America

First printing 2008
⊗
Library of Congress Cataloging-in-Publication Data

Conversations with Ursula K. le Guin / edited by Carl Freedman.
     p. cm. — (Literary conversations series)
  Includes index.
  ISBN 978-1-60473-093-7 (cloth : alk. paper) — ISBN 978-1-60473-094-4 (pbk. : alk. paper) 1. Le Guin, Ursula K., 1929-—Interviews. 2. Authors, American—20th century—Interviews. 3. Science fiction—Authorship. I. Freedman, Carl Howard.
  PS3562.E42Z596 2008
  813'.54—dc22   2008015524

British Library Cataloging-in-Publication Data available

Books by Ursula K. Le Guin

Novels:
Rocannon's World. New York: Ace, 1966.
Planet of Exile. New York: Ace, 1966.
City of Illusions. New York: Ace, 1967.
A Wizard of Earthsea. Berkeley: Parnassus Press, 1968.
The Left Hand of Darkness. New York: Ace, 1969.
The Lathe of Heaven. New York: Scribner's, 1971.
The Tombs of Atuan. New York: Atheneum, 1971.
The Farthest Shore. New York: Atheneum, 1972.
The Dispossessed: An Ambiguous Utopia. New York: Harper & Row, 1974.
The Word for World Is Forest. New York: Berkley-Putnam, 1976.
Very Far Away from Anywhere Else. New York: Atheneum, 1976.
Malafrena. New York: Putnam's, 1979.
The Beginning Place. New York: Harper & Row, 1980.
The Eye of the Heron. New York: Harper & Row, 1983.
Always Coming Home. New York: Harper & Row, 1985.
Tehanu. New York: Atheneum, 1990.
The Telling. New York: Harcourt, 2000.
The Other Wind. New York: Harcourt, 2001.
Gifts. New York: Harcourt, 2004.
Voices. Orlando: Harcourt, 2006.

Story Collections:
The Wind's Twelve Quarters. New York: Harper & Row, 1975.
Orsinian Tales. New York: Harper & Row, 1976.
The Compass Rose. New York: Harper & Row, 1982.
Buffalo Gals. Santa Barbara: Capra, 1987.
Searoad. New York: HarperCollins 1991.
A Fisherman of the Inland Sea. New York: Harper Prism, 1994.
Four Ways to Forgiveness. New York: Harper Prism, 1995.
Unlocking the Air. New York: HarperCollins, 1996.
Tales from Earthsea. New York: Harcourt, 2001.
The Birthday of the World. New York: HarperCollins, 2002.
Changing Planes. New York: Harcourt, 2003.

Poetry:
Wild Angels. Santa Barbara: Capra, 1974.
Hard Words. New York: Harper & Row, 1981.

Wild Oats and Fireweed. New York: Harper & Row, 1988.
Blue Moon over Thurman Street [with Roger Dorband]. Portland: NewSage Press, 1993.
Going Out with Peacocks. New York: HarperPerennial, 1994.
Sixty Odd. Boston: Shambhala, 1999.
Incredible Good Fortunes. Boston: Shambhala, 2006.

Books for Children:
Leese Webster. New York: Atheneum, 1979.
Adventures of Cobbler's Rune. New Castle, Virginia: Cheap Street, 1983.
Solomon Leviathan's Nine Hundred and Thirty-first Trip around the World. New Castle, Virginia: Cheap Street, 1983.
A Visit from Dr. Katz. New York: Atheneum, 1988.
Catwings. New York: Orchard, 1988.
Catwings Return. New York: Orchard, 1989.
Fire and Stone. New York: Atheneum, 1989.
A Ride on the Red Mare's Back. New York: Orchard, 1992.
Fish Soup. New York: Atheneum, 1992.
Wonderful Alexander and the Catwings. New York: Orchard, 1994.
Tom Mouse. New York: DK Pub., 1998.
Jane on Her Own. New York: Orchard, 1999.

Criticism:
The Language of the Night. New York: Putnam, 1979.
Dancing at the Edge of the World. New York: Grove, 1989.
Steering the Craft. Portland: Eighth Mountain, 1998.
The Wave in the Mind. Boston: Shambhala, 2004.

Translations:
The Twins, the Dream/Las Gemelas, El Sueño [with Diana Bellessi]. Houston: Arte Público Press, 1996.
Lao Tzu: Tao Te Ching: A Book about the Way and the Power of the Way. Boston: Shambhala 1997.
Kalpa Imperial by Angelica Gorodischer. Northampton, MA: Small Beer Press, 2003.
Selected Poems of Gabriela Mistral. Albuquerque: U. of New Mexico Press, 2003.

Edited Volumes:
Nebula Award Stories 11. New York: Harper & Row, 1977.
Edges [with Virginia Kidd]. New York: PocketBooks, 1980.
Interfaces [with Virginia Kidd]. New York: Ace, 1980.
The Norton Book of Science Fiction [with Brian Attebery]. New York: W. W. Norton, 1993.

Contents

Introduction

Perhaps the first thing that should be said about this volume is that it lives up, abundantly, to its title: the pieces that follow are in the most genuine way *conversations* with Ursula Le Guin. For not every interview is really a conversation. All too often, the interviewer limits himself or herself to short, simple, deferential queries, and the interviewee responds with a series of (frequently prepackaged) sound-bites. The interviewer tends to disappear from sight, and the interview becomes an occasion not for vigorous dialog or the generation of ideas but merely for the statement or, more likely, the restatement of the interviewee's established positions on a variety of subjects. One or two interviews of this sort may be of interest, but the inevitable repetition means that reading a large number of such interviews with the same interviewee tends to yield diminishing returns.

By contrast, one could read through many more of the interviews in which Le Guin has participated than this volume has space to include without growing a bit fatigued by repetition. As the following pages make clear, Le Guin takes every interview not as an opportunity to recapitulate long-held views but as an occasion for authentic intellectual discourse, with all the unpredictability that this implies and all the attendant dialectical give-and-take. She never hesitates to challenge an interviewer's assumptions when they seem to her inadequate to the issues at hand, and at least some interviewers return the compliment—that of conceptual seriousness—by issuing challenges of their own. As with any authentic intellectual conversation, the fundamental project of a Le Guin interview is *learning*, on the part of both parties to the interview and, of course, of the reader as well; and the topics about which one can learn are varied indeed, from U.S. foreign policy to the history of architecture, and much else besides.

Despite this variety, it is, naturally enough, Le Guin's accomplishments as a writer that give rise to most of the questions that her interlocutors ask— and that thus constitute a kind of organizing principle structuring these quite various conversations; and one can hardly appreciate the material in this volume without some concrete sense of Le Guin's literary oeuvre and stature. Her achievement is much too large, rich, and heterogeneous to be presented in more than outline form here; but the following device may be useful in introducing Ursula Le Guin's work to the reader.

If you were to ask a big group of knowledgeable scholars of the field to name the very best of all American science-fiction authors, you would, of course, receive a variety of answers; and probably the most common answer would be that one cannot meaningfully select any particular writer as the "best" of such a large and heterogeneous cohort. Still, there are certain writers whose names would figure prominently in the discussion. The name of Philip K. Dick would be frequently mentioned, and so would that of Samuel R. Delany. Some of the older and more conservative scholars might nominate Robert Heinlein, and a few scholars with a special passion for cyberpunk might suggest William Gibson. Those with a particular interest in the genealogy of the genre might name the first significant figure in American science fiction, Edgar Allan Poe. It is a safe bet, however, that, of all the names that would come up, none would be proposed more often or more enthusiastically than that of Ursula Kroeber Le Guin.

Science fiction is by no means the only area where Le Guin has major achievements to her credit. But she remains best known as a science-fiction author and looms larger in science fiction than in any other particular kind of writing. In order to understand her prominence—and arguably preeminence—in the field, it is necessary to rehearse some literary history that is well known to professional scholars and serious fans of science fiction but remains only dimly grasped, at best, by the general reading public; and the general reading public has responded to Le Guin more favorably than perhaps to any other science-fiction writer of her time.

Despite the long and varied history of American science fiction—which goes back at least to the periodical publication of Poe's "MS. Found in a Bottle" in 1833—there is one watershed event that remains more aesthetically consequential than any other in the formation of the genre: namely, the transition, during the 1960s and 1970s, from the so-called "Golden Age" of science fiction, typified by the work of writers like Heinlein and Isaac Asimov, to a new kind of science fiction. The latter is sometimes called "new wave" after somewhat similar innovations in French cinema and in British science fiction, but it lacks any generally accepted appellation; it has, however, throughout many further developments, dominated the field ever since (certainly in literary terms, though not always in commercial ones). There are many ways that this transition can be described. In terms of the apparatuses of literary production, distribution, and consumption, the main shift was from the pulp magazines—which had dominated American science fiction since the founding of *Amazing Stories* by Hugo Gernsback in 1926, and had found their single most important instance in *Astounding Science-Fiction* under the legendary editorship of John W. Campbell from 1937 onwards—to the publication of books. During the "Golden Age," even such now classic volumes as Asimov's *I, Robot* (1950) and his *Foundation* (1951) were compiled mainly by reprinting stories from the pulps; afterwards, science fiction, like most other varieties of American fiction, became mainly a matter of book-length novels. In terms of readership, "Golden Age" science fiction was consumed largely by adolescents and pre-adolescents, and overwhelmingly by males. The newer sort of science fiction appealed increasingly to adults, and many more women began to read (and to write) science fiction than ever before. In aesthetic terms, the newer science-fiction writers grew dissatisfied with the merely competent, unadorned prose with which "Golden Age" authors had usually contented themselves, and took to composing works of genuine stylistic interest and distinction. Likewise, the newer writers began to create characters of considerably more psychological depth than their "Golden Age" predecessors had usually even attempted; and they also began to explore complex political and sexual issues in ways that had generally been taboo before.

Maybe the most succinct way to sum up the transition is simply to say that, between about 1960 and about 1980, American science fiction became a branch of American *literature* in a full-fledged and unambiguous sense that (the work of Poe excepted) had never quite applied before. The science-fiction writers and readers of the "Golden Age" were usually (though not always) people of little *general* literary background; and they often displayed little or no interest in modern literature beyond their chosen generic ghetto. Professional literary critics typically returned the (dis)favor, taking almost no serious interest in science fiction and referring to it, on the rare occasions they did so at all, in tones of contemptuous dismissal. After 1960, however, American science fiction is increasingly written and read with concrete awareness of the larger context of modern literature generally; and its best and most characteristic products become fully comparable, by nearly all generally recognized aesthetic criteria, to the best and most characteristic work being done in any other section of American fiction. Despite the inevitable temporal lag between literary production and critical perception, it was not long before eminent and influential American critics like Leslie Fiedler, Robert Scholes, and Fredric Jameson were devoting significant attention to work in the genre. Today it is increasingly difficult—indeed, in some areas of American literary and intellectual culture it now seems merely quaint or reactionary—to claim a serious knowledge of the important American fiction produced over the past half-century that does not include a knowledge of science fiction.

Any such cultural sea change is, of course, necessarily the work of a great many individuals. But no individual is more central to the shift described above than Le Guin, and only two others—Dick and Delany—are comparable to her in importance. Perhaps the quickest way to indicate Le Guin's stature is by pointing to some of the external marks of literary recognition: the enthusiastic praise she has attracted from Harold Bloom, the most energetic and influential canon-building critic of the age; the entrée she has gained to such prestigious literary and critical forums as *Critical Inquiry* and *The New Yorker*; and such general accolades that she has won as the National Book Award, the Living Legend Award from the Library of Congress, the PEN/Malamud Award, and the (shortlist for the) Pulitzer Prize—not to mention the numerous prizes she has won *within* the science-fiction scene. Indeed, the current volume bears particular witness to the perhaps unparalleled attention that Le Guin's work has attracted from readers not otherwise specially devoted to science fiction. Though many interviews with her have appeared in periodicals internal to the science-fiction world, many of the best—and hence a disproportionate number of the interviews reprinted here—first appeared in more general forums.

More important than such extrinsic markers of distinction, however, is, of course, the actual quality and influence of her work; and here, despite the considerable bulk of her oeuvre, there remain two titles that should be singled out for having done at least as much as, and perhaps more than, any other particular novels to bring American science fiction into its modern era.

The first of these is *The Left Hand of Darkness* (1969). Perhaps never, before or since, has a single text had such a profound and immediate impact on the field. A decade after its publication, Baird Searles and his colleagues at New York City's renowned Science Fiction Shop summed up the matter accurately, if inelegantly, when (in *A Reader's Guide to Science Fiction* [1979]) they

proclaimed Le Guin to be, on the strength of that novel, one of the "few writers in the genre that have in one or a few works figuratively goosed s-f into
a quantum leap in quality and sophistication." They approvingly quote a re-
viewer who decided, after reading fifty pages or so of an advance copy, "Science fiction will never be the same." Similarly, Brian Aldiss, for many years
the most informed British observer of American science fiction, had already,
in 1973, recognized that *The Left Hand of Darkness* established Le Guin as a
major talent; and (in *Billion Year Spree*, his history of the genre) Aldiss quotes
a substantial passage from the novel in order to show that "Le Guin is a rarity
in that she writes beautifully. Not prettily. Beautifully."

   It is, indeed, the perhaps not quite unprecedented but certainly highly unusual quality of the novel's prose that accounts for much of its success. The
daring of its subject matter, however, and the disciplined seriousness with
which it is treated, are no less important. The narrative is set on the planet
Winter, whose inhabitants are sexless and ungendered—except during certain
estrus-like periods, when each individual may become either male or female.
This ambisexuality is unnerving to the novel's viewpoint character, the in-
terplanetary visitor Genly Ai, who, like earthly men, is continuously male;
conversely, his unchanging gender and sexual identity seems like a shocking perversion to the natives. Though *The Left Hand of Darkness* is a quest
story—like much earlier science fiction and, indeed, much earlier literature
from the *Epic of Gilgamesh* and the *Odyssey* onwards—its intelligent concern with the psychic and sociocultural consequences of gender amounted
to a groundbreaking innovation for the genre. Highly influential, too, was its
quasi-anthropological mastery at describing an entire invented culture not
merely with a few broad strokes but in patient, plausible detail (an achievement that seems appropriate for a writer whose father, Alfred Kroeber, was an
important figure in the development of academic anthropology in the U.S.).
It speaks well for the science-fiction community that its members responded
to so radically original and in many ways shocking a novel by giving *The Left
Hand of Darkness* the field's two most coveted prizes for Best Novel of the
year: the Hugo Award from the fans at the World Science Fiction Convention
and the Nebula Award from the professionals of the Science Fiction Writers of
America. Decades after its original publication, the novel continues to receive
a good deal of critical attention; and, as the reader of this volume will see,
probably no work inspires more questions in Le Guin's interviewers.

   Le Guin became the first writer ever twice to win both the Hugo and the

Nebula for Best Novel simultaneously when, several years later, *The Dispossessed* (1974) also received both prizes. Though the triumphant success of *The Left Hand of Darkness* necessarily prevented the later novel from appearing as quite such a bolt from the blue sky, *The Dispossessed* (1974) is probably to be counted as ultimately an even more consequential text. As I have myself argued in print before now, it may be the most prominent and unavoidable landmark in the entirety of modern science fiction. Like the earlier novel—whose stylistic brilliance it at least equals and perhaps surpasses—*The Dispossessed* (1974) displays an anthropological interest in "thick" cultural description, in this case of two twin but radically contrasting planets: Urras, an earthlike world that is dominated by the American-style monopoly-capitalist superpower A-Io, but that also includes the competing, quasi-Stalinist nation of Thu; and Anarres, a physically much poorer but socially more progressive world whose civilization, founded several generations before the time present of the novel by a group of political refugees from Urras, is organized along anarcho-socialist lines. The novel is itself anarcho-socialist in viewpoint, and its treatment of Anarres is sympathetic and supportive—but by no means uncritical. Indeed, the political intelligence at work in *The Dispossessed* is among the subtlest and most searching to be found anywhere in modern fiction; one apt tribute to the novel is that in today's university it is widely taught not only in literature courses but in political science courses as well. At the same time, *The Dispossessed* is far from being political in a merely programmatic way: Le Guin's ultimate interest in her invented societies is in the kind of people they produce. For instance, the novel's protagonist Shevek—an Anarresti physicist who attempts to promote intellectual and social exchange between the twin worlds (and who is said to be in part a fictionalized portrait of Robert Oppenheimer, who was friendly with Le Guin's parents)—is one of the most memorable and vividly realized characters in science fiction.

The incomparable success of *The Left Hand of Darkness* and *The Dispossessed* has perhaps somewhat unfairly overshadowed Le Guin's other achievements in the genre; so that it is worth stressing that, even if these two novels were left out of consideration, the quantity and quality of Le Guin's science fiction would still make her one of the field's major stars. Two novels that seem to me especially worth stressing in this regard are *The Lathe of Heaven* (1971) and *Always Coming Home* (1985). The former—about a psychiatrist who attempts to direct a patient's ability to alter reality by dreaming about it—is one of the most original and provocative variations on the Frankenstein theme since Mary Shelley's 1818 novel, the founding text of science fiction. Le Guin's novel also serves to remind us that she was among the first to recognize the genius of Philip K. Dick, whom she famously described as "our own homegrown Borges." Today Dick's influence is everywhere in science fiction and is found well beyond the precincts of the field as well; but *The Lathe of Heaven* remains, I think, the finest Dickian work by anyone other than Dick himself.

As to *Always Coming Home*, it is sometimes described as Le Guin's most "postmodernist" work, though the adjective may, as often, create more confusion than illumination. It is perhaps more useful to recognize the book (it somewhat begs the question to call it a novel) as the most thoroughly *anthropological* of Le Guin's science fiction: the sociocultural description of the Kesh, a gentle people imagined to live in the distant future near what is now the northern Pacific coast of the United States, is among the "thickest" of any imagined society in literature. The richness and complexity of the description is partly a function of the multigeneric composition of *Always Coming Home*, which includes not only various literary forms in both prose and verse but also visual art (in the form of drawings that are something more than mere "illustrations" of the text) and even music (the original edition of the book came with an audiocassette of Kesh songs). Some have argued that the radically nonlinear structure of *Always Coming Home* helps to make it also the most deeply feminist of Le Guin's writings.

The Left Hand of Darkness, The Lathe of Heaven, The Dispossessed, Always Coming Home—to appreciate these volumes is to have made an excellent *beginning* at understanding the character, scope, and importance of Le Guin's science fiction. But anything like a full account of her work in the genre would require much more space than is available here. It would, for example, require consideration not only of a number of other novels but also of a large number of science-fiction short stories, which collectively establish her as one of the foremost practitioners of that form after Dick and Theodore Sturgeon: "The New Atlantis" (1975) and "The Day Before the Revolution" (1974)— the latter a Nebula-winning "prequel" to *The Dispossessed*—are outstanding examples here. Yet, as I have already noted, Le Guin's science fiction, for all its importance to the field, does not exhaust her own importance in modern American literature.

Science fiction apart, Le Guin's most noteworthy achievements have doubtless been in fantasy. Admittedly, the two genres are often associated with one another: but more, I believe, because of the marketing habits of booksellers and commercial publishers than because of any profound aesthetic similarities between these two extremely different varieties of fiction. In any case—though many science-fiction writers have written some fantasy, and a much smaller percentage of fantasy writers have written some science fiction—it is extremely rare for anyone to do major work in both genres. There are a few arguable exceptions, but, barring Delany, it may be that almost the *only* writer who has incontestably done so is Le Guin herself.

The Earthsea sequence is generally accounted the most important of Le Guin's fantasy works. Though it originally gained renown as a highly successful (in both critical and popular terms) trilogy of novels—*A Wizard of Earthsea* (1968), *The Tombs of Atuan* (1970), and *The Farthest Shore* (1972)— nearly two decades later Le Guin began expanding the sequence with (so far) a further three volumes of novels and stories (*Tehanu* [1990], *Tales from Earthsea* [2001], and *The Other Wind* [2001]). The Earthsea books have often been compared to J. R. R. Tolkien's *Lord of the Rings* trilogy (1954–1955)— the name "Earthsea" itself may be, at least in part, an echo of Tolkien's Middle-earth—and the affinity between the two series is genuine enough: the Earthsea sequence is squarely in the world-building Tolkienian tradition, and Le Guin has often expressed admiration for and indebtedness to *The Lord of the Rings*. But Le Guin's is in many ways the more mature and the more concrete creation, and is likely to prove the more enduring. Though Le Guin's series certainly contains important elements of heroic fantasy, it is not so unrelievedly martial as Tolkien's. Earthsea is considerably more balanced and varied than Middle-earth, including daily life and suffering as well as action and adventure. One might say that it feels more like an actual social formation, a place where individuals really live, whereas Middle-earth (apart, perhaps, from certain episodes in the Shire) too often feels like a mere stage set for fantastic exploits. Similarly, Le Guin's protagonist, the wizard Ged, is a far more memorable and vividly realized character than any of Tolkien's. Even Le Guin's use of magic—probably the main staple of this sort of literary fantasy—is significantly different from Tolkien's. Whereas magic in *The Lord of the Rings* (most prominently displayed, of course, with regard to the rings themselves) is for the most part a mere inexplicable given, sorcery in Earthsea is developed with such precise and quasi-rigorous detail that it almost counts as an alternative science. In this way it provides a precedent for "thaumaturgy" in China Miéville's great Bas-Lag series of novels; and, in general, the Earthsea books can be understood to look forward to Miéville's expressly anti-Tolkienian project as well as backward to Tolkien himself. As the interviews in this volume help to illustrate, perhaps none of Le Guin's achievements is more widely or intensely loved than the Earthsea sequence.

A further interesting distinction of the sequence concerns its readership. The original trilogy seems to have been intended mainly for younger readers and was certainly received in this way. *The Tombs of Atuan* won a Newbery Silver Medal (the Newberys being the most prestigious set of literary prizes designed specifically for children's literature), and "Children's Books" was the category in which *The Farthest Shore* won a National Book Award. Over the years, however, the series (and not only the later additions but also the original trilogy itself) has attracted an increasing number of adult admirers, so that today it is probably enjoyed about equally by readers of all ages. The "children's literature" classification now seems a fact more about the origin of the Earthsea books than about their current status. Such, indeed, is often the progress of the finest works of fantasy written for young people. Obvious examples include Tolkien's *The Hobbit* (1937) and the Alice books (1865–1871) of Lewis Carroll; and it may be that similar processes are today ongoing with regard to Philip Pullman's *His Dark Materials* trilogy (1995–2000) and the Harry Potter novels by J. K. Rowling (1997–2007). Le Guin is a rare American presence in this predominantly British company.

Even after one has recognized Le Guin's immense contributions to science fiction and to fantasy, there remains much to say about her oeuvre. A significant number of her works—especially her shorter works—of prose fiction are not precisely fantasy *or* science fiction, though they belong to a genre that may have certain elements in common with both. The frequently discussed Hugo-winning tale "The Ones Who Walk Away from Omelas" (1973), for instance, might be counted as an example—one among many in the Le Guin oeuvre—of the modern parabolic allegory of the sort invented by Kafka and developed by Borges and others. Indeed, I have always thought that Le Guin's comparison of Borges to Dick—though a generous and welcome boost for Dick at a time when he had very little general literary reputation—would apply with greater precision to Le Guin herself.

Yet even a capacious multigeneric term like "speculative fiction" or "arealistic fiction" is inadequate to Le Guin's achievement. She is, in fact, a master of realism itself. The most prominent example here is perhaps the Pulitzer-shortlisted *Searoad* (1991), a cycle of related short stories that, somewhat in

the tradition of Joyce's *Dubliners* (1914), explores the ordinary lives of both
tourists and permanent residents in Klatsand, Oregon, a fictional beach resort
town. The anthropological interest in *place* so important for Le Guin's fantasy
and science fiction is fully active here too. The town of Klatsand is in a way
the largest and most important "character" in the book; but the overall cultural portrait is built out of many small, interrelated particulars in the lives
of a good many individuals. As with Joyce—but also as with so many earlier
writers in the American grain—one conclusion that *Searoad* suggests is the
always-scandalous Thoreauvian discovery of how large a role quiet despera-
tion plays in the existence of men and women.

There is still more that is worthy of note in the immense Le Guin oeuvre.
She has produced many books for younger children, and these—especially,
perhaps, the four in the Catwings series—must count as among the relatively
few works that can be enjoyed equally by kindergarteners and by their parents (or grandparents) ever since "Dr. Seuss" (Theodor Seuss Geisel) set the
undisputed gold standard in this regard. Not content only with being an all
but unanimously acclaimed master of English prose, Le Guin is also a poet of
genuine achievement; and the seven volumes of verse she has published over
the past three decades would make a perfectly respectable literary career all by
themselves. She has also done notable work as a literary translator. Here her
best-known publication is probably her 1997 rendering of the *Tao Te Ching* of
Lao Tzu. Hailed by some as the most compelling version of this ancient Chinese text available in English, it is certainly an appropriate accomplishment
for a writer who—as *The Left Hand of Darkness* and many other works illustrate, and as she discusses in the conversations that follow—has been deeply
influenced by Taoist spirituality for decades.

Nor should we forget Le Guin's contributions as a critic, editor, and
teacher. *The Norton Book of Science Fiction* (1993), of which she is senior
editor, has been controversial since its first appearance, but is by long odds
the most influential academic anthology of science fiction ever published. No
other particular volume has done so much to promote the teaching of university courses in science fiction, which today constitute one of the "growth
industries" of American higher (especially undergraduate) education. No
less consequential, in a somewhat different way, is Le Guin's own critical
prose. Indeed, it seems clear that, with the lone exception of Delany, no other
science-fiction author has had a greater or more deserved impact as a critic.
Included in her several volumes of essays are such already classical efforts

as "From Elfland to Poughkeepsie" (1973), one of the most important state-ments yet made on the importance of literary style for fantasy fiction; "Why Are Americans Afraid of Dragons?" (1974), a manifesto-like defense of the creative imagination that memorably argues "the ultimate escapist reading" to be "that masterpiece of total unreality, the daily stock market report"; and "Science Fiction and Mrs. Brown" (1976), which ingeniously applies Virginia Woolf's defense of modernism and the psychological novel to the study of science fiction.

Le Guin's ready critical intelligence—exercised in a long and successful career of academic teaching positions as well as in her published works—makes her an excellent subject for interviewers; and her history of excep-tional generosity with her time, despite an always heavy work load, means that the editor of this volume has had quite a few conversations from which to choose. Those that follow represent only a selection of the many inter-views Le Guin has given over the years and decades: a selection that has been heavily weighted toward the longer, more intellectually substantial pieces. As noted above, discussion of Le Guin's writings naturally constitutes the basic agenda of the pieces in this volume. But the richness and, especially, the con-ceptual seriousness and inventiveness of those writings means that conver-sation about them inevitably leads to a great many more general topics as well. Though it is unnecessary to attempt a thorough inventory of the top-ics discussed in the pages that follow, it may be useful to mention a few of the themes that the reader will most frequently encounter.

Perhaps the most basic issue to be encountered in these interviews—and one on which Le Guin has been utterly consistent throughout her career—is the matter that she has most famously engaged in "Why Are Americans Afraid of Dragons?": namely, the absolute importance of the artistic imagi-nation. It is no surprise to find her, in one of the interviews collected here, an ardent admirer of William Morris, for Morris, perhaps more compellingly than any other modern figure, showed by both precept and example how art is not a mere pleasant decoration to life but an integral part *of* life, and an indis-pensable requirement for psychic health and balance: and not merely for a mi-nority of especially "artistic" types, or on special "artistic" occasions, but for all men and women on a daily basis. Such is Le Guin's viewpoint as well. Also like Morris, Le Guin sees, and argues, that a proper understanding of the cen-trality of the imagination to human existence must caution against any ex-cessive or too exclusive valuation of realism as a literary genre (though, as we have seen, she has produced first-rate realism herself). One might say of her what Brecht suggested of himself, that she is more concerned with *reality* than with realism: and in a particularly memorable turn in one of the conversations below, she notes how much more reality is to be found in the wildly arealistic science fiction of Dick than in a feeble work of conventional (and entirely unreal) "realism" like *Peyton Place*.

The reader will also find in the pages that follow a good deal of discussion of the belief systems that have meant the most to Le Guin, notably Taoism and, especially, feminism. With regard to the latter, there has been an evolution in Le Guin's art and thought that is reflected in her interviews. Born in 1929, she was thus already in her late thirties, and a published author, by the time that second-wave feminism really began to work its revolutionary transformation in American consciousness; and some elements in her early work (for instance, the heavy preponderance of male over female fictional characters) reflect this fact. But she was quick to take the pressure of feminism as it emerged onto the U.S. sociocultural scene. In sharp contradiction to the familiar pattern by which people become increasingly conservative as they age, Le Guin has, indeed, become only more trenchant and committed in her feminism over the years; and, as the reader will discover, she can be a skillful polemicist for the cause. She is especially good, I think, at making clear the essential *modesty* of the basic feminist claim—that women should be treated and valued equally with men—and she shows how sexism too often, and in bad faith, misreads this simple demand as denoting all manner of "anti-male" hostilities.

Finally, we might note that, though Le Guin is by no means a "confessional" writer or interviewee, she does not hesitate—when it seems pertinent to the issues under consideration—to discuss various aspects of her personal life and background; and these interviews, taken together, supply a fair amount of autobiography. Perhaps the most interesting revelations here concern her early life and, in particular, the way that the childhood of this radical artist not only seems to have been generally happy—one may think, in contrast, of those who experience noisily "troubled" childhoods and in adult life settle down to conservative philistine respectability—but provided essential training for the sort of writer she was to become. The fact that Le Guin was the daughter of a famous scholar is of course unsurprising in a writer for whom ideas have always played so important a role. But, more specifically, Alfred Kroeber's pioneering role in academic anthropology combined with the personal attitudes and values that both parents established in the family home to provide the ideal background for an author who would go on to take a comparative, holistic interest in entire cultures, actual and invented, and who would pursue such matters in an unswervingly non-essentialist and non-ethnocentric way. Even the construction of the house in which Le Guin grew up—which she fondly recalls, in one of the interviews below, as a building of great beauty—seems to have played a part in the early shaping of the writer committed to the necessity of creative imagination.

One could easily note other subjects that Le Guin illuminates in the conversations that follow. Indeed, the variety of topics covered in these selections, along with the combination of sharp intelligence and clear, accessible presentation, should make the volume an ideal introduction to Le Guin for those still unfamiliar with her work. But I think that even the many readers who have followed her output eagerly and with great care since the 1960s will also find much to interest them in these interviews with one of the outstanding literary and intellectual figures of our time.

It remains only to acknowledge those who have helped me in the preparation of this volume: such as my friend and colleague Robin Roberts, herself a science-fiction critic of considerable note, who read and commented on an earlier version of the paragraphs above; and my old friend from high school days, Carl Gardner, who did the same—and who also, a great many years ago, introduced me to the works of Ursula Le Guin by giving me the copy of *The Dispossessed* that still contains most of my marginal notes and to which I most often refer when teaching or writing about the novel. There are three other individuals whose contributions need to be described in a bit more detail.

Seetha Srinivasan, the director of the University Press of Mississippi, originally suggested this project to me: a suggestion that forms part of Seetha's admirable effort to recognize the importance of science fiction in modern literature by including science-fiction authors in the justly renowned series in which the current volume appears. I acknowledged Seetha's efforts in my Introduction to *Conversations with Isaac Asimov*, which Mississippi published in 2005; and once again her support and encouragement have been indispensable.

My most obvious debt is to Ursula Le Guin herself; and for me the most rewarding aspect of editing this book has been getting better acquainted with

Ursula personally. I had been reading and admiring her works for about a quarter century before I developed any personal acquaintance with her. When I did, I found—contrary to a well-worn commonplace about the relation between authors and their books—that the intelligence, friendliness, strength, and generosity displayed on the pages of her works are precisely the qualities that also characterize her in "real life." Her cooperation and helpfulness to me while I was putting this book together have been exemplary: not only in her willingness to take time out of a very busy schedule in order to participate in the interview that concludes the volume, but also in giving me much sound and useful advice in preparing the editorial material. Having said that, I should, however, immediately add that neither Ursula nor I ever had any notion that this book should be in any way "authorized" by her. Responsibility for the editorial material rests with me and me alone; and it is not to be assumed that Ursula would necessarily agree with my comments.

Finally, my greatest debt of all is to Rich Cooper, my student and my friend, and also, while this volume was in progress, my research assistant. Rich proved to be virtually the Platonic ideal of what a research assistant ought to be: smart, energetic, conscientious, well organized, imaginative, and never afraid to take the initiative in our joint labors. Equally adept in dealing with documents and with human beings, Rich inspired such confidence that it was with an entirely easy mind and a clear conscience that I delegated to him virtually all the work that *can* be properly delegated in the editing of a book like this one. All final decisions were mine: and so any blame that attaches to shortcomings that may be found in the editing must be assigned exclusively to me. With this qualification, however, *Conversations with Ursula K. Le Guin* should be considered a product of our collaborative efforts.

CF

Chronology

1929   Born Ursula Kroeber on October 21 in Berkeley, California, daughter of Theodora Kroeber and the anthropologist Alfred Kroeber.

1951   Receives B.A. *magna cum laude* from Radcliffe College.

1952   Receives M.A. in Romance languages from Columbia University.

1953–54   Fulbright Fellow in Paris. Meets and marries the historian Charles Le Guin.

1954–56   Instructor in French at Mercer University and at the University of Idaho.

1959–61   Begins publishing poetry in various periodicals.

1961   "An die Musik," first published work of prose fiction, appears in *Western Humanities Review*.

1962   "April in Paris," second published work of prose fiction, appears in *Fantastic*.

1966   Publishes first novel, *Rocannon's World*.

1969   Publishes *The Left Hand of Darkness*. It wins both the Hugo and Nebula Awards for Best Novel.

1971–2002   Holds teaching positions as Lecturer, Guest Lecturer, or Writer-in-Residence at many institutions, including Portland State University, University of Reading (England), University of California–San Diego, University of California–Santa Cruz, Kenyon College, Tulane University, Bennington College, Stanford University, and San José State University.

1972   Receives Newbery Silver Medal Award for *The Tombs of Atuan* and National Book Award for Children's Books for *The Farthest Shore*.

1974   Publishes *The Dispossessed*.

1975   *The Dispossessed* wins Hugo and Nebula Awards, making Le Guin the first writer ever twice to win both Best Novel awards simultaneously.

1979   Receives Gandalf Award as Grand Master of Fantasy.

1985	*Always Coming Home* shortlisted for National Book Award.
1992	*Searoad* shortlisted for Pulitzer Prize.
2000	Receives Living Legend Award from the Library of Congress and Robert Kirsch Lifetime Achievement Award from the *Los Angeles Times*.
2001	Receives Lifetime Achievement Award from the Pacific Northwest Booksellers Association.
2002	Receives PEN/Malamud Award for Short Fiction.
2003	Named Grand Master by the Science Fiction and Fantasy Writers of America.
2004	Receives Margaret A. Edwards Award from the American Library Association for Lifetime Achievement in Young Adult Literature.

Conversations with Ursula K. Le Guin

Ursula Le Guin

Anne Mellor/1980

A public dialogue between Le Guin and Anne Mellor, Professor of English, Stanford University, November 6, 1980. From *Women Writers of the West Coast: Speaking of Their Lives and Careers* (Santa Barbara, CA: Capra Press, 1983). Reprinted by permission of Anne Mellor.

Ursula Le Guin is a distinguished writer of science fiction, the only woman who has thus far been recognized as a master of the genre. Her audience includes readers of various nationalities and children of all ages, for whom *The Earthsea Trilogy* and *The Beginning Place* are memorable landmarks in the world of fantasy. Her sizeable audience at Stanford, sprinkled with a large number of young men and women who identify themselves as "science fiction freaks," sat enthralled as she expounded her ideas on "World Making."

"The idea of world-making makes me think of making a new world, a different world, something like middle-earth or the planets of science fiction—that is the work of the fantastic imagination. Or you can turn it around and say, what about making the world new, making the world different? That is the mark of the political imagination. Then you've got utopia, dystopia or whatever. But what about making the not-new? What about making this world, this old world that we live in? The old world is made new at the birth of every baby and is made new every New Year's Day. In a day-to-day living sense, we make the world we inhabit. But I have to leave it to the philosophers to decide whether we make it from scratch. It tastes like a scratch world. That's Bishop Berkeley's cosmic mix.

"What artists do is make a skillful selection of fragments of the cosmos, unusually useful and entertaining fragments of the cosmos, arranged to give an illusion of coherence and permanence. An artist makes the world, her world; an artist makes her world *the* world for a little while. Like a crystal, a work of art seems to contain everything and to imply eternity, but I think it's a fake. It's an explorer's sketch book; it's a chart of the shorelines on a foggy coast. To make something is to invent or discover it. Michelangelo cuts away the extra marble that hides the statue, right? Now I tried reversing this, which I think we do less often. To discover something is to invent it. Julius Caesar said, 'The existence of Britain was

3

uncertain until I went there.' We can safely agree that the ancient Britons probably were fairly certain that Britain was there. But it does depend upon how you look at it, and as far as Rome was concerned, Caesar *did* invent Britain. He made it because he got there.

"Think of Alexander the Great . . . I don't suppose anybody here is old enough to have read *Fifty Famous Stories.* I don't know who wrote it. It's a little tiny book you read when you're about six, and my entire knowledge of world history comes from it. And now I will tell you a story that comes from *Fifty Famous Stories.* Alexander the Great sat down and cried (and as far as I can figure, he was somewhere in the middle of India) because there were no new worlds to conquer. What a stupid, silly man! There he was, sitting and sniffling half way to China, and then he turned back. Alexander the Great was a conqueror. Conquerors are always running into new worlds and then they are running out of them. Conquest is not finding and conquest is not making. Our culture, which conquered what is called the New World and which sees the natural world, the world nature, as an adversary to be conquered, look at us now! We are running out of everything. I have been thinking about 'Lost Worlds and Future Worlds' and realize that I can't get to the future worlds without the lost worlds. We are the children of the conquerors. We live here in the Americas; we are the inhabitants of a lost world. It's totally lost, even the names are lost. The people who lived here on these hills where we are now—10,000 or 20,000 or 30,000 or 40,000 years ago—we haven't got the carbon dating down yet—how are they remembered? They are remembered in the language of the conquistadores. They are the Santa Claras, the San Franciscos; they are remembered by the names of foreign demigods. Sixty-three years ago my father wrote that the Cossano Indians are extinct so far as all practical purposes are concerned. A few scattered individuals survive. This period of sixty-three years has sufficed to efface even traditional recollections of the forefathers' habits except for occasional fragments. Here is one such fragment preserved in my father's book. It was a song which they sang somewhere around the San Francisco bay under the live oaks. Originally there weren't any wild oaks here, these oaks are European. There were different weeds on the hill. 'I dream of you, I dream of you jumping rabbit, jack rabbit, and quail. . . .' Then in the same chapter on the Cossano Indians, there is one line from a dancing song. 'Dancing on the brink of the world.' When I was a kid and when I was a young writer, I knew I had to have a past to make a future with, and I didn't know where to go for it. I went to the European culture of my own forefathers and my own mothers. I took what I could from them and I learned as I went on to filch, to steal, to grab anything I could—from China, from Japan, from India, the idea of the wave from China, the dancing god from India, anything I could use to patch together a world. But what I'd like to say now is that there is still a mystery in the place where you are born, the place where you grow up, and Berkeley is where I was born and grew up. My world, my California, it still isn't me. To make a new world you've got to start with an old one. I don't think there is any question about that. To find a world, maybe you have to get lost. The dance they danced in California, the dance of renewal, the dance that renewed the world every spring, was always danced on the brink, on the edge, on the foggy coast.

"California has influenced me totally and utterly! I went East to college and I think in some ways I felt more alien in the Northeast than I did even in France where I went after college for graduate work. I had planned to be a college teacher of French and Italian language and literature. I don't want chauvinism to creep up on me from behind, but I feel very Western. You'd think growing up in Manhattan would force you to utopia. I love New York City, that's a good city. It's next best to London. But living there is hard. It's just so much easier to get along on the West Coast.

"When I talk about my parents, I always feel like I'm boasting. I happened to be born, luckily enough, to my father, Alfred Kroeber, who was an anthropologist. He grew up in Manhattan and got his doctorate under Franz Boas at Columbia and happened to get a job in California, which was way-out at that time, about 1904 or 1906, and he lived the rest of his life out here, first writing at the museum in San Francisco and always affiliated with U.C. Berkeley. He did his ethnology mostly among the Indians of California and his archeology in Peru. He had an early marriage and his first wife died very young of tuberculosis before the First World War. Then getting on to fifty, he took a second wife who was Theodora, my mother. She had had two children of her own earlier and then she had two children with him; so I have two older half-brothers and a brother. There were four kids in the family and when they got us all raised and married and sent off, then my mother, Theodora, started writing and wrote a best seller, somewhat to her own surprise and immensely to the surprise of the U.C. Press which published *Ishi, In Two Worlds* and didn't know what to do when it appeared on the *New York Times* best seller list. I think they were sort of humiliated."

Although Theodora was not an anthropologist by training, she had taken a course in anthropology with Professor Kroeber as a part of her work for a Mas-

ters in Social Psychology. That classroom encounter led to the marriage and produced the family whose shared interest in cultures was to exert a profound influence on Ursula Le Guin's life and writing.

"I grew up amongst anthropologists, Indians, refugees from Nazi Germany,
crazy ethnologists. The best family friend was an Indian who came to stay with
us for six weeks every summer. He was just a member of the family. I actually
thought I was related to Juan. You know how kids are, they take all of this for
granted. Obviously, something seeped through, a kind of cultural relativism, a
kind of nobody really has the word but everybody's word is worth listening to.
And then I think something genetic also happened because I don't know about
my mother—my mother is so sneaky, I can't put my finger on her at all. She is beyond me, entirely. As for my father, I physically resembled him and I'm interested
in artifacts, just as he was. He liked to know how a thing was made, what it was
made for, why it was made that way. This comes into my fiction all of the time.
It's where my fiction often starts from, small artifacts. I know I inherited this, but
my father did it with real things while I make them up.

"I guess I had a fortunate upbringing, an incredibly lucky childhood. I've
been told that Tillie Olsen recently talked here about luck in a writer's life, and
that touched me very much because, God knows, I was lucky. If I can draw on
the springs of 'magic,' it's because I grew up in a good place, in a good time even
though it was the Depression, with parents and siblings who didn't put me down,
who encouraged me to drink from the springs. I was encouraged by my father, by
my mother. I was encouraged to be a woman, to be a writer, to be any damn thing
I wanted. Even by my brothers, although they sometimes did put me down because they were older, but only to a certain extent.

"My writing started when my next oldest brother taught me how to write. I
think I more or less started when I learned the alphabet, at five. You wouldn't believe how awful it was. I started sending things out for publication at about eigh-
teen. I got some poetry published in little poetry magazines. That was partly because my father kept kicking me and saying 'come on, come on, you can't keep
putting everything in the attic. If you're a writer, you're a writer. People have
to read what you write.' He really goaded me and in fact acted as my agent for a
couple of years.

"It's a lot of work sending writing out, it's a *lot* of work! You have to keep a
record of whom you're sending to, what you've sent, and when it comes back,
what they said, and then whom you send it to next. He was a methodical person
and he rather enjoyed this and he taught me how to do it; until I got a literary

agent I used his system. Anyway, when I was in my early twenties, I got a little
poetry published. I sent things out for about ten years before I got anything published that I got paid for. Then they discovered I was a science fiction writer. What
do you know! I was in like Flynn. I had a label and I could get published.

"By that time I was getting pretty hungry for a market. You get on towards
thirty and you've written all these years and you haven't published anything except bits and pieces and one short story in an academic journal. There comes
a point when you either publish or you stop, and I was getting near that point.
Then I realized that science fiction was different from when I had stopped reading
it at twelve. There were some very neat new writers and new science fiction magazines, and I said, 'maybe these magazines would take my stuff.' And sure enough
they did—so I came in as a science fiction writer and God bless science fiction because I probably never would have gotten published. They wouldn't have known
what to call me because I wrote such weird stuff, and publishers and book sellers
need labels. They have to know what section to put it in in the bookstore. That's a
fact of life.

"By now I have written science fiction, hard science fiction, soft science fiction,
juvenile fiction, truly juvenile. I've got a kid's picture book out. I've got young
adult fiction. When I was reviewing Doris Lessing's last two books from the
Shikasta series, I found that she has discovered what I, to my great joy, had discovered a little earlier: that (a) if you're writing what they call science fiction, you're
absolutely free—you can write anything you damn please, and (b) that if you
take seriously the science fiction premise, you are furnished with an inexhaust-
able supply of absolutely beautiful and complex metaphors for our present situation, for who and where we are now, and I think it's not only women who have
found this out. Angus Wilson was one of the first to do this with *The Old Man in
the Zoo* years ago. That is a science fiction novel, if you look at it closely. Several
of the writers who interest me most are doing this sort of thing, but Lessing has
done it wholeheartedly and courageously. I love her introduction that says academics put science fiction down and to hell with them! That's really nice coming
from Doris Lessing.

"I'm getting awfully choosy in my science fiction reading at this point; I have
read too much. It's not science fiction's fault, it's my fault. I've O.D.'d on it. I'm
full up. I know all the plots. But there are some writers I can read without question and with pleasure and joy, like Vonda McIntyre. Or Gene Wolfe. The current
Gene Wolfe in print is a collection of short stories called *The Island of Dr. Death
and Other Stories*. I think Gene is one of the major novelists of the eighties. He's

working on a trilogy which is going to be called *The Book of the New Sun*. I think we have something inexhaustible being written under our very eyes. And, with a kind of bitterness in my heart, I have to say that I think probably the best American science fiction writer alive is still Philip K. Dick, although he let me down really badly when he turned against abortion rights and women. He still is a superb artist, one of the best novelists we have got. My favorite is *Martian Time Slip*. This is a man who has never been recognized by any critic of any stature. He has never had a decent edition of any of his books. They come out in these ratty little paper backs with gaudy covers and go out of print again, but I tell you, he is one of the best we've got going.

"I think the critics are lagging. There's an awful lot of schlocky science fiction, God knows, baloney ground out from the baloney factory. Let's have another sword and sorcery book, which is about the level the movies have just reached. But the critics are lagging in that they have ignored Philip K. Dick and McIntyre and Wolfe. They're just not looking at the stuff. They're taking the easy way out and saying 'that's science fiction, I won't read it.' That's stupid. You should never dismiss any book because it happens to have been published with a certain label on it. My God, you could publish *Wuthering Heights* among the gothic romances. It *is* a gothic romance. You could reissue it and would the critics pay any attention? No."

Le Guin was asked to say something about how feminists might proceed in the creating of new worlds.

"Since Tuesday, election day, when Ronald Reagan was elected, I'm wearing my ERA button everywhere. We have got to come awake again. We've got to work really hard. That's all I know, but in what exact ways, I don't know."

Mellor commented that we could do worse than follow what Le Guin called Odonanism in *The Dispossessed* and wondered whether Le Guin still felt the society founded on Anarres is a viable utopian vision for us.

"Odonanism is roughly identifiable with anarchism. I think it is a fairly identifiable form of the anarchist lineage of Kropotkin, Emma Goldmann and, to a large extent, Paul Goodman. It's pacifist anarchism, an identifiable tradition, not Bakhunism. It's just that nobody else had ever used it for fiction—it seemed such a pity. Well, the problem of anarchism, as the Marxists have consistently pointed out, is how do you get there? It's lovely once you're there. You know, the only place it has been wisely and seriously tried is Spain, and look what happened to Spain in the 1930s. Once you ask how we can practice it, I'm afraid my realism takes over.

"I made the proponent of Odonanism a woman. Do you want to know some-thing humiliating? In a partial first draft of the novel Odo was male, and I was consistently uncomfortable and uneasy with Odo. Then I realized: 'you're not a man at all,' and then it all just flowed like milk and honey, but I was obeying my cultural imperatives which say that people who invent things, who get large ideas and spread them, were men, and it took an act of will to get around it."

In response to a question about the relation between the sexes on Anarres, Le Guin said that it was "egalitarian." Then she exclaimed, "God, how can you do anarchism in a few sentences! Men and women are people; they meet on equal ground; approach each other on equal ground. All choices, all options are open. The point about anarchism is that you don't close any doors, and this of course demands a great deal of the people who try to live by it.

"About the couple relationship, I guess I'm fascinated by marriage in the larger sense of the word. Human beings do seem to sort themselves out into pairs as their life goes on, and yet at age fifty-one now, I'm very much caught between two cultural norms, one which was a pair-bonding one since I grew up in a very closely pair-bonded family and this is, to some extent, still an ideal to me. Two people who are really happy together is a lovely thing, and I guess I was interested in showing that. And because I was trying to write a utopia, a happy place, a good place, I wanted a happy couple in it."

In *The Left Hand of Darkness* Le Guin explores the possibility of biological an-drogyny, as opposed to an egalitarian society.

"To put it extremely crudely, it's as if human beings were cats or dogs, and we went into heat once a month, but in between heat, you're asexual or nonsexual and in heat you can go either male or female every time. One time you might sire a child and the next month you might become pregnant and nine months later bear one, and these options are open until menopause. Of course, what that means is that in the society in which those androgynes live, there are no sex-linked occupations since everybody can be male or female at any time."

Although the androgynes are biologically both male and female in *The Left Hand of Darkness,* they are invariably referred to in the masculine, by use of the generic "he." Le Guin was asked if she would now change anything in the book to cope with this linguistic problem.

"Actually, in my feedback from it, I found a strange variation on that. Most men happily accept all the Gethenians as male, but women vary about it. If I wrote it again, I would change a lot of things I couldn't do then. You can't go fiddling around with something you wrote fifteen years ago before there was a women's movement. I would play a lot more with the children. That's what I left out. I got so fascinated with my political plot that I left the kids out. Stupid. I would not change my use of pronouns. I did that, you may know, when I was given the opportunity of reprinting a short story called *Winter's King* which was a prelude to *The Left Hand of Darkness*. It was before I really noticed they were all called 'he' and when I got to reprint it, I refer to the King and others as 'she.' I called it 'King' and then I called it 'she,' and this was a lot of fun. I've had a lot of feedback from that edition, but I don't honest to goodness think it makes much difference. It's always a gamble whether my imagination works. Every novel is a collaboration between the writer and the reader, right? And I had to ask a whole lot of the readers of *The Left Hand of Darkness* to try to put themselves into the shoes of an androgynous person throughout the book. I gave men a very easy out. I had this kind of callow male earthling hero. Women, I didn't give an easy out. I thought that they, like me, would find it very easy to be androgynous and actually, to a large extent, that's true. And to a certain extent, men have identified not with Genly Ai, the male, but also with Estraven, the androgyne. It was a gamble, it still is a gamble."

Both *The Dispossessed* and *The Left Hand of Darkness* are set in extremely barren climates. Anarres is set on the moon where it is dusty and sterile and nothing grows, and in *The Left Hand of Darkness* it's always freezing. Le Guin was asked why she had placed those potentially feminist utopian societies in such harsh environments.

"I don't know. I honestly don't know. I've been asked this before. I have tried to think about it before. It's my utopia, my place where I want to be. I don't know why. All I can say is this: the South Sea islands, the place where everybody dreams of going, where the fruits drop off the trees and men and women are both available and everything is warm, comfortable, and easy, has always absolutely revolted me. Somehow, I crave the other. Maybe because I'm a Californian. I grew up in utopia. I've moved north. I moved to Portland where it snows a little, and I like it."

In most of Le Guin's novels, the major protagonists are not, in fact, female, but male. Le Guin was asked if she found herself thinking through male protagonists or whether she used them ironically.

"Again, I don't know and again it's something I've given enormous thought to because I wrote a couple of my major books before the women's movement was going. When it came up in the late sixties and through the seventies, it forced me to question everything I had taken for granted, everything about myself, everything about my writing. And I have not come out with very satisfactory answers. I know one reason I use males is the same reason that I use aliens in alien planets— I like to distance. There is something evasive, apparently, about me that wants to write through a distanced protagonist. When I have written books with a female protagonist, I feel totally different about the book. I feel a curious vulnerability and unsureness about the book always. In other words, I'm more vulnerable if I'm writing as a woman and there's a lot of defensiveness going on. It could be that I'm working towards being able to write as a woman, who knows? I really don't know."

Referring to another book, *The Lathe of Heaven*, in which dreams become effective, Le Guin was asked what relationship she saw between our dream life and the real world.

"It's all the same thing. There is no distinction. Western culture has tended to discount the dream, to a really psychotic extent. It's time that the dream was reoccupying its proper kingdom." Le Guin admitted that she sometimes used her own dreams in her writing. "Not like Robert Louis Stevenson, who actually called upon them and summoned them. Jekyll and Hyde came from a dream zone. But usually when I'm writing, I don't dream very much because it's all going into the writing."

Although Le Guin tended to discount the distinction between dream-world and "real" world, she made a sharp distinction between the real world and the world of science fiction. When asked if there is really a difference between what we call reality and science fiction, she retorted decisively: "You bet you there is. You keep that firmly in mind. It's a fiction. You know what Marianne Moore said about imaginary gardens with real toads—sometimes there are real gardens with imaginary toads in them. But it's a mixture. Fiction writers write fiction, particularly in science fiction. People forget this and say they are describing reality or they are predicting reality. But the very most that a fiction writer can do is offer an option."

Dialogue with Ursula Le Guin

George Wickes and Louise Westling/1982

Originally appeared in *Northwest Review* 20.2–3 (1982). Reprinted by permission of *Northwest Review*.

Raj Lyubov is a typical figure in Ursula Le Guin's fiction, an anthropolgist whose mission is to report on higher intelligence life forms (hilfs) on another planet. In this case the planet is populated by a peaceful race of furry human beings three feet tall who live in harmony with the lush forest that covers their world. The men from Earth who have come to log the planet are led by a military macho who regards these "creechies" as subhuman and treats them brutally. Le Guin has explained that she wrote *The Little Green Men* (as she entitled it) in protest against the Viet Nam war in which the landscape was defoliated and noncombatants of a different race were callously slaughtered in the name of peace and humanity. Characteristically in this novel she subordinates science fiction to her liberal humanitarianism and her concern for the natural world of which humanity is but a part.

Anthropology came naturally to the daughter of the great Berkeley anthropologist Alfred Kroeber and his wife Theodora, a writer best known for her biography of Ishi, the last surviving Indian of his tribe. Writing also came easily to Ursula Le Guin, but success did not come until she turned her talents to science fiction and fantasy. Then she published in rapid succession three novels set in the universe she was to explore in later novels, and the first volume of *The Earthsea Trilogy* which introduced still another world, this one an antique world of wizards and dragons and legends. Since 1966 Le Guin has published more than a dozen novels and won some of the most prestigious literary awards. Her most highly acclaimed novels are *The Left Hand of Darkness* and *The Dispossessed*.

The interview was conducted in the Le Guin family home in Portland, a comfortable old wooden house on the edge of Forest Park. The neighborhood seems an appropriate setting for the author who created the forest world of Athshe. In collecting her stories for publication in *The Wind's Twelve Quarters* she discovered "a certain obsession with trees" in her writing and concluded that she is "the most arboreal science fiction writer." She talks about this dendrophilia in the interview.

George Wickes: When did you first know that you were going to be a writer?
Ursula Le Guin: I don't know. I sort of took it as an established fact.

Wickes: From infancy?
Le Guin: Yes. When I learned how to write, apparently.

Wickes: What do you suppose it is that makes people write fiction?
Le Guin: They want to tell a story.

Wickes: There's much more than story in your fiction.
Le Guin: But I think the basic impulse is probably to tell a story. And why we do that I don't quite know.

Louise Westling: Did you write lots of stories as a child?
Le Guin: Some. I wrote a lot of poetry. They've always gone together. But I started writing stories somewhere around eight or nine, I think, when I got an old typewriter. Somehow the typewriter led me to prose—although I don't compose on the typewriter now.

Westling: What kinds of books were your favorites in early life?
Le Guin: I grew up in a professor's house, you know, lined with books. My favorites as a child were certainly fiction or narrative, novels and myths and legends and all that. But I read a lot of popular science, too, as a kid. Altogether, pretty much what I read now.

Wickes: If you were asked to compile a list of the books that have been most important to you, not only as a writer but also in your thinking, what would be the first half dozen?
Le Guin: I've tried to do it, and it goes on and on. It's insufferably boring, because I've read all my life, and I read everything. I've been so influenced by so much that as soon as I mention one name I think, "Oh, but I can't say that without saying that." I think there are certain obvious big guns, but I really hate to say any one, or six, or twenty. But you could very roughly say that the English novelists of the nineteenth century and the Russian novelists of the nineteenth century were formative. That's where my love and admiration and emulation was when I started. But then I read all that other junk, too. And I did my college work in

French and Italian literature. I never much liked the French novelists. I can tell you what I *don't* like. I don't much like "the great tradition," the James-Conrad thing that I was supposed to like when I was in college. I've revolted against that fairly consciously. Flaubert I really consider a very bad model for a fiction writer.

Wickes: Stendhal?

Le Guin: Stendhal's a good novelist, but I think the limitations of Stendhal have been rather disastrous. I think you'd do better with Balzac. If you have to imitate a Frenchman.

Westling: Proust?

Le Guin: You can't imitate Proust. And in modern writing, for instance, Nabokov means nothing to me. I have great trouble reading him. I see a certain lineage there which I just don't follow, don't have any sympathy for.

Wickes: How about more philosophical books, like some of the Oriental thinkers, or Thoreau?

Le Guin: You'll find him buried around in poems and novels fairly frequently, but I don't know Thoreau very well. You have to be a New Englander to really read Thoreau. There was stuff around the house, again. My father's favorite book was a copy of Lao Tzu, and seeing it in his hands a lot, I as a kid got interested. Of course, it's very accessible to a kid, it's short, it's kind of like poetry, it seems rather simple. And so I got into that pretty young, and obviously found something that I wanted, and it got very deep into me. I have fits of delving further into Oriental thought. But I have no head for philosophy.

Westling: You've said that you now associate some of your ideas with Jung but that you probably came to these yourself first before you ever read Jung.

Le Guin: My father was a Freudian—he was a lay analyst—so the word *Jung* was a four-letter word in our household. After the Earthsea trilogy was published, people kept telling me, "Oh, this is wonderful, you've used Jung's shadow." And I'd say, "It's not Jung's shadow, it's my shadow." But I realized I had to read him, and then I got fascinated. Then he was extremely helpful to me as a shaman or guide at a rather difficult point in my life. At the moment I wouldn't want to read Jung; you have to need him, like most psychologists. But it was amazing to me to find how parallel in certain places his imagination and my imagination, or his observation and my imagination, had run.

Westling: Well, part of it could be your absorption with mythology, because he came to his thinking by saturating himself in mythology.

Le Guin: I didn't have an absorption with mythology, but I had a child's curiosity, and there were Indian legends all over the place. My father told us stories that he had learned from his informants, and my mother was interested, too. The books I read were mostly children's editions, but what's the difference? The stories are there.

Westling: Yes, it doesn't matter, the pattern is what counts.

Wickes: How do your books come to you? Is there a particular process, or is it different every time?

Le Guin: It varies from book to book. For some of them it's very neat, and I can describe the process, but then for another one it's utterly different. *Left Hand of Darkness* is the nicest one because it came as a vision, a scene of these two people pulling something in a great snowy wilderness. I simply knew that there was a novel in it. As Angus Wilson describes it, his books come that way, with a couple of people in a landscape. But some of them don't come that way at all. *The Dispossessed* came with a perfectly awful short story, one of the worst things I ever wrote. There it was, all about prison camps, everything in it all backwards, a monstrosity of a little story. Then I thought, ``You know, it's really terrible that you could write anything that bad after writing all these years; there's got to be something in it." And sure enough, there was, after about two years' work and reading all these utopists and all the anarchists and thinking a lot. That one took real homework. But sure enough, the idea had been there all along; I just hadn't understood it. Yes, I worked like all blazes on that one. And for *Left Hand of Darkness* I had to plan that world with extreme care, writing its history, roughly, before I could do a good solid novel.

Wickes: It seems to me there's a good deal of geography in your writing, too.

Le Guin: I like geography and geology. You may notice the other thing besides trees is rocks.

Wickes: Yes, and landscapes, weathers, climates—you go into these things a great deal.

Le Guin: It's one reason I adore Tolkien; he always tells you what the weather is, always. And you know pretty well where north is, and what kind of landscape you're in and so on. I really enjoy that. That's why I like Hardy. Again, you always know what the weather is.

Westling: You said you liked trees and you liked rocks, and that expresses a dichotomy I've felt in your fiction, between lush forest worlds and desolate places where people have to struggle. I wonder whether you are simply a creechie but are restrained by pioneer impulses.

Le Guin: You know, I've had this mad fascination with Antarctica ever since I was sixteen or seventeen and first read Scott, and that's where all that snow and ice comes in. I believe all the sledge trips in *Left Hand of Darkness* are accurate. That was very important to me, that I didn't give them too much to pull and make them go too far.

Westling: That's the heart of that book, the most fully realized thing in it.

Le Guin: Sure, that's where it started. But that is also my Antarctic dream, my having followed Scott and Chapel and Wilson on those awful trips for years. Every now and then I have another binge, going back to Antarctica. I have a story coming out in *The New Yorker* about the first women who got to Antarctica. Actually they got to the Pole first. But they didn't leave any traces.

Wickes: You mean they got there ahead of everyone else?

Le Guin: They got there just a little bit ahead of Amundsen. A small group of South American women. I think I enjoyed writing that story more than anything in my whole life.

Wickes: Now that brings up something else. You have all these journeys in your fiction; people are always traveling around. That's a great way to see your geography, but it often becomes the plot. We go on a journey, not always an ordeal or quest, but we always go on a journey.

Le Guin: You've just hit a very significant note here. Actually I'm terrible at plotting, so all I do is sort of put people in motion and they go around in circles and they generally end up about where they started out. That's a Le Guin plot.

Westling: Well, who says you have to go straight ahead and then stop?

Le Guin: I admire real plotting, the many strands and real suspense. But I seem not able to achieve it.

Westling: Have feminists commended you on this fact? They should. That's supposed to be feminine, just as Eastern culture is supposed to be feminine because it emphasizes the circular.

Le Guin: But complexity surely is neither masculine nor feminine, and I see the line of my stories being awfully simple. It's not that I want to write mysteries, I'm talking about something more like what Dickens did, pulling strands together, weaving something—I'm not very good at that. I just plunge ahead. Or I do it by trickery, by zig-zagging.

Wickes: How long have you lived in Oregon?
Le Guin: Since 1959.

Wickes: Do you think Oregon has had an influence on your work?
Le Guin: Sure. It's the place I've lived longest now.

Wickes: Has it made you a dendrophile, or were you one already?
Le Guin: I must have been one already, but I didn't even notice until I was looking over that bunch of short stories I was supposed to write an introduction for and suddenly realized, "My God, this thing's crawling with trees." I think living on the edge of a forest has had some influence. And we've managed to plant a forest, without really intending to. The kids won't let us cut anything down: "Oh, what a sweet little seedling!" So now we have a garden towering over us. And every summer when I was growing up in northern California, I lived in a forest, up in the foothills of Napa Valley, and going out in the woods was what I did.

Westling: Were you a tomboy?
Le Guin: I had three older brothers, so I tagged around after them. I wasn't brave, and I didn't climb trees—I've been terrified of climbing and so on—I was not a tomboy in the sense of being brave and courageous, but my parents made no great distinctions between boys and girls, so I had the freedom of the woods.

Wickes: Would your feelings about nature have something to do with your feelings about what we might loosely call civilization or more exactly call technology? How do you feel about technology—for or against?
Le Guin: Oh, for. I don't know, it's such a large question, every answer turns out sounding like a fortune cookie, but you don't get civilization of any kind without technology. If you want a tool to do something with, you've got to figure out how to make it and how to make it best. And all that aspect of life I enjoy very much. I am really interested in things and artifacts, doings and makings and objects. So in the very simplest sense I enjoy technology. I love a good tool or a well-made thing.

Wickes: Yes, but there's a difference between craftsmanship and technology.
Le Guin: Well, craftsmanship is just good technology. Now, if you're talking about the excesses of the industrial West, then obviously we have taken some-

thing too far too hard. But to say that I'm against technology would make me a Luddite, and that I detest and abhor and am afraid of. People who think they can get on without the things that we now know how to do are kidding themselves. I would last five days in the woods without a good deal of technology. And besides, I like houses and cities.

Wickes: Yet it seems to me that your ideal state is the one you describe in *City of Illusions,* for instance, a comfortable old Maybeck house in the forest, with modern conveniences that nobody has to look after, where life is rather simple.
Le Guin: No, no, not at all. That's a total dead end. That's why he had to get out of that place. It was fun to describe it, to give it the solar cells and stuff so that they had this nice, low-level dream technology, but I'm a city person.

Wickes: I'm surprised to hear you say that because I thought the city was a bad place in your fiction. There's the one in *City of Illusions,* which is a bad place, or the one on Urras in *The Dispossessed,* which is beautiful and luxurious but ultimately evil.
Le Guin: But what about the other city in that book, the one on Annares? It's a kind of Paul Goodman city.

Westling: And yet dangers lurk there, because of the political conniving.
Le Guin: A city is where all dangers come together for human beings, where everything happens to human beings. I use "city" in a fairly metaphorical sense. A city is where culture comes together and flowers. A pueblo is a city.

Westling: The idyllic moments in many of your stories, though, seem to occur outside of cities. It's the pastoral problem. People need to escape the corruption of urban life and find renewal in an idealized natural setting, but they have to go back.
Le Guin: Yes, people are always going back and forth. But in my fiction the place they're going to end up and do their work and live their lives out is the city. As at the end of *The Beginning Place,* which is, of course, much fresher in my mind than *City of Illusions* is. If I might say so, *City of Illusions* is rather a bad book to use for anything; it's my least favorite and certainly the one with the most just plain stupid mistakes and holes in it.

Wickes: Still, quite often you present this antithesis between the modern city and the natural world, and my impression is that your fiction doesn't show very much interest in technology. By technology I mean hardware, gadgetry. This side of science fiction doesn't seem to interest you very much, and though you've got the convenience of space travel which will permit you to visit all these wonderful different worlds, you're not really interested in how the contraption works.

Le Guin: Not at all. Because I don't believe in it. If you ask me, do I believe that we will have space-flight of the speed necessary to get outside the solar system in any *foreseeable* future, I'd say no. We have nothing leading to such technology. So the whole thing is a metaphor, and you play around with making it look realistic, because that's part of the fun of a novel. And I put limitations like they couldn't exceed the speed of light. I like that part of it; I like playing with theory and what science I am able to absorb, which is pretty limited. But the engineering part is where I draw the line. I like my washing machine, and I treat it well, but I don't really yearn to know what's inside it.

Westling: How do you go about mapping out an imaginary world like that of *Malafrena*?

Le Guin: You certainly have to have maps. You have to know how far it is from there to there, or you get all mushy in your mind. Don't all the novelists draw maps? Jane Austen did it, when she needed to, and the Brontës did.

Westling: But when Joyce wrote back to Dublin and had people measure the time it would take to walk from one place to another and whether Bloom could jump over the railings, wasn't he being awfully literal-minded?

Le Guin: Well, of course. A novelist has to be really, stupidly literal about these things.

Wickes: But that's very different from inventing a country, as you do in *Malafrena*.

Le Guin: Whether it's real Dublin or invented Dublin, it's got to be right. Whether it's really there and other people can walk it, or whether you're building it for them to walk in the mind, it's got to be absolutely solid.

Westling: When you got ready to write *The Lathe of Heaven,* did you wander around in downtown Portland to see exactly where the parking structure was in relation to the other places?

Le Guin: I checked a couple of things, because my memory's so terrible. There are deliberate red herrings there. For instance, I could show you the house George lives in, but it's not on the street I say it is, it's one down. And Dave's Delicatessen never was on Ankeny Street. When they moved it, I went into an absolute panic. I thought, If they put it on Ankeny, I'm leaving this town.

Wickes: Why did you choose Portland as the setting instead of some imaginary place?

Le Guin: Oh, that wasn't an imaginary place type of story. That was about America now. That story came close to home, literally.

Wickes: Is this your vision of what's going to happen in the next twenty years?

Le Guin: The book's a dream, quite a bad one. If I had a vision of what's going to happen, I'm sure I would be unable to speak it. And I don't see why I should. I don't see what right I have. I'm not a prophet. I do not predict. I certainly hope I'm wrong.

Wickes: Are you more interested in the past or in the future? Your fiction goes both ways.

Le Guin: It's all mixed up together for me. You don't get one without the other. It's a Gordian knot which I have no wish to cut. It's obvious there's going to be no future without the past and no past without the future. I get rather Chinese about the whole thing.

Westling: Well, in a way then, real time doesn't matter because what you're doing is establishing metaphors within which problems can be explored. Is that right?

Le Guin: Yes. And I think the way of talking about time that makes the most sense to me and within which I work most happily is to connect what it's now fashionable to call waking-time and dream-time. There are two aspects of time, and we live waking in one; but western civilization has announced that there's only one real time, and it is that one. This I more or less consciously reject, and I am perpetually attempting by one metaphor and device or another in my books to reestablish the connection between the dream-time and the waking-time, to say that the one depends upon the other absolutely.

Westling: Well, then, do you see the writer as a dreamer?

Le Guin: Any artist goes back and forth between the two times, trying to speak one to the other, as a translator or interpreter.

Wickes: One of the most interesting things that keeps turning up again and again in your fiction is "mindspeech" and telepathy. Do you believe in ESP or anything like that?

Le Guin: I have to give the agnostic's answer. I certainly have never experienced it. But it was a very convenient metaphor for what I needed to do in the stories. I am not sure what it's a metaphor for. I've read some critics who have had some ideas about what I was trying to say and have left that to them because I really don't know what I was babbling about. I just know I needed it in certain stories

Wickes: I think it works very well.

Le Guin: It certainly is another way of talking about double vision. There is more than one way to see, more than one way to speak, more than one aspect to reality.

Westling: Its also a way to indicate the closeness of the two travellers across the ice.

Le Guin: Sure, it's a lovely emotional metaphor. You can play with it endlessly. That's what's so neat about science fiction. It gives you the opportunity to say, "All right, there is such a thing as telepathy, and you can learn it as a technique." Then you play with it novelistically. That's why I've enjoyed writing science fiction.

Westling: Have you ever lived in a desolate place like Anarres?

Le Guin: No. I never really lived in a desert, although I'd been across it in a train, until we went to French Glen years ago; just overnight. A whole book, *The Tombs of Atuan,* came out of that one trip into the Oregon desert. And I'm absolutely addicted to the desert now. Both of my parents liked the high desert country; they liked the Southwest and went there when they could.

Westling: Your new story in *The New Yorker* makes me think of another question, which I'm sure you've been asked *ad nauseam,* but I'll just ask it one more time. Why is it that most of your protagonists are male?

Le Guin: I don't know. Yes, I've certainly been asked it, and I've tried and tried to answer it, and I've given up trying to answer it. In the crudest sense it's that all protagonists doing the kinds of things that I had mine doing were male, and it took an effort of the imagination which I wasn't cabable of making until very recently to change that. This is going to look rather odd in print, but it really doesn't matter to me very much what sex people are, and this is my main problem as a feminist. Every now and then I forget to be upset.

Westling: Well, Flannery O'Connor said that she always knew there were two sexes, but she guessed she behaved as if there were only one.

Le Guin: Yes, I'm afraid this happens to a lot more of us than has either been fashionable or even right to admit, but I think now we can admit it. I think the Movement has gone far enough, given us strength enough that we can say it. Sometimes it just doesn't bloody matter.

Westling: I used to be quite disturbed when I thought of myself in front of a classroom. For years I saw a man in a tweed coat with a pipe. And that bothered me. I've been working on it for ten years, and I'm still not able to see me up there yet, but it's not the man in the tweed coat any more. I wonder whether you've had to make that kind of conscious effort.

Le Guin: Oh, yes. And I am so grateful to the whole women's movement for giving me the intellectual tools to make the effort with. Sometimes it's almost gimmicks—making yourself change the sex of a pronoun to see what happens, for example.

Westling: So sex does matter, ultimately, doesn't it?

Le Guin: Of course it does. But it doesn't always matter in everything.

Westling: Well, if one grows up with adventure stories, they're always about boys, and one's imagination gets formed by that.

Le Guin: That's it. But you see, I happily identified totally with the hero—if it was Jane Eyre, I identified with her; if it was a hero in Zane Grey, I identified with him—and I never thought a thing about it. And so I didn't think anything about it as a writer. My conscience had to be raised a lot before I saw that. As of about the early '70s, it does matter. Now I can't do this innocently any more, that innocence is gone. So now it matters a lot what one's protagonist is. I would defend my earlier books, because then it didn't matter. But now it does.

Westling: So you wouldn't agree with Virginia Woolf that there is such a thing as a woman's prose style.

Le Guin: I don't know. I am not going to disagree with Virginia Woolf about anything. I see her style, which is wonderful. Now there's the kind of complexity that I envy with my whole heart, that kind of weaving. But is there anybody besides Virginia Woolf who can do that particular sort of thing? You see, that way of thinking slides so easily into a sort of sexism that it worries me a little bit.

Westling: But many of your stories are about heroic adventures in the vein of the old military epics with hardly any participation by women.

Le Guin: Are they? Well, particularly the earlier ones. There's nothing like a good vicarious adventure.

Wickes: Speaking of one of the later ones, when did you write *Malafrena?* At the time it was published, or was this a book you'd written earlier?

Le Guin: No, it wasn't a book I'd written earlier, but parts of it are very old. The idea and some bits of it go back to the mid-fifties or late fifties. And it shows in the way it's put together; it creaks a little. It's a very old-fashioned novel. It's a nineteenth-century novel.

Wickes: We would have guessed that it was your apprentice work.
Le Guin: Well, there's apprentice work in it.

Wickes: Of course its entirely appropriate that it should be a nineteenth-century novel; it's right in the tradition of Stendhal.
Le Guin: If you're going to write about the revolution of 1830, you might as well do so in a style appropriate to the subject.

Wickes: You majored in Romance languages in college. What other languages do you know at least something of? The reason I ask is that you have these names that seem to be part Germanic, part Slavic, part Scandinavian.
Le Guin: Well, I've got a little linguistic facility which I haven't done much with. I'm trying to teach myself Spanish now, but that's no great trouble for someone with French and Italian. I didn't learn any other languages. But my father was an ethnologist. There were books about language around, and he talked with informants in the languages he knew, like Yurok. The house was always full of people with funny accents. I'm comfortable with foreign languages, and I enjoy them, so it's a lot of fun making them up. Word-making is one of the roots of fantasy. It reaches its peak in Tolkien, who said he wrote *The Lord of the Rings* so that they could say "Good morning" in Elvish.

Wickes: How do you choose your names? It seems to me you have a hodgepodge, or is that deliberate?
Le Guin: I don't think you'll find too much hodgepodge in the phonemes of any language that is implied by the names in a certain island or a certain country in my books. I tried to have fairly clearly in mind what pool of sounds they used because it bothers me very much in other people's fantasies when they have a hodgepodge of sounds that don't go together. One name obviously resembles German and the next something totally different, like Chinese, and then you get an 'X', which you don't know how to pronounce. I tried for a certain coherence in implied language, and also for something that looks pronounceable to the reader so that he doesn't have to stop every time he comes to it.

Wickes: In Earthsea you've got quite a variety in the names.
Le Guin: Well, there are four languages going in Earthsea. There's Kargad; there's Hardic, the main one; there's the Old Language, and then there's the language they speak up in Osskil.

Wickes: Then in *Malafrena* you have characters with names taken from several different languages. I spent a lot of time trying to figure out where Orsinia was, and whether you agree or not; I know it's Hungary.

Le Guin: Well, it isn't Hungary; but it must be pretty near Hungary. I'll tell you something funny. I've been told quite authoritively by several people what it is and where it is, and nobody has ever mentioned Czechoslovakia, which is incredible to me because it seems fairly obvious that there's a lot of resemblance. Could I throw Romania at you? That's the language.

Wickes: Well, I figured it should be Romania, but it doesn't fit. For me the real clincher is that when Luisa goes to Vienna she stays in the Hotel König von Ungarn.

Le Guin: You know why? Because I stayed in the König von Ungarn. It was right behind the Dom. It's closed now, but it was a real hotel that Mozart and Beethoven stayed in, so I could use it with total assurance. I knew it was there in the 1820s and 1830s.

Wickes: Do you attach any particular significance to the names in *Malafrena?* For instance, Valtorskar and Paludeskar seem to be landscape names. Is there a significance to those landscapes? Is Luisa a swamp?

Le Guin: There's a touch of swampiness in the Paludeskar family. I like Luisa, though. Now that was one of the parts of that book that was old. Luisa was an incredible villainess as I first thought about her, the *femme fatale,* when I was trying to write that book way back when.

Wickes: One final question. What are you writing now?

Le Guin: I have just been working on a television screenplay of one of my short stories for PBS. This is a new venture for me, screenwriting. Last year I was working on a screenplay for *Earthsea* with Michael Powell. He's an old British director—have you seen *The Red Shoes?*—and he was determined to make *Earthsea* into a movie.

Westling: And what's its fate?

Le Guin: Its fate is Hollywood. We wrote a perfectly beautiful screenplay that would make a beautiful, serious fantasy, finally, in the movies. But then Hollywood said, "Oh, yes, this is wonderful, yes, we want to do this, but actually what we need now is a movie about immortality." And so Michael and I said, "Well, yes, but you see, what we have is not a movie about immortality. We have a movie about this here wizard, and this young lady." We did the whole thing backwards.

You never start with a script. What we should have done is gone down to Hollywood together, Michael and me, and said, "Here we are, you're going to buy us, for $200,000, and two years from now we will give you the script that you always wanted." What idiots, we arrived with a script! And so now they want to rewrite it. And it's going to be our movie or no movie. So it will probably be no movie. But we are both rather obstinate people, and we believe in our screenplay; so who knows?

An Interview with Ursula Le Guin

Larry McCaffery and Sinda Gregory/1982

From the *Missouri Review* 7.2 (1984). Reprinted by permission of Larry McCaffery.

The following interview took place on June 7, 1982, in Ursula K. Le Guin's home, a lovely two-story house located in one of Portland's older neighborhoods. From the dining room window, there was a postcard view of the Columbia River, the many bridges and highways that crisscross it, and of the smoky Portland skyline. Following some initial difficulties in figuring out how to work the pull-top tabs on three beers, Ms. Le Guin settled us in her living room for an afternoon-long discussion which frequently was punctuated by the flow of the household around us.

Ursula Le Guin is probably as responsible as any other living writer for changing our notions of what science fiction and fantasy are capable of doing. As with the works of Italo Calvino, J.L. Borges, Philip K. Dick, and Stanislaw Lem, Ms. Le Guin's fictions defy genre definitions. Typically they are a sophisticated blend of myth, fable, political inquiry, and metaphysical parable, with all elements carefully controlled in terms of their anthropological implications. Hers is art that takes us on a circular journey to the future and back again, for not only is Le Guin a wonderful spinner of fantastic tales, she is also able to make us take note of the words and cultural assumptions with which we construct our present. What Le Guin does perhaps better than any other writer is to create a world apart from our own and then explore its premise, its prevailing metaphor, to its fullest implications. Once that's accomplished and we put down her fiction to take up those fictions around us that order the "real world," we are left with her craft's insidious aim: to make us examine with alien eyes our commonplace truths.

Although she was writing novels and short stories during the 1950s, it wasn't until the early 1960s that Ursula Le Guin found in science fiction a publishing home. From the time of her first published novel (*Rocannon's*

World in 1964) onward, Le Guin has been both highly prolific and widely praised. Her fourth novel, *The Left Hand of Darkness* (1969), won both the Hugo and Nebula Awards (Le Guin is the only writer to have won both of these prestigious awards twice, having won four Hugos and two Nebulas) and immediately established Le Guin as an important writer in the field. Her Earthsea trilogy—*A Wizard of Earthsea* (1968), *The Tombs of Atuan* (1971), and *The Farthest Shore* (1972)—has been compared with Tolkien's *The Lord of the Rings* and is often considered her most successful work to date; it also garnered for Ms. Le Guin the first stirrings of mainstream recognition, winning the Newbery Honor Book Citation (for *The Tombs of Atuan*) and the National Book Award for Children's Literature (for *The Farthest Shore*). *The Dispossessed* (1974), which again won the Hugo and Nebula Awards, reflected her increasing understanding of physics and her growing interest in anarchism as a political theory. Although the 1970s saw Le Guin continue to publish science fiction and fantasy successfully, there also began appearing various mainstream works of fiction (*Orsinian Tales,* 1976, and *Malafrena,* a novel, 1979), poetry (*Wild Angels,* 1975) , and essays (*The Language of the Night,* 1979). Her other major works include: *The Lathe of Heaven* (1971), *The Wind's Twelve Quarters* (stories, 1975), *The Eye of the Heron* (1978), and *The Beginning Place* (1980).

McCaffery: As an anthropologist, your father spent a great deal of his professional career trying, in a sense, to recreate other peoples' cultures. Is that one of the attractions of science fiction for you—that it allows you to reconstruct, imaginatively, other cultures and get outside your own?

Le Guin: Yes. Science fiction allows me to help people get out of their cultural skins and into the skins of other beings. In that sense science fiction is just a further extension of what the novel has traditionally been. In most fiction the author tries to get into the skin of another person; in science fiction you are often expected to get into the skin of another person from another culture.

Gregory: You've said that when you turned to science fiction writing in the early 1960s that it was partially out of a desire to find a publishing "niche"—a place which would allow you to publish the unclassifiable things you were writing at that time. But why this particular niche? Why not, say, detective fiction, or historical romances, or any other genre?

Le Guin: The answer to that is simple: science fiction was what bought me. The other genres weren't interested. Whatever it is that I write—this general, odd area which seems hard for others to define, although I know in my own mind what it is—didn't sell until it was given to a science fiction editor. Today my work sells in other areas, because once you get published it is easier to get published again and again and to enlarge that pigeonhole you've been put in. But in all honesty, my entry into the field of science fiction was largely a matter of chance or circumstance. It finally occurred to me that this kind of editor might buy whatever it was that I was writing.

Gregory: There's a story about your interest in science fiction becoming rekindled about this same time by your being given the works of Cordwainer Smith. Did that really happen?

Le Guin: Yes, I realized that if there was a place for him, there must be a place for me.

Gregory: What did you find in Smith that got you re-interested in science fiction? I understand you had been an avid science fiction fan as a kid but had given up the field in favor of more traditional forms of fiction.

Le Guin: Smith had a highly original imagination expressed in original language. His works were certainly much better than the pulp stuff I had been reading when I quit looking at science fiction back in the '40s. He is not a "literary" writer, but he knew what he was doing as a short story writer—in fact, he was an excellent story writer. And yet here he was, working in the science fiction mode. To me encountering his works was like a door opening. There is one story of his called "Alpha Ralpha Boulevard" that was as important to me as reading Pasternak for the first time and realizing that one could write a novel the way he wrote *Dr. Zhivago*. There are these moments in most writers' careers when you discover that someone else has actually written down some of these things that have been going on in your own head; you realize that this isn't just a private experience.

Gregory: Could you talk a bit about the effects your remarkable parents had on your writing or your imagination.

Le Guin: I find it almost impossible for me to analyze the effects my parents and their friends had on me. I wasn't exactly a dumb kid but I was such an unaware kid. I don't think I was as conscious of things going on around me as other kids might have been. I was a nice serious little Germanic girl, a good girl. I have always liked to work. I was very introverted. And I was the youngest and the only girl. My parents never pushed any of us in any particular direction intellectually. They wanted us to be intelligent, and to be intellectuals if we wanted to be.

It was important to them that we be educated people. This was during the war; my three brothers went away to the service, which meant that their education was all fouled up. I was the only one who had a normal progress through school. But my parents made absolutely no distinction between the boys and the girl. It never occurred to me that because I was a girl I was expected to do less or do other than my brothers. That was enormously important to my whole attitude. The intellectual milieu I grew up with was, of course, high-powered in a kind of easygoing way. A kid doesn't recognize how unique the situation is, because a kid doesn't have anything to compare it to. I thought that every kid lived that way, and had these impassioned, intellectual conversations around the table. To me that was just how it was, I didn't question it, it didn't seem strange. It was a very articulate family—my brothers and I were always encouraged to talk a lot—and there were books all over the place. It was no holds barred, as far as what we could read or talk about. There were also a lot of refugees around the house, and academic friends of my father. One Indian who always came and stayed with us every summer, Juan Dolores, was like a member of the family. As I look back on it, I suppose that was the kind of thing that must have influenced me later on. It's not every child who is lucky enough to have a Papago uncle!

McCaffery: I've heard the suggestion that the Napa Valley country place where your family spent its summers must have been one of the sources for your later wilderness settings. Did you and your brothers ever invent fantasy worlds while you were there, like the Brontë children?

Le Guin: Nothing so elaborate as that. We were a close-knit family and we did what most kids do when they play together. When, for example, my nearest brother was doing *Julius Caesar* in junior high, we'd do our own version at home. We did build some forts, and I had to be the Germans attacking. So we basically played the kind of imaginative games all kids play. When my brothers were off in the war, there were several summers when I was there more or less alone. This was a different experience, since I had the woods to myself. Entirely to myself.

McCaffery: When you said that you had the run of the house as far as books were concerned, it occurred to me that you must have run across a lot of mythology because your works so often seem fascinated with the myth-making process. And *Rocannon's World,* your first novel, was directly based on Norse mythology. That doesn't seem like a coincidence.

Le Guin: No, it certainly wasn't. My mother was the mythology book collector in my family, partly because she liked mythology and partly because she liked it for us. So by the time I came along (I was the fourth kid), there was a lot of my-thology around, mostly in kids' versions, but what's the difference. Beautiful big books with lots of illustrations. I plunged around in those books and in every-thing else; the Norse myths were my favorite. Sometime in here I also came across Dunsany's *Dreamer's Tales,* which proved to be another revelation. Dunsany was important to me because he was the first writer I had come across who wrote what I would call "pure fantasy." Today his works probably seem old-fashioned— I know my kids didn't take to him at all. He wrote in a Biblical-grand-Irish-Romantic language, a very mannered style. But as a kid in the 1930s, I wasn't so far from that early-twentieth-century mannerism. What I saw in Dunsany were these absolutely pure invented fantasies: a mythology that one person had made up. The idea that people could invent their own myths, use their imagination to the limit was a wonderful discovery.

McCaffery: So it wasn't just the mythic quality of the work but the fact that it was completely made up, not handed down but invented on the spot, that in-trigued you so much. . .

Le Guin: That was the magical quality. After all, that's the basis of our modern notions of the difference between myth and fantasy: in myth the story is handed down while in fantasy one person is inventing things on his own. This can be quite a revelation for kids. They use their imagination a lot this way—as with the stories they tell themselves or tell each other before they go to sleep—but they may not realize that adults engage in this fantasy-making activity and are will-ing to share it. Of course, nowadays fantasy and children's books have become an enormously bigger industry than they were in the '30s and '40s, so probably children often make this discovery a lot earlier than I did; it probably doesn't hit kids with quite the air of glorious revelation as it did me, an introverted kid who needed an *outlet* for a strong imagination.

Gregory: When I first read *Rocannon's World* I didn't realize that it was so elabo-rately based on Norse mythology. When you were conceiving that book were you using these mythic parallels more or less unconsciously or were you more system-atic about it?

Le Guin: Oh, quite systematically. I was still fairly young when I wrote that novel and rather uncertain of what I was doing—I thought it was science fiction I was writing, but now I'd say it's more a fantasy. I initially plotted it myself, but some-where in the building I began to see the parallels with Odin's adventures. So I thought, all right, I'll just use these parallels more systematically. Then I went

back and read Padraic Colum's Norse legends, *The Children of Odin,* and I stole
various things like the episode where Odin is standing in the fire—only I put him
in that stupid impermasuit . . . I was a beginner, and *Rocannon's World* is really
a beginner's piece. With the charms and many of the limitations of a beginner's
piece.

Gregory: I can't recall any of your other works using specific myths like this.
Le Guin: I never consciously borrowed in that way again, although obviously unconscious residues appear. I must admit that I'm made uncomfortable when a fiction writer systematically uses myth. Oh, Joyce's borrowing—one major writer to
another—is all right; but when writers base a fantasy or science fiction piece directly on some myth, there is often an intellectualization that trivializes both the
myth and the novel. I have tried to avoid that and get down far enough inside my
own head, where I can at least believe I'm creating while I'm writing. Later on, a
critic may get a look at what I've come up with, and point out some parallels and
explanations, and I say, Oh, that's what I was doing . . .

Gregory: Rumor has it that you wrote your first story at the age of nine and had it
rejected by John Campbell's *Astounding.* That's a pretty early start.
Le Guin: Writing was never a hobby for me. Writing has always been what I've
done. Actually, I was so pleased to be getting the same kind of rejection slip that
grownups did that I wasn't cast down at all.

Gregory: Did you take creative writing classes in college?
Le Guin: I took one at Radcliffe out of curiosity and a sense of duty. I'd said to
myself, Look here, you consider yourself to be a writer, now take a class in writing. But the class was a disaster. I got an "A" and all that, but I didn't belong there.
I was also very arrogant. Nobody could teach me nuttin'.

McCaffery: I was intrigued with your reply to the special issue of *Science Fiction
Studies* that scholars might do well to go back and check some of your critical
work in college which dealt with Renaissance literature.
Le Guin: I was being facetious with that remark. I doubt there's anything of interest in the critical work I did in college. I was training myself to make a living
and I knew I couldn't do it writing, at least not for a long time.

McCaffery: What I found interesting about that comment, facetious or not, was
that a number of recent writers, like Barth and Coover, have said that they went
back to Renaissance literature and studied it when they were starting out as writers. Both say that they found this area interesting for formal reasons—these pre-

novelistic, pre-realistic forms opened up all sorts of possibilities for them. The other thing that occurred to me is that Renaissance literature is filled with fantastic voyages, landscapes that fuse inner and outer states, and several other motifs that have found their way into your works. Did your immersion in that area have much of an effect on your work?

Le Guin: Undoubtedly it did because it was such a long and loving immersion. I found that I had an affinity with writers like Ariosto and Tasso, at least to the extent of loving their poetry. But my motivation was basically opposite to that of Barth's. I knew I had to earn a living but I didn't want to try and earn it by writing because I wanted to write what I wanted to write—not what some editor wanted. What I was most suited to earn a living by was scholarly work in literature, and so far as I was concerned it had *not* to be English literature, because I didn't want my studies to get near what I was doing with my writing. So I focused on literature in a foreign language from the relatively distant past. One of my hangups before I left graduate school was that I was going to have to take my orals in twentieth-century French literature and I didn't want to do that reading; I wanted to read only the contemporaries I wanted to read, not be forced to read anybody. In retrospect I can see that I was protecting my own integrity, my selfhood as a writer, against contemporary writers who might threaten me because they were doing what I knew I couldn't do, or confuse me by excellence into an effort to imitate. I was also trying to protect myself against an intellectualization of what I did. Being an intellectual, I'm extremely aware of the dangers of that. So what I did in school was turn back, in a sense, to an area of literature that seemed safely remote.

Gregory: So you weren't looking for pre-novelistic sources for your own works, the way Barth was doing?

Le Guin: Exactly. But of course what happens is that you do find sources, only you distance them enough so they don't overwhelm you. It is a matter of respect for yourself and for the older artists. At twenty-one or twenty-two, both my arrogance and my modesty as an artist led me to work with stuff written in a different language by people who had been dead for four hundred years.

McCaffery: I haven't found much information about Jehan Le Maire de Belges, the subject of your unfinished Ph.D. thesis. Who was he?

Le Guin: He was a fifteenth-century Frenchman. Just before the Renaissance. A little after Villon, who was totally medieval, and just before the Pleiade, the great court poets who flowered during the Renaissance. You can tell by his work that he knows something's coming, but he doesn't know what. I found him a touching figure in literary history—there's this young imagination trapped in the out-moded armor of medieval imagery and allegorical forms. Pivotal people are always rather touching. I think any artist will identify with someone struggling to get out of a cocoon. Of course, he never made it—he's a thoroughly and deservedly unknown figure.

McCaffery: Those allegories of Ariosto and Tasso were in some ways very futuristic with those fantastic voyages—they were almost like science fiction without the science.
LeGuin: Of course they didn't really have science to use. But they had a similarly disciplined imagination.

Gregory: Even in your early works that preceded your entry into science fiction—like the 1950s pieces that would later be incorporated into the *Orsinian Tales*—you were doing something quite different from the fairly narrow brand of social realism that most writers were pursuing back then.
Le Guin: That's maybe why I didn't get published during that period. When it comes to writing I do not think in abstract terms, such as, "Am I going to write a traditional or a non-traditional work?" I was in college when I started the pieces that eventually became the *Orsinian Tales*. I was trying to write fiction rather than poetry, which is what I was mainly doing up to that point, and I was stuck in that old formula that everyone always tells you—to write about what you know, what you've experienced. This is a terrible thing to tell an eighteen-year-old. What does an eighteen-year-old know? I remember thinking finally, "To hell with it, I'll just make up a country." And since most of what I knew came out of books at that point—I'd read a lot more than I'd done—I made up a place that was like the places in books I liked to read. But as soon as I began work in Orsinia, I realized I didn't have to imitate Tolstoy. I had created a place I could write about in my own terms; I could make up just enough of the rules to free my imagination and my observations. This was a big breakthrough for me—to say, "All right, I don't give a shit whether I get published or not; I'm not going to write for anybody but myself; I'm going to make these stories good by standards I set for myself." It was a step out of the trap of feeling that I had to get published right away. It was a step inwards that finally led me out.

McCaffery: The *Orsinian Tales* seem very "literary" in an almost nineteenth-century European sense.
Le Guin: They had a literary origin, as I said. I was soaked in the Russian novels from the age of fourteen on. I read and reread Tolstoy and Dostoyevsky, and it's

obvious to anyone who's familiar with their work that I've been tremendously influenced by them. Another thing important to Orsinia's development was that I
became aware politically. The first thing I really noticed and took personally, from
a political standpoint, was the invasion of Czechoslovakia in 1947 by the Russians. That's when I came of age, and realized I had a stake in this world. And of
course if there's any country Orsinia is like, it's Czechoslovakia. It's puzzled me
that everyone says Orsinia is like Hungary, but nobody mentions Czechoslovakia. Writing about Orsinia allowed me to talk about a situation that had touched
my heart, yet I could distance it, which was very important at that time. This was
during the McCarthy period, and you can't imagine what the McCarthy era was
like. Well, maybe you can, these days, because we seem to be trying hard to bring
it back. But in a political climate like that, one's imagination begins to look for
ways to say things indirectly, to avoid the polemic, the soapbox. You have to decide whether you're going to be a preacher or a novelist.

Gregory: Was *Malafrena* written during this same period?
Le Guin: I got the original idea for that book in the early 1950s but for a long time
it never worked itself out. I would occasionally find myself doing a bash at it, but
it wasn't right and I'd put it away again. I had eventually put it away in despair
when some editor asked for something, and so I thought I might as well have another look at it. I had to rewrite it almost totally. This time it seemed to work.

McCaffery: It's amusing that so many reviewers kept saying things like, "With
Malafrena Le Guin has at last decided to work her way into the literary mainstream."
Le Guin: I was surprised and amused as well. There are whole paragraphs and
passages which are very old and hadn't been changed at all. But there were things
I needed to rethink entirely. Getting the women characters right. Itale was always
okay, the men's story was easy, but I had a terrible time with the women. I didn't
understand them. I especially didn't understand what was happening to Piera, the
heroine. I know now why: I needed to become a conscious feminist to understand
why my women were acting this way and what was happening in their relationships. Without the teaching of the Movement of the '70s, I would never have got
the book unstuck. So although the general conception of the book was twenty
years old and bits and pieces of it remain intact, I can't say *Malafrena* was like one
of those books found in the bottom of a trunk; it kept coming out of the trunk
and being worked on, and then hurled back in despair. Until I finally grew up
enough to write it.

Gregory: In one of the science fiction journals, you list literary influences, but the only science fiction writers included were Philip K. Dick and Italo Calvino.

Le Guin: That's why I'll refuse to give you a list—there's so many people I'd be sure to leave out. Wasn't Borges on that list? How could I have left him out? What I've started to do when people ask who influenced me or who I like is to say whom I *don't* like. That list is much shorter.

Gregory: Well, whom *don't* you like?

Le Guin: I don't like Nabokov. I'm told I have to read *Ada* because it's a science fiction novel, but I can't read it. Boring.

Gregory: The reason I brought up that list of influences was to see if you'd say that your main literary influences were from outside science fiction.

Le Guin: I wouldn't say that. It would be silly. Obviously I have been influenced by science fiction writers in my science fiction books. If you're going to write science fiction, within even a moderately narrow definition of the term, you must have read it. If you haven't, you're wasting your time and everybody else's. There are several mainstream writers who have happily launched themselves into the sea of science fiction because they see what a glorious field it is; and since they haven't read any science fiction, they do things that were done forty years ago and have been done a hundred times since. A situation embarrassing for everybody. I've read a lot of science fiction and enjoyed a lot of it, been influenced by it. I'm an omnivorous reader, except for mysteries which I can't seem to get anything out of; I can enjoy a Harlequin romance. And, of course, only snobbery or ignorance apologizes for liking science fiction anymore, with writers like Philip K. Dick and Gene Wolfe around.

McCaffery: *The Lathe of Heaven* obviously owes something to Dick . . .

Le Guin: Of course. You could almost call it, "Homage à Dick." I was openly, I trust, acknowledging the influence. My approach was like saying, "This is one great way to write a novel, invented by Philip K. Dick." That's one thing about science fiction: writers in the genres are less uptight about imitation and emulation than "mainstream" people. Writing should really be more like music, with its healthy spirit of borrowing—as in the period of Bach, as in all healthy artistic periods. Everybody borrowing from each others' tunes and ideas like crazy and nobody worrying. There's plenty of music to go around.

McCaffery: After you listed your literary influences, you mentioned that music may have had as much to do with affecting your works as fiction. Music occurs in your works in many ways, both directly and, I think, structurally. Could you talk a bit about the way music may have affected your literary sensibility?

Le Guin: I made that comment partially because when people ask you for "influences," they almost inevitably mean literary ones. How silly. It's very probable that listening to Beethoven might influence a writer far more deeply than anything read, but only musicians are asked about Beethoven. The same thing is true, of course, with painting. We really ought to run the arts together more.

McCaffery: We talked with several writers who have made much the same point—that various media, like painting, music, television, the cinema, affect the way they think about fiction.

Le Guin: Right. These other media all shape your aesthetic sensibility, your intellectual perception of things. Most of my cognition is via art. I think as an artist. I don't think as a thinker. Very often I don't think in words at all. Cognition often comes to me visually or is heard. The trouble is that we don't have a vocabulary for talking about these things. But except for the very purest types of art, these various inputs are bound to have an effect on the creative process.

Gregory: Let's talk about the specific creative process that allows you to invent whole universes over time and space. For example, when you began the Hainish cycle did you have a grand vision in mind? Or did you just invent as you went along and not worry about consistencies, linking things up, until later on?

Le Guin: The so-called Hainish cycle wasn't conceived as a cycle at all: it is the result of a pure economy of imagination. I'd gone to the trouble of creating all these planets in that insane universe ("insane" because nothing alive can go faster than light), and had discovered that it's a lot of work to invent a universe. I certainly didn't want to do that work all over again; it would probably have come out pretty much the same since it's all out of the same head. So each succeeding book was placed in a different time but in the same universe.

McCaffery: So you never sat down and charted things out precisely, the way we assume Asimov or Heinlein did with their macro-histories?

Le Guin: No. My history is really pretty scroungy. I'm certainly not like Asimov, who I've heard has an office full of charts. Of course, when I'm writing a novel I'm very careful about that world. *The Left Hand of Darkness* and *The Dispossessed* both took a year or so of research and planning. I work out the details of the individual world very carefully beforehand. But I'm not very careful about the connections between the different novels. Those connections have never struck me as important; it's merely entertaining for people to have a reference here or there to other books. On the other hand, I created a very detailed map of Orsinia for myself, with all the distances; I had to know, for instance, how long it would take a coach-and-four to get from one place to another. That sort of internal consistency is, I think, important to most novelists. When you build a world you are responsible for it. You don't want a coach traveling too far in one day. I want these details to be right. They have to be.

Gregory: Was the map the first thing created for *The Earthsea Trilogy*?
Le Guin: Yes. At first the map could be adjusted to fit the story. This is the beauty of fantasy—your invention alters at need, at least at first. If I didn't want it to take two weeks, say, to get from one island to another, I could simply move the islands closer. But once you've decided that the islands *are* that far apart, that's it. The map is drawn. You have to adjust to it as if it were a reality. And it is.

McCaffery: Obviously you must have had to think about the geography of the universe in your Hainish works very differently than the more limited worlds of the *Orsinian Tales* or *The Earthsea Trilogy.*
Le Guin: Actually there's no geography at all between the worlds in those books; there's only time. The only thing that's interesting is when each book happened, whether events are taking place before or after other books. Time moves closer and closer to now, after starting way in the future. A critic was the first person to point this out to me. I hadn't seen it, nor do I have the faintest idea of why I've been developing the books in that way.

McCaffery: One critic suggests that you deliberately don't set things too close to the here-and-now to distance yourself and your readers from painful subjects. But your two novels, *The Lathe of Heaven* and *The New Atlantis,* and quite a few of your stories, are set right here in Portland—and take place not too far in the future. Is there any conscious reason why you might choose to use a real rather than an invented setting?
Le Guin: First off, that critic was on the wrong track. One thing I've noticed about my settings is that when I have something I really don't want to say but which insists on being said I tend to set it in Portland. *The Lathe of Heaven* and *The New Atlantis* are among the saddest things I've written, the nearest to not being hopeful, and they're both set right here. I don't know the reason for this.

Gregory: In your National Book Award acceptance speech, you said, "I think that perhaps the categories are changing like the times: Sophisticated readers are accepting the fact that an improbable and unimaginable world is going to produce an improbable and hypothetical art. At this point, realism is perhaps the least adequate means of understanding or portraying the incredible realities of our existence." Are you dissatisfied with realism because you feel the world is itself, in a sense, less "realistic," more fantastic? Or does this view have more to do with the formal restrictions that realism imposes on writers?

Le Guin: That statement is several years old. I made my comments aggressive to combat the patronization suffered by the fantastic arts and the critics' tendency to undervalue or brush them aside. My comments were therefore deliberately provocative—science fiction has been spat upon a great deal—and I was getting back at an attitude I deplore. Anybody who loves Tolstoy as much as I do obviously has a strong respect for realistic fiction. Let me pursue your question, since it's an important one. I do indeed think that at this point the world is in a degree of flux, is more fantastic than the world of the great nineteenth-century realistic novel. Consequently the description of what's right here in front of us can end up reading more fantastic than any fantasy. That's surely what Garcia Marquez is doing: simply describing what's happened. So in the National Book Award acceptance I was also trying to say, "Don't worry about categories, they're becoming irrelevant, or maybe have always been irrelevant."

Gregory: One other quote I'd like you to respond to: "Science fiction has inherent limitations which may keep it always on the fringe of the greatest potentialities of the novel." What did you have in mind there about "inherent limitations?"

Le Guin: That quote goes even further back. I was thinking of science fiction in a fairly narrow definition, the way it was conceived about 1967 or '68. I wasn't talking about fantasy in general. What I was driving at was simply that science fiction has certain inherent limitations because no genre is going to break all the barriers the way absolutely unlimited art forms can do. But I no longer believe first-rate science fiction can be categorized as genre fiction at all. Take Gene Wolfe's *Book of the New Sun.* He calls it "science fantasy." Is it science fiction? Is it fantasy? Who cares? It is a great novel.

McCaffery: But when you're at work on a novel, isn't it useful for you to make distinctions between science fiction and fantasy? *Some* sort of definition would seem to be necessary for the artist to know what the boundaries are, what can be done and what can't be . . .

Le Guin: Yes, I've found that I have to make certain distinctions of this sort for myself. When I failed to do this, as with *Rocannon's World,* I wound up with an uncomfortable hybrid between fantasy and science fiction. Later on I discovered that I personally do much better when I clearly separate straight science fiction, like *The Left Hand of Darkness,* from straight fantasy, like *The Earthsea Trilogy.* But that's not true for all writers, many of whom work very comfortably within hybrid forms. And as far as critics are concerned, even Darko Suvin's very intelligent attempts to create a classification system for science fiction and fantasy don't seem very useful.

Gregory: While we're on the subject of the ambiguity of labels, the importance of true names runs throughout *The Earthsea Trilogy.* This insistence seems a further extension of the idea in your other works that words are slippery and misleading, and that they can lock people into modes of thought that often are removed from the essence of experience. This view of language, which may have some connection with your familiarity with anthropology, must occasionally strike you as paradoxical since as a writer you must try to have language serve your purposes as precisely as possible.

Le Guin: I'm constantly struck with the paradox you're talking about. George Steiner says that language is for lying. What language is for is not merely to say that what I'm sitting on here is a "chair"—if that's all we did with language, what the hell good would it do us? Language is for saying what might be, what we want to be, or what we wish wasn't. Language is for saying what isn't. That is paraphrasing Steiner rather boldly, but I think it's a marvelous approach to the use of words. As for what it is that fiction writers do: I tell lies for a living.

McCaffery: You've said that *The Left Hand of Darkness* began for you with an image of Genly and Estraven pulling a sled . . .

Le Guin: No, it wasn't as particularized as that. It was just an image of two people (I didn't know what sex they were) pulling a sled over a wasteland of ice. I saw them at a great distance. That image came to me while I was fiddling around at my desk the way all writers do.

Gregory: At what point in your planning of *The Left Hand of Darkness* did you realize that the inhabitants of Winter were androgynous? They weren't that way in "Winter's King," the story that you based the novel on.

Le Guin: I didn't realize their androgyny until early on in the planning of the novel, long after I'd written that short story. At that point I was trying to figure out what exactly this novel was going to be about, what was going on, who these people were, and so on. I had a vision or mental plan and I was beginning to think about the history of the countries, that sort of thing. As I was going through this planning process, I realized there was something strange about the people on this planet—were they all men? At that point, I said to myself "These aren't all men; they're neither men nor women. And both. What a lovely idea . . ."

McCaffery: Have most of your books and stories begun with the kind of visual image that began *The Left Hand of Darkness?*

Le Guin: They've all begun differently. That image from *The Left Hand of Darkness* is a good one to talk about, though, because it's so clear. Angus Wilson says in *Wild Garden* that most of his books begin with a visual image; one of them began when he saw these two people arguing and he had to find out what they were arguing about, who they were. That fits in beautifully with the kind of visual image that started *The Left Hand of Darkness*. But the others have come to me totally otherwise: I get a character, I get a place, sometimes I get a relationship and have to figure out who it is that's being related.

Gregory: The sexual implications of *The Left Hand of Darkness* seem to have a lot in common with what feminists have been writing about. Were you much aware of these writings while you were developing your conception of what you wanted to do with that book?

Le Guin: This was back in the sixties before I'd read any of the feminists, except for Virginia Woolf. *The Second Sex* was out, but I hadn't read it yet, and the rest of the American feminists were just writing their books. *The Left Hand of Darkness* served as my entry into these issues—issues that all we proto-feminists seemed to be thinking about at the same time. Of course, if I wrote that novel today I'd do some things differently, perhaps handle certain issues more effectively and dramatically. But that's no big deal. I did it as best as I could at the time.

Gregory: A number of feminist critics, including Joanna Russ, criticized *The Left Hand of Darkness* for being too "masculine" in its presentation. How do you respond to that sort of criticism?

Le Guin: As I said, I was writing that novel back in 1967 and 1968, and we've all moved on a long, long way since then. When I'm at work on a novel I'm not trying to satisfy anybody who has a specific program they want propaganda for. I dissatisfy a lot of my gay friends and I dissatisfy a lot of my feminist friends, because I don't go as far as they would like.

McCaffery: You've mentioned in several places that you don't so much plan your books consciously as "find them" in your subconscious. Could you talk about what you mean by this?

Le Guin: I'm given something like a seed, a beginning. After that the planning, the intellectualizing, and the plotting take place. Let me try and make this process a bit clearer by going back to that vision that started *The Left Hand of Darkness* because it's fairly easy to talk about. I had this vision of the two people with a sled on the ice—that was the generating seed. Well, I already had found out a lot about the Antarctic by years of reading journals from the Scott and Shackleton expeditions; so first I had to figure out if that vision was occurring in that Antarctic. I realized it wasn't the Antarctic, so I had to find out where they were. And I had to find out who they were. As I began to find that out, I began to think: what exactly am I talking about here? Is this a novel? A short story? A novel starts relating to everything and getting bigger and bigger; if it's a story then it's self-limited and intense, it comes as a whole, so that I have to write it all down as fast as possible.

McCaffery: One of the impressive things about your writing is the way you work out the full implications of the premises of your fictions. I mean, if you have a world in which there are tiny people living in forests—as in *The Word for World is Forest*—then you carefully work out what the implications would be about these people's language, culture, mythologies, and so on. How do you proceed in developing these details?

Le Guin: It's fiddle, fiddle, fiddle, trying to get all the pieces to fit together. It's an enjoyable process, but one you can't work with very fast. What does it really imply that beings exist in a forest? Are they going to clear it? Cut it? Eat it? When I'm developing a novel, which may take two years of planning, everything's a constant jiggling and resorting and figuring out. This means a lot of note-taking for me because I forget details easily. I also lose notes.

Gregory: What kinds of "fiddling" were required in *The Dispossessed*?

Le Guin: That book took me the longest. It began as a crappy short story, one of the worst I've ever written. But I sensed that buried in that ten pages of garbage there was a good idea. I can't even remember now what the story was, but the beginning of the character of Shevek was in it; he was a man on a sort of prison planet. This was before I had done any reading of the Anarchists; but somehow that failed story led me to them. I read Goodman and Kropotkin and Emma and the rest, and finally found a politics I liked. But then I had to integrate these political ideas, which I'd formulated over a good year's reading, into a novel, a utopia. The whole process took quite a while, as you might imagine, and there were hundreds of little details that never found their way into the novel.

McCaffery: *The Dispossessed* seems different from your other books in that it presents a vision of society that you seem to want your readers to consider as an actual possibility. Can anarchism work on this planet?

Le Guin: First off, I don't agree with the distinction you're making—I'm completely in earnest in *The Left Hand* and others in the same way that I am in *The Dispossessed*. But in terms of anarchism, the problem is how to get there. As Darko Suvin has pointed out, all utopias tend to be circular and isolated. They tried an anarchist utopia in Spain in the 1930s, and look what happened there. The only trouble with an anarchist country is going to come from its neighbors. Anarchism is like Christianity—it's never really been practiced—so you can't say it's a practical proposal. Still, its a necessary idea. We have followed the state far enough—too far, in fact. The state is leading us to World War Three. The whole idea of the state has got to be rethought from the beginning and then dismantled. One way to do this is to propose the most extreme solution imaginable: you don't proceed little by little, you go to the extreme and say let's have no government, no state at all. Then you try to figure out what you have without it, which is essentially what I was trying to do in *The Dispossessed*. This kind of thinking is not idealistic, it's a practical necessity these days. We must begin to think in different terms, because if we just continue to follow the state, we've had it. So, yes, *The Dispossessed* is very much in earnest about trying to rethink our assumptions about the relationships between human beings.

McCaffery: You chose to set your utopian society, Anarres, in a bleak, harsh landscape. Were you trying to suggest that any utopian society is going to have to abandon the dream of luxury and abundance that we take for granted here in America?

Le Guin: The way I created Anarres was probably an unconscious economy of means: these people are going to be leading a very barren life, so I gave them a barren landscape. Anarres is a metaphor for the austere life, but I wasn't trying to make a general proposal that a utopia has to be that way.

Gregory: Your use of names has intrigued me ever since I saw your comment that to know the *name* of a person or a place is to "know" that person or that place. Could you talk a bit about the process that's involved in selecting these names? Obviously with a name like "Genly Ai," there must be a lot of conscious decision-making going on.

Le Guin: Genly's name is *Henry,* evolved in time. What happened to the "h" is what the Russians do, and then the "r" became "l." He first came to me as "Genly

Ao," but I thought that sounded too much like "ow"—as when pinched—so I decided this isn't right. This selection process sounds mysterious, but it isn't really.
One listens. You listen until you hear it, until it sounds right. You go: Eye, I, Aye,
Ai . . . and "ai" is *love* in Japanese. What more could you ask for in a name? When
something like that comes together, you grab it. But it's not really as if I chose it
in a truly volitional, deliberate, intentional sense. It's more as if I opened something and then waited until something came out. A box. Pandora and her box?

McCaffery: You've gone on record a number of times suggesting that the specific "meaning" or significance of the incidences in your works is unconscious. Yet
when one looks closely at your books, they usually seen extremely carefully put
together—for instance, the mythology or background sections in *The Left Hand*
seems to have been created with specific intentions in mind. When you're at work
on something, are you really not conscious of the specific implications you're developing?

Le Guin: The tricky bit in answering that question is what you mean by *unconscious.* What I mean when I say that I'm not conscious of certain elements
or implications of my work is that I don't have an intellectual, analytic understanding of what I'm doing while I'm doing it. This doesn't mean that I don't
know what I'm doing; it does mean that there are different modes of knowing,
and the analytic mode is inappropriate to the process of making. As the old song
says, "I know where I'm going . . ." I've got a good intellect, and it was fairly highly
trained, long ago. But the intellect has to be kept in its place. As the emotions and
the ethical sense and intuition have to be kept in theirs. For me, personally, the intellect plays its major part in *revising.* And also at the very beginning, in disallow-
ing an idea which is inherently stupid or self-contradictory. But once it's served
there, the analytic mind must serve other functions during the first draft of a
piece of fiction; it cannot be the controlling function. If I were thinking while I
wrote of whatever it is the Antarctic means to me, let's say, all those snowy wastes
that this California kid is always dragging her readers through, if I were thinking of it as a symbol of something else, let's say Snow is Loneliness or whatever—
zonk, I might as well drop it and go garden. And once I know what Antarctica
means to me, I won't need it any longer, and will have to find a new metaphor.
I'm not saying that self-knowledge destroys creation. I'm saying that for me, self-
consciousness vitiates creation. A writer like John Barth deliberately plays with
self-consciousness; I doubt that Barth thinks much of my writing, and I don't
take pleasure in his, but I know he knows what he's doing and I respect him for it.

But I don't work that way. My mode is not to intellectualize about what I'm doing until I have done it. And when it's done, I don't want to, because it's done and I want to get on with the new work, with what has to be done next.

Gregory: I'm among those who feel that *The Earthsea Trilogy* is your best work to date, despite being aimed at a young-adult readership. Did you approach these works differently, in any fundamental sense, from your adult novels?
Le Guin: *Earthsea* is the neatest of all my works. In purely aesthetic terms, it seems to me the best put together. When I started out I said to myself that I didn't see why this kind of book had to be different from any other, except for the commonplace that the protagonist had to be young, or there had to be a young viewpoint character. This viewpoint is simply standard for books slanted for the juvenile, but it wasn't hard at all for someone like me, who can drop back into adolescence without noticing it. After an initial self-consciousness, as soon as I began to see the characters and the plot, I wrote the same way I always had done. I don't know of anything you "do" for kids that is different than you do for adults; there's maybe a couple of things you don't do: there are certain types of violence, for example, that you leave out, and there's a certain type of hopelessness that I just can't dump on kids. On grown-ups sometimes; but as a person with kids, who likes kids, who remembers what being a kid is like, I find there are things I can't inflict on them. There's a moral boundary, in this sense, that I'm aware of in writing a book for young adults. But that's really the only difference, as far as my feeling goes.

Gregory: One of the things that surprised me about *Earthsea* was the way you explore the function of death in human life—I guess I'd assumed I wouldn't find that subject in a young adults' novel. And your exploration of death is done in what seemed such a sensible, reassuring manner. Was that the artist talking? Are you personally that accepting of death?
Le Guin: Not at every moment. Not many critics have been willing to notice that the view presented of life and death in *Earthsea* is not only non-Christian but anti-Christian. This can't be as reassuring as any view of death that includes a real personal immortality. But, sure, that view was written out of personal conviction. Sometimes the idea of becoming grass is pleasant, sometimes it's not. We all have our night terrors. Those night terrors are one of the things you can't dump on a kid. You can share them—if you're able to—not dump them. Kids want to talk about death. They are often more willing to talk and think about it than adults.

McCaffery: And of course a lot of fairy tales deal with death and violence, although usually in disguised forms.

Le Guin: Disguising things, presenting things metaphorically, is the way you generally do it. You don't force, you don't scream. You don't treat kids that way. The metaphor is the means and the end in one. By metaphor we may evade dishonesty.

Gregory: At what point in your life did you become interested in Taoism, whose influence seems everywhere apparent in your work?

Le Guin: The old Paul Carus translation of the *Tao Te Ching* was always on the downstairs bookshelf when I was a kid, and I saw it in my father's hands a lot. He was an anthropologist and an atheist; I think this book satisfied what other people would call his religious beliefs. He clearly got a great lifelong pleasure out of this book, and when you notice a parent doing something like this it's bound to have some effect on you. So when I was twelve years old I had a look at the thing and I reacted the same way my father had—I loved it. By the time I was in my teens I had thought about it quite a lot. I was never in the position of most kids in having to break with any church. My father was quite strongly anti-religious—his generation of anthropologists more or less had to be. He was respectful towards all religious people, but he counted religions as essentially superstitious. There was a certain feeling among intellectuals of my dad's generation that the human race was done with religion, that religions belonged to the past. That, of course, has not proved to be true.

McCaffery: Despite your disavowal of propaganda, your works can often be seen as responses to specific political and social concerns—the elaborate critiques of current political and sexual attitudes in *The Dispossessed* and *The Left Hand,* the satire of the arrogance of many scientists and politicians in *The Lathe of Heaven,* the Vietnam analogies established in *The Word for World Is Forest.*

Le Guin: Sure, I care about what's going on, and my books reflect these concerns. I just hope my ax-grinding doesn't intrude too much. Haber in *The Lathe of Heaven* is an almost allegorical figure of what I most detest in my own culture: people who want to control everything and to exploit for profit in the largest, most general sense of exploit and profit. He's the ultimate, controlling man. And Vietnam was very central to *The Word for World Is Forest,* obviously. I was living in London when I wrote that novel. I couldn't march so I wrote. I prefer, though, to keep my activism out of my art; if I can march downtown with a banner, it seems a lot more direct than blithering about it in a novel. When I was in London I couldn't do anything and I had an anger building up inside me, which came out when I was writing that novel. It may have hurt that book from an artistic stand-point.

Gregory: So you feel there's a contradiction between aesthetic aims and moral ones?
Le Guin: No. Art is action. The way I live my life to its highest degree is by writing, the practice of art. Any practice, any art, has moral resonances: it's going to be good, bad, or indifferent. That's the only way I can conceive of writing—by assuming it's going to affect other people in a moral sense. As any act will do.

McCaffery: How does your worry about "ax-grinding" fit in here?
Le Guin: That's different. By that I mean that I don't want to get on hobbyhorses in my fiction, saying that this is "good" in my works and that is "bad." That kind of moralizing is a bad habit and, yes, I wish I were free of it forever. Such approaches are always simplistic and are usually uncharitable. Taken as a whole, overt moralizing is not an admirable quality in a work of art, and is usually self-defeating.

Gregory: Science fiction seems to appeal to a lot of Americans today who are concerned about the things you write about, who feel that something drastic needs to be done before we blow ourselves up or completely destroy our environment.
Le Guin: We have to thank Reagan and friends for this mood, maybe. They've scared us. Poor Jimmy Carter, who was perfectly aware of what World War Three would be like, couldn't get through to the public. We let him do the worrying for us, and then blamed him for our problems.

Gregory: What happened to Carter seems to reinforce the point you make in *The Dispossessed* that even idealistically-oriented programs will inevitably become contaminated by the same power-structures they're fighting against.
Le Guin: That's what history, unfortunately, seems to teach us. An anarchistic society inhabited by real people. The imaginary garden inhabited by real toads. As soon as you get real people involved in something, no matter how idealistically motivated they are, everything is eventually going to get mucked up. With people, nothing pure ever works quite right. We're awful monkeys.

McCaffery: Is that why all utopias are, as the subtitle to *The Dispossessed* suggests, inevitably "ambiguous"?
Le Guin: I think so. Besides, I'm rather afraid of purity in any guise. Purity doesn't seem quite human. I'd rather have things a little dirty and messy. Mixed up. Mucky.

Interview

Irv Broughton/1988

From *The Writer's Mind: Interviews with American Authors, Volume II* (1990).
Reprinted by permission of University of Arkansas Press.

1974

Irv Broughton: When did you first feel confident about your writing?

Ursula Le Guin: I tried to publish from age nineteen on, rather lackadaisically and timidly. I was urged by my father into publishing some of my early poetry; he acted as my agent. He was then about eighty and leading a full life as an anthropologist. He said, "It's time you got something published; you're just writing for yourself, really." But it did become a necessity to me to publish. I began to realize that I must publish, I must communicate if I call myself an artist. When I was about twenty-six or twenty-seven, then I really made an effort to get published. But up to then my stuff wasn't terribly good, and I really wasn't eager to publish it.

IB: Writing is, for many, a process.

UL: Writing is simply a major part of the way I live . . . like having kids or being a member of a family or cooking meals. It's one of the things I do, one of the important things I do. But of course one tries to do it well, and since it's an act of communication, a public act, one is obliged to try to do it well because other people are involved in it. After all, the readers—you owe them an obligation.

IB: What about personal growth?

UL: Well, I started out writing poetry, then I wrote short stories, then I wrote novels—that's all part of growth. Novelists, you know, don't usually start until rather late. Some of them didn't start writing until they're forty or over. And I have also learned something, thank God! The only excuse for getting older is that you do keep learning.

IB: What do you think about the hacks in the field?

UL: Kill . . . kill . . . I don't like hacks. I don't like hack musicians, I don't like hack painters, and I don't like hack writers. I do take art seriously and I don't like people using it cynically. It really makes me very mad. Very mad indeed.

IB: Cynically?

UL: Yes, to make money out of it, to make fame out of it—using it as a device for their profit. Now very great writers do this, of course—Dickens used his art in that sense for fame and fortune. But to use it and *not try to make it good,* that's hacking and that's what I hate.

IB: What about writing as self-expression, pleasure? People are entitled to that, are they not?

UL: People are entitled to do absolutely anything, so long as it doesn't do harm to others. To write, paint, or play the fiddle—for one's own pleasure is a lovely thing, a truly human act. The difference between the amateur and the artist is one of degree, not of kind. It is, however, a very great difference. The difference between the amateur and the "professional" is one of kind, not of degree: it is an economic difference—the professional gets paid. That does not, however, make him an artist. It may make him a hack.

IB: Stanley Hyman did a tribute to his late wife Shirley Jackson and noted how surprised people were that the author of disturbing and grim fiction should be a wife and mother and an apparently happy one.

UL: Being a wife and mother is supposed to be a consuming occupation, therefore you couldn't do anything else. And then the fact that Shirley Jackson wrote the kind of books she did. I suppose people think: I wonder if she strangled her children.

IB: How can the science fiction writer be believed today?

UL: It may be easier to believe science fiction writers than it is to believe normal fiction writers, because science fiction can reflect this incredible, exorbitant world we live in much more faithfully than a novel which tries to pretend that the old social norms still exist, or that what happens in *Peyton Place* really matters. For example, one of the American science fiction writers I admire most is Philip K. Dick, and Philip K. Dick's world involves immense tracts of pure insanity. It's a world which is always in danger of falling to pieces. It is an accurate picture of what is going on in a lot of people's heads and how the world actually does affect us—this weird, disjointed, unexpected world we're living in now. Well now, Phil

Dick reflects that by using a sane, matter-of-fact prose to describe the completely insane things that happen in his novels. It is a way of mirroring reality. *Peyton Place* is a fine trivial example of non-realism. What reality is that reflecting? Nothing. A literary pseudo-reality where everybody goes to bed all the time with each other. It doesn't exist, you know; it has no relevance. It is escapism. Whereas serious science fiction is a modern literary device for handling this insane world we live in.

IB: A literary device?
UL: Yes, a tool fitted to the job. Like the right size of screwdriver.

IB: You consider yourself a feminist?
UL: Yes, I have all my life. A more or less unconscious one until 1974.

IB: How do you mean that?
UL: Well, in sixty-seven or sixty-eight there was no feminist movement. It died as a movement after the First World War. My feminism before the women's movement started consisted simply of the fact that I wasn't going to let any men put me down because I wasn't a man.

IB: Your book *The Left Hand of Darkness* was used a lot by the women's movement.
UL: It still is. Women's studies groups often read it as a textbook in a course or as a discussion subject for a group. Because one of the things I was trying to do in the book was to get away from stereotyped roles of manhood and womanhood. I did so by the "simple" trick of making the characters both men and women.

IB: I understand your initials got you in trouble.
UL: My agent sent *Playboy* a story before I was a well-known writer—as "U. K. Le Guin." They accepted the story, contracted for it, paid me for it, and then she told them that my name was Ursula K. Le Guin. So they wrote me a letter asking to use my first two initials only—I believe this is a direct quote—"Because many of our readers are frightened of stories by women." And I felt somewhat bound by the fact that my agent and I had in a sense deceived them; they had a right to continue our deception. I came to them as U. K.; they could present me to their readers as U. K. So I said, "Sure." Since then I have felt that, had the women's movement been going then, I don't think I could have done that in conscience. I would have realized that I was copping out. But at the time I thought it was funny. And I wrote them—you know in *Playboy* they have a little blurb about the writers in it—and they sent me this form to fill out. They wanted to know my hobbies, my

interests, and so on. Well, anything I said would give away the fact that I was the wrong sex. So I wrote for them across this whole space—"The stories of U. K. Le Guin are not written by U. K. Le Guin but by another person of the same name," and they printed that. I gave them an out.

IB: The women's movement has been helpful to you?
UL: It could help me help other people. I've never felt that I much needed help, because I had an extremely good start in life from my parents who simply weren't sexist. They weren't prejudiced for boys and against girls or the other way around either. They just set us all off on equal footing—sons and daughter. And so I have been able to hack it without worrying about it very much. But a lot of other people aren't. A lot of women, particularly, are hassled. They need all the help they can get, because they've been set off on the wrong foot and have to pretend to be something they aren't. And here's where you get the solidarity, as in any movement—any even slightly evolutionary movement. And then to allow myself to come out as "U. K. Le Guin" was letting them down, letting the others down; therefore, I feel bad about it now. And doubt I would have done it had my consciousness been raised a little bit.

IB: For a long time it was said that science fiction was going to do in the psychological novel.
UL: There are very few writers capable of writing psychological novels in any field of fiction. I don't know quite what you mean by psychological novels. You mean one where the characters have real emotions? Yes. Oh, it's being done in science fiction—occasionally.

IB: You've criticized science fiction for not being imaginative in terms of the social movements.
UL: In terms of society. The man-woman thing's a perfect example of it. In most science fiction until quite recently, women either didn't exist, or if they existed, they were these little stereotyped figures that squeaked. Or conceivably, the very ultimate possibility, there was an elderly woman scientist that never married and wore glasses. And that was fifty-three percent of humanity, represented either by absence or by these few stock figures. Well, this is not looking at the world as it is and society as it is. Then when we get into social imagination, we've thought up a lot of fancy hardware in science fiction but have not been imaginative about society. The society usually presented in stock classic science fiction is an extrapolation of free enterprise capitalism, or an extrapolation of the British Empire of the

1880s, and nothing further. There's no Marxism; often there's not even any democracy. This is American science fiction I'm talking about, by the way, not science fiction from the rest of the world. American imagination thinking about getting to another world. When they get there, they find a feudal society, they find an intergalactic empire exactly like the British Empire, or they find the Rotary Club. There's a current reaction going on against the squeaking female carried off by the monster, saying "Oh captain, save me." Some of us are using rather extraordinarily courageous, independent women characters.

IB: In the science fiction story isn't it difficult to have to set up a whole world and then people it? There's an inherent difficulty, it seems, in setting that great construct up and then making human people.
UL: Well, you may not be setting up a whole world. You may very well be using this one a few years in the future, but, yes, it's very difficult to write a real novel which is also science fiction. It's what I try to do, and I am aware of the difficulties. In science fiction writing, if your interest is technological, then your hardware's going to occupy so much space, you're going to be spending so much time on that, and perhaps on the social and political system, that it's hard to develop your people as well. Whatever your science fiction element is, it's always going to be rubbing elbows with the novelistic parts of it, and perhaps crowding it to the side so that there's a sort of combat going on within. It's hard to do, but I do think it's worth doing. I think some of the most interesting novels of the 1960s have been science fiction novels. And most of the least interesting novels of the 1960s have been non-science fiction novels.

IB: Why would you say that?
UL: What, the latter part of my statement? People talk about "the novel is dead"; well, it seems to me they're talking about what we in science fiction call the "mainstream novel," which does seem to be in a poverty-stricken condition at the moment.

IB: Have you ever written diaries or anything like that?
UL: I keep a journal—I think most writers do—where you write down sometimes thoughts, sometimes ideas, sometimes what's going through your mind. And when you'd like to write a letter to the newspaper—but it's too much trouble, you write it down, get rid of it.

IB: I heard a professor say female writers were, as a rule, more concerned with description than men.

UL: I don't think that's true. It's interesting that in a writing workshop or contest where authorship is concealed nobody can usually tell whether a woman or man wrote the story.

IB: C. S. Lewis talks about how science fiction separates from the ranks of the novel and sometimes becomes a new form which he refers to as a pseudo-history. He feels that there's the same quality of texture and so on—broad general movements and tones.
UL: That's very nice. That isn't true of all science fiction, but there's Cordwainer Smith with his future history, which was clearly worked out on paper and in his mind. He only gives you a glance of it in each story, but you get this exciting sense of reading a history of a people you never knew about, and it gives you this sort of resonance which a good history book does. The sense of space and time being large which is very exciting and beautiful.

IB: Is that what you like about science fiction?
UL: That's one of the things I like, yes. The expansion, the opening doors, instead of being shut in a small closed room. You're in a room with all the doors open and you can see the sky.

IB: Which do you think science fiction is more important in defining: the infiniteness or the finiteness of the universe?
UL: I don't know. I think I could argue both. I think one of the most interesting things science fiction has done and is doing, in Stanislaw Lem for instance, is showing the infiniteness of the universe and the fact that we are not going to be able to understand everything—that we cannot assume that our mind is of the same potential size as the universe. Lem thinks it's not. He thinks that we will not be able to understand everything no matter how long we go on with thinking and using signs. And he gives to me a most exhilarating picture of a fairly incomprehensible universe but a very beautiful one, which of course is what we all are faced with right here and now. Terrifying, but also beautiful.

IB: How much do you have to know about science to write science fiction?
UL: It is good to know something about at least one field, so that you know how scientists think and how science is done, if you're going to have any science or even any pseudo-science in your stories. But there is a requirement: that a science fiction writer be *interested* in science. He may hate it; I think Ray Bradbury hates it. I know he hates technology, and I rather think he hates science. But he's interested in it. It's got down into his subconscious and it comes up in the form of hor-

rors and monsters. But he takes it seriously. My main criticism of much modern fiction is that it doesn't involve science and technology, socially and in personal terms; in other words, it excludes most of the actual, physical world we live in, and the relationships of human beings to their world. By concentrating exclusively on people it becomes irrelevant to people. Whereas good science fiction includes us in the universe.

IB: Do science fiction fans get a kick out of finding flaws in science fiction writers' logic?
UL: Yes, the logic and the details, oh yes. If you make a mistake, you're going to get letters about it.

IB: Has this happened to you?
UL: It would have happened to me—now let me put in a good word for *Playboy* here. In the story that *Playboy* published, I had made a bad mistake in my genetics. *Playboy* apparently sent it to a genetics expert, because it had to do with cloning, and he or she caught this thing. And there wasn't time for me to rewrite the sentence, so they rewrote it and airmailed it to me and said, "Is this all right?" I said, "Yes, yes, of course, thank you!" That was neat. I appreciated that, because I would have got some angry geneticists on the telephone or something. "You got your x and y's mixed up, kid!"

IB: What do you think of the confessional kind of writing?
UL: I haven't read much of it because it is not my meat. The ego that fills the universe is very boring, really. The novels of the great writers are not confessional. They are deeply *personal*—profoundly individual.

IB: Do science fiction writers worry about being "scooped" by the morning papers?
UL: Yes, we worry, and unless one is very knowledgeable in some field, one is scooped. I wrote a book, *The Lathe of Heaven,* which involved sleep and dream research. Well, I was up on my sleep and dream research, fine. I loved to read about that stuff and I was well educated in it when I wrote the book. But I had a machine in the book called the "Augmentor" which had a kind of feedback effect to the brain, which augmented certain things the brain was doing in sleep. Then I found out the Russians and the Israelis had been using it for seven years already when I wrote the book, so I had to improve my Augmentor a little bit.

IB: Isn't it a dangerous occupation, that places everything on words?
UL: Yeah, it's a mug's game.

IB: It seems like there's at times a self-indulgence in some science fiction writing that's a little difficult to appreciate.

UL: You mean the wish-fulfillment type thing where you get the hero defending us from the alien fleet single-handed? Sure. And that's part of this hangover from the pulp days. It's also because an awful lot of teenage boys read science fiction. I think what a lot of the writers don't realize is that a lot of teenage girls do too. Those wish-fulfillment sort of things tend to be very male-oriented, and it turns the girls off a lot. I ceased to read science fiction partly for that reason—because I was tired of bureaucratic heroes.

IB: C. S. Lewis, referring to science fiction, once said, "If you have a religion, it must be cosmic; therefore, it seems odd to me that this genre was so late in arriving"—at the theological area.

UL: I am an atheist and I always have been; I have a great deal of trouble with C. S. Lewis, with the way his mind works. I don't really know what he's talking about. I admire the first book of his trilogy, as a novel. He was one of the first writers to invent alien creatures who were truly alien and truly sympathetic. I think those Martians of his are magnificent. And the second two books of his trilogy I consider an abomination, because he started preaching. I do not like to preach, or be preached at.

IB: What qualities of science do you find in yourself? Any?

UL: If I have any relation to the scientific temperament, it's probably some genetic inheritance from my father. I like solid facts and solid artifacts. I like to know about things, where they came from and what they are.

IB: He was in anthropology? What did he do?

UL: He was a professor at the University of California, a cultural anthropologist. He worked in Peru and in California and wrote some standard texts.

IB: Did you travel with him?

UL: No, he was in his fifties when I was born, and his traveling was mostly earlier. But we had Indian friends who would come and stay and many anthropologists circulating around, so I was fairly well plunged into anthropological life in that sense.

IB: How does this come out in your writing?

UL: Well, I think in the sense I just said. I'm interested in other cultures. I have this great advantage of not being brought up ethnocentric, of not being culture-bound. Of course, we're all culture-bound in that we grow up in one culture. But I grew up amongst people who spent their life thinking about other cultures and about the way others thought—different races, different people. I thought this was the way everybody was. The world came as kind of a shock when I realized everybody wasn't an anthropologist or an Indian and wasn't interested in facts and artifacts and the structure of society. All this shows up very clearly in my books. My father did the real thing; I make it up.

IB: Would you agree with Isak Dinesen's idea, "All sorrows can be borne if you put them in a story"?
UL: That's nice, and I like Isak Dinesen. Yes, but it is kind of a tautology, because if you can put them in a story, it means you're already bearing them. You are bearing them as a woman bears her child.

1988

IB: You spoke years ago of being in awe of poetry. Are you still in awe of poetry?
UL: Sure. I started out writing poetry. I've always written poetry. My awe of it is related to the awe I feel for music. Poetry partakes more directly of the irrational than most prose. It's uncanny. It's taken me a long time to find my voice as a poet. I feel I'm still and always will be trying to find it more clearly.

IB: What does your poetry owe your science fiction writing or vice versa?
UL: I don't know. I suppose one of the most useful things about writing serious science fiction or fantasy—repeat, if you're taking it seriously—is a kind of discipline. Things have got to be coherent if you're inventing a world, whether in science fiction terms or in fantasy terms. It's got to hang together. You're not relying upon the coherence of the everyday world to hold your invented world together, you have to do it yourself, and so this gives one a certain discipline in making sure everything does hang together in whatever it is you're writing.

IB: There seems to be a strong feminine thread in your poetry. It comes out in your novels, but also in your poetry. Do you think a poem is an extra good vehicle for that?
UL: I'm leery of saying that one chooses to express something in such and such a form because then you get into this thing of writing as self-expression which is a very low form of writing. I find myself tongue-tied, (as you can see) if you talk about "expressing"—as if one were an orange and the juice was being squeezed

out. As I have increasingly found my voice as a woman, thanks to feminism and feminist theory and criticism and feminine solidarity during the last ten to fifteen years, as I've been able to speak less as a kind of genderless object in the male mode and more directly as a woman and a woman writer, a lot of it has come out as poetry. It is one of the things that made me feel my poetry really grew up: I could write from the body out.

IB: Has feminism affected your self-concept?
UL: Yes, it's given me more confidence to be a woman. It has helped women be women and not just reflections of men, particularly, as Virginia Woolf said, "magnifying reflections" of men. And it's not easy on either women or men to have this new kind of consciousness, because men feel something is being taken from them, and that's true. When women refuse or cease to serve as "magnifying mirrors," men have to find their own self-image. So a lot of people have felt kind of frightened and lonely in the process of this—what you might call—gentle revolution.

IB: Your mother influenced you, didn't she?
UL: What the literary influence was, God knows. She started writing long after I did, but she was successful well before I was, so it was interesting catching up to each other. Women are often interested that a woman who had four children and was a classic housewife could start writing in her fifties and become a genuinely good artist and successful writer.

IB: Did you compare notes?
UL: She saw my work mostly when it was pretty near finished, because I don't show first drafts. She was the other kind of writer—she would show things that weren't finished yet and say "What shall I do? What shall I do?" and we would sit around and talk. Actually, what you do with that type of writer is let them talk about it until they see where they want to go next. And my mother sometimes did that. She had some very hard books to write. *Ishi* was terribly hard.

IB: Anything you learned from her?
UL: No. She was fifty—she was thirty when I was born—so I was finding my own way by then.

IB: How did it feel when she came to you to show you something?
UL: Oh, it was lovely. I mean, here we were doing the same thing, fighting the same difficult word battle and able to talk shop with each other. It was absolutely lovely.

IB: Do you ever second-guess an ending of a book?

UL: If you mean you think you know where a book's going and it isn't going there, it has happened. I think generally one learns fairly early as a novelist, particularly as a novelist because a novel is a commitment of a month or years to a job, that you've got to know the general direction of your work. If you start off without knowing where it's going, or with a total mistake, you're likely to waste several weeks or months and find yourself at a dead end, because it really had no direction in the first place. But one can make a mistake. My book *The Eye of the Heron* is a fairly simple science fiction story, a little planet upon which there are two colonies—one a bunch of pacifists and the other a very patriarchal and macho culture—a thought experiment. OK, we've got these aggressive people and these Gandhian pacifists, and both of them think that their way is right. Both of them think that they know what they're doing. All that seems very straightforward. What I didn't know when I planned out the book was that the hero was going to have to be killed by the middle of the book, and that he wasn't the hero, that the hero was actually a girl from the aggressive culture, only she isn't really a hero either. So the writing would go along for a while and then stop and I would be stuck. "What on earth? What's wrong? It isn't going right." And then I would have to painfully figure out what had to happen. And it really was painful that I had to kill Lev off, that he was insisting upon getting himself killed. It's a hard thing to do to a nice young hero, to a person who is, after all, a part of yourself. That is the one case I can think of where the book knew where it was going, and I was unable to accept it.

IB: Ever run into a hero or character you genuinely don't like?

UL: There's a voice character, a viewpoint character, in *The Word for World Is Forest* whose name is Davidson. He was a pretty terrifying voice for me to write because he's a highly aggressive, sadistic man. But then, he is part of me, obviously. I wrote him and accept him as part of myself.

IB: How do you find yourself dealing with that?

UL: I just let him talk. You're kind of inside his head and essentially you're listening to his thought so it was kind of like, "OK. That's how Davidson thinks."

IB: You're a political being.

UL: Aren't we all? I deny that I'm more political than anyone else. I happen to practice an art which lends itself to being clearly political—writing, an art which cannot hide its political grounds the way a nonverbal art can. I have to *defend* my politics more than a dancer might, for instance, or a composer.

IB: We live in a world of massive forces. Do you draw on these?

UL: Well, of course. To pretend that writing could be nonpolitical, could be non-motivated by the forces that move our society and our world—to pretend that is mere self-deception. To pretend that there is some kind of pure art that rises above politics in the larger sense, I think is a fraud. All art is political. And I think consciousness of this is a rather good thing. Unconsciousness, pretense that one can be nonpolitical, somehow escapes commitment, and I think that damages art in the long run. An example of this is the place of women in art. Take painting—the endless painting of naked women. This is not supposed to mean anything. They're just painted because they're beautiful. But, of course, it does mean something politically: It means we have a clothed man painting a naked woman. It means that women are seen as objects by men who are perceiving subjects. This is a good example of artists saying, "But I'm not political," and saying it in all good faith, believing it, but not admitting the fact that we are working within a politics of the relationships between men and women.

IB: Where did you learn to read a novel?

UL: I don't know. I've written all my life. I devour books. As soon as I literally learned to read I was reading narratives, and I do it continuously. To me, it's a central part of my being a writer—to read the same kind of thing that I write, poetry, narrative fiction, and nonfiction.

IB: Some writers speak of having trouble reading certain types of books when they're writing.

UL: Oh, absolutely. Most novelists don't read novels when they're engaged upon a novel because if you read a powerful style, it's going to derail you, either consciously or unconsciously. "Oh shit, I wish I could write like that." Then if you start doing it, it'll derail what you're doing, you'll lose your own voice. It has to be a pretty good book to do that to anybody as old as I am.

IB: Did that used to happen to you?

UL: Oh, when I was a kid, of course. I would read D. H. Lawrence and then I would turn out an absolute dreadful ten pages of D. H. Lawrence, or Tolstoy, or what have you, but only when I was a kid. The process of becoming a writer is the process of learning your own voice, and how to speak in your language, not somebody else's. It was along in my mid-to-late twenties that I began to get the skill to talk my own language.

IB: The concept of thought experiments is interesting. I guess it's a physicist's concept, isn't it?

UL: Yeah, right. I came upon that reading physics for peasants. I think Schrödinger is who I learned it from, in talking about his own famous quantum
thought experiment with the cat in the box. I wrote a story called "Schrödinger's
Cat." I won't go into the whole experiment, but it was obviously an excellent
metaphor for a certain kind of science fiction.

IB: Ever gotten so involved in mixing fact and fiction that at some point, maybe
for just a moment, you lose track of which is which?
UL: Well, one has a longing to stay in the book. This isn't only true of the book I
may be writing. It can be true of the book I may be reading. But I would say that
a genuine confusion there would be very dangerous and would be verging upon
lack of control as an artist. It's something that an artist would have to be careful of.

IB: I guess I'm talking about the magic one likes to be led by.
UL: Confusing the fictional world with the real world is really bad stuff. I've had
people who believed my novels and that's one reason I have an unlisted phone
number. They are confusing fiction with their lives, and their lives tend to be
somehow slurred by drugs and stuff. These people are frightened and sometimes
frightening. But there's another aspect to this. In a mystical sense, there is a su-
perior reality to a great work of art, to a real solid work of art, a very good novel
or poem, and that heightens one's ordinary reality. It makes life more real. We're
talking two very different things here. A mere confusion of fiction with life is to
me flying saucer country—I don't go there.

IB: You refer to yourself as "the most arboreal science fiction writer." Tell me
about this.
UL: Trees are interesting to write about because, particularly in the Pacific Northwest, we are so surrounded by them. They are these presences that many people
don't even see. They don't realize trees have different leaves, even. And here are
these lives standing silently all around us, amongst which we exist.

IB: We see icescape in your work. Ever go up to the mountains for stimulus when
writing something like that?
UL: I'm a Californian. My ice and snow is basically of the mind. I didn't see snow
fall until I was seventeen years old and went east. So it's always been magical. If
I'd grown up with it, I'd possibly despise it. To me snow is always a miracle, but I
don't need to go where it is.

IB: Talk about *Always Coming Home.* You invented a complete culture in that.
What was the day-to-day nuts and bolts of that? That was pretty exhaustive.

UL: Yes, it took a long time. I had to think myself into these people's minds—people who perceive the world very different from the way we do. It was a sort of mental archeology, mental anthropology. I couldn't just decide, "Oh, they think this and they think that." It was a process of growing it all together, because their attitude on one thing was going to influence their attitude on everything else. And that had to be *my* attitude because I was writing their literature. So it was a very long process of thinking myself into their skin. In this case, by the way, going to the place where it actually happens was not only helpful but probably essential. The Napa Valley's a place I've known all my life, but being there during the central four months of writing the book was necessary. I had to be there to be writing on that ground because it was centrally important to me that the book be grounded in real earth, real dirt—adobe dirt.

IB: So what was the hardest thing about it?

UL: Trying to put it all together. Trying not to leave things out. You know, a novelist's job is largely leaving things out. Getting the story flowing clear of all the junk around it—the river banks. Well, in this book, I wanted to include the river banks. Not only the river, but the banks of the river and the bed of the river and the trees over the river. So in some ways I had to unlearn everything I'd learned about writing a book.

IB: Wasn't *Always Corning Home* a kind of quest for self-knowledge? Did you feel it that way?

UL: No, I don't feel it that way. I just wanted to write that place. I wanted to write it right; therefore, it had to be inhabited by the right inhabitants. There are a lot of neat people in Napa Valley, but the present day agriculture is kind of criminal—it's all one crop. It's all high-money vineyard, isn't it? That's no way to use that valley. It's one way but not the right way.

IB: How long did the book take to write?

UL: Well, the actual writing was probably a year and a half, but the getting ready to be able to write it was three or four years, roughly. I was kind of getting my head in place.

IB: How did you do that?

UL: I don't know. It's underground material. It's what Gary Snyder calls "composting." You know, stuff has to go down inside of you, get into the dark and turn into something else, before you can use it in art. If you use raw experience, straight experience, you're doing journalism which is another discipline.

IB: Talk about the origins of the music tape that accompanied the novel.

UL: Well, I was, oh, halfway—better than that—through the book. I was long-ing to hear the music of the songs that I was able to write by then, because a lot of the poetry was obviously sung. I was doing a radio play for KSOR in Oregon, an original radio play, and they got some original music for it. And the guy that did it was Todd Barton, the music director of the Ashland Shakespeare Festival. Todd and I got on well and I liked his music, so I got up my courage and said, "Would you be interested in writing music for a nonexistent people?" And he didn't think very long; he said, "Yeah." And I could not have found a man better qualified, be-cause he's not only a good composer, but because of doing music to all those plays, Todd is savvy about any number of musical styles. So he didn't fall into the trap of writing music like anybody else—like the Javanese or the Koreans or whatever. He is sophisticated enough that he could develop a genuinely different musical style and a very pleasing one, I think.

IB: Did the music feed your writing?

UL: Yes, when we started working together, and of course, when Peggy, the art-ist, got in on it too. I was in control, I was the big honcho, because somebody had to be able to say, "Yeah, this is right. This is the way they would do it." Or, "No, I don't think this is quite right, you know." Somebody had to coordinate all our work—the music, the visual, the textual. And that was me. But it became very much a collaboration. Peggy's pictures would feed my sense of what things looked like there, and Todd's music would make me feel as the people felt. And I had to invent the language for Todd's singers to sing in. We couldn't have them singing in English. So very late on, essentially when the book was written, I had to go back and invent the language. I had until then been translating from a non-existent language. Then I had to make a partially existent language, so we could have our songs. That was fairly hard work, but fun.

IB: I guess! So that would be the hardest book to write.

UL: I guess it was the biggest undertaking.

IB: Did you ever want to actually *live* in one of the worlds you've created?

UL: No, no. I live here.

IB: Do you use dreams in your writing?

UL: I have done it. While I'm actually writing a book, I tend not to have very vivid dreams. It's as if the material were going into the writing. But I have started several poems and a story or two from dream material.

IB: For example?

UL: There are dream poems in a couple of my books of poetry. They are titled "Dream Poem."

IB: And the story?

UL: I don't know a good example. It would be simply something in a story that a dream helped me solve or see my way clear. Actually, rather than dreams, the most useful time, the really sacred time to me is between sleeping and waking in the morning. It's not dream state. It's waking state when one is still in touch with the unconscious, but the conscious mind is able to direct the seeking a bit. And that, that is my most useful time as an artist.

IB: Isaac Asimov says he isn't a good sleeper because he wakes up and starts thinking—writing in his head.

UL: Right. But I wouldn't put it that way. I'm a good sleeper, and I need sleep. But if I can wake really, *really* early in the morning and be undisturbed for half an hour or so, as I was saying, that is a very, very good thing. That's a time when a lot of work can be done.

IB: How many hours do you work a day?

UL: It varies enormously, but essentially all morning. From seven to noon is pretty much my real writing time. Letters and crap take up the afternoon.

IB: Do you ever get on a roll and go all day or all night?

UL: Well, since my children are grown, I can do that. It used to be impossible. You know, I'm nearly sixty, and I don't have that kind of energy anymore. Very seldom. I've been surprised lately that I *could* actually write all day sometimes, because normally three or four hours of real writing is enough for the day. But I have spent eight and nine hour days writing this year.

IB: I would think just creating the names that you create would be a full-time job for some writers.

UL: Well, that's just a gift, I guess.

IB: Did you used to make up a lot of names when you were a child?

UL: Oh yeah. I made stories with my brothers. We played narrative games with stuffed animals, with toy soldiers, or acting out parts ourselves. The way kids do, you know. And most of those would involve names.

IB: So how do you make up names?

UL: It's a process of listening. You have to just sit around and listen to it until it's right. Some of them come easily. If I can't get a character's name, then I know there's something wrong with the character, or with the conception of the story. And this is just as true in mundane fiction or non-sci-fi, or whatever you want to call it. In my stories that *The New Yorker* has been publishing, these are about absolutely ordinary people in an ordinary world, but their names are just as important. If I don't know that she's called "Jane," I can't write about her. It's the same thing exactly as making up an exotic or invented name.

IB: Do you ever change a character's name halfway through if you feel the character isn't going right?
UL: No. That's got to *be* right.

IB: Do you track your characters like a bloodhound, as Faulkner was said to have done?
UL: My characters are more within me than that. I don't know where I would track them to. This thing of tracking, as though something were going away from you and you had to follow it—that simply makes no sense. That has no resonance to me. The character is something that happens as I write.

IB: Do you take notes and keep notes and things?
UL: I write so many kinds of books; in some of them notes would be appropriate. For instance, in *Always Coming Home* I didn't know how many kinds of oak grew in California. I had to make a considerable study and indeed I took notes. It's a small example of the kind of research or reading that I did for that book. Educating myself to the flora and fauna and climate and geology of California, because I wanted to get it right. In a book like *The Beginning Place,* what would I take notes about? I know supermarkets and I know the imagination, and it takes place in the ground between a supermarket and Elfland, so there was nothing to research. Nothing to take notes about.

IB: In 1942 you wrote an origin-of-life-on-earth story that was rejected. How did you feel?
UL: At age twelve?

IB: You were twelve then?
UL: I was twelve in 1942. I was delighted to have a genuine rejection slip. (Laughs.) It meant I was a real writer, with a real rejection slip. At twelve years old, I think that was fairly natural.

IB: Did you put it on your wall?
UL: I had it for years. I have no idea what has become of it.

IB: The scientist in your stories is frequently a lonely type. Is that kind of a metaphor, mixing of metaphors with science, or is that kind of the plight of the artist to the lonely trade?

UL: I think my scientists often could be seen as artists, to some extent, when I was writing with male protagonists.

IB: John D. McDonald one time asked me a kind of rhetorical question which I think is interesting. He said, "Could the writer write something if they didn't think it was unique?" What are your views on that?

UL: Well, earlier you asked me something about "hacks." My response then was that a hack writer is a person who is writing something that they know isn't original or they haven't put their mind and heart into. And that's what makes a second-rate writer, or a "hack." To me, writing is my central way of being. It's the best way I know how to *be*. How to live my life. My life is my writing, so I'm going to try to do *my* writing, not somebody else's.

IB: Do you have a favorite story?

UL: No. Well, it's always the one I'm working on.

IB: One of your characters, Shevek in *The Dispossessed,* delights in the "verbal splendor." What is your view on "verbal splendor" as a writer? I mean, you obviously write with a beautiful flair . . .

UL: Well, I enjoy it. You know, that's a huge question, and you're opening a can of worms about a yard around. Are we talking prose here or are we talking poetry?

IB: We're talking prose.

UL: OK. I essentially grew up in the, I would say, Tolstoyan school of trying to make the writing transparent. The most important thing is that the writing be almost transparent, that the person reading the novel or short story not be aware of the writing as "beautiful," in the sense that that beauty brings you out of the narrative. The narrative is the dominant thing in the story. And clarity of style is probably the first virtue of style. I still believe this, more or less. But I've always had kind of an oral approach to my writing. I do hear it. I hear the sound of it. Many people go straight from eye to brain. I don't. That's why I'm now so interested in oral literature and poetry for tape and stuff like that. But it's always influenced my prose style in that if the sentence doesn't have a kind of cadence, if it doesn't read aloud well, it's not a right sentence to me. And the same with a paragraph. I can tell you the kind of writing I *don't* like, that might be more useful. Vladimir Nabokov—to me, his is not a good prose style. It is self-conscious, self-reflective, rather posturing, goes in for a lot of fancy vocabulary; it is always bringing me up short. I want to say, "Oh, stop showing off, Vladimir, get on with it." It's a rather intolerant position to be sure. But then a writer like Kipling comes to mind, whose style is very idiosyncratic, rather strange, and, particularly in his finest things, in some of the children's books, is deliberately rather splendid and very rhythmical and totally oral. I love it. Well, maybe because being a native English speaker, he did it better than Nabokov. Anyway, it depends on the writer how I respond to verbal splendor in prose.

IB: You first tackled a mainstream novel with *Malafrena?*
UL: First published one.

IB: Did that feel different to you?
UL: *Malafrena* was begun earlier than any of the other published books. The early versions or sketches for it go back into, oh, really just post-college days, I guess. I'm a little dim about it now. And I think one can see it's a very old-fashioned novel. It's written like a nineteenth-century novel because that is largely what I was reading, particularly the English and Russians.

IB: What do you owe Jane Austen?
UL: Endless pleasure. Years and years of delight.

IB: What did you learn from Jane Austen?
UL: A great deal about life.

IB: For example?
UL: I can't give you an example. You don't get fortune cookie maxims from a great novelist. You learn what life is like and what people are like.

IB: Gertrude Stein said, "I'm writing for myself and strangers."
UL: (Laughs.) That is nice. That is funny!

IB: You say you are anti-progress. Can you talk about that?
UL: (Laughs.) Did I say that?

IB: Yeah.
UL: I was probably driven to it. Anyway, thank you for the chance to clarify it, because "anti-progress" sounds silly. Sounds like destroy the machinery and return to the land with a wooden hoe. This is not quite my style. But the myth of progress, the idea that we *must* progress and that progress is continual economic growth and continual technological complication, oh, I think that is a very de-

structive myth that has long outlived its time. We need new understandings of
how we live in the world.

IB: Frank Herbert said something about time being literal in our particular
culture.
UL: I don't know what he meant. But in *Always Coming Home,* I was trying to get
a different sense of time than our clock-bound one. I wonder if he was talking
about the fact that we think time is a thing because we have the clocks to measure
it by. We think that our measurement of the process and existence of time, we—
what's the word—we reify it. I bet that's what Frank was talking about. And I was
trying to get clear away from that in *Always Coming Home.* To perceive time in a
more cyclical, bodily sense, than we generally do.

IB: He said there was this conception we held of the future. We refer to it as "the
future" as if there was *one* future.
UL: That's sweet. He had a lovely mind, Frank did.

Ursula K. Le Guin's Life and Works:
An Interview

Rebecca Rass/1991

From angelfire.com/ny/gaybooks/lefthandofdarkness.html#interview. Reprinted by permission of Rebecca Rass.

Ursula K. Le Guin draws a sharp line between herself as a person, woman, wife and mother, and herself as a writer. An introvert, she jealously keeps her private life to herself, shielding her family and her private self from the limelight.

In her entire body of stories and novels nothing is autobiographical. Her friends and family members will not find themselves in her books as is so often the case with fiction writers. Although the integration of polarities emerges as a central theme in her writing, it seems that hers is a sharply divided world between the private and the professional.

Her answer to my request for a telephone interview came in the form of a short letter, with a don't-call-me-I'll-call-you provision, ardently defending her telephone number as others defend their valuables.

Is this one reason why she writes science fiction, for the distancing effect that creates the maximum remoteness between Le Guin the writer and Le Guin the woman? Is science fiction the best way to guard her privacy? "I don't want to write autobiographies," she said once. "I want to distance myself from my books. That's one of the reasons I write science fiction. I write about aliens."

So I was truly surprised to hear a warm and melodious voice over the telephone. She apologized for not calling the day before as agreed. I was happy she had not called then because on the previous day I had joined other writers in a demonstration for freedom of speech concerning the Salman Rushdie affair. "Oh, that's what we did here!" she exclaimed. (Rushdie's novel *The Satanic Verses* had provoked Iran's Ayatollah Khomeini to order his assassination.)

Here was a glimpse of Le Guin the person, after all. It was typical of her, putting her writing aside and throwing herself into a social or political cause she believes in. In the 1960s she became involved in the peace demonstrations and campaigned for Eugene McCarthy and then George McGovern in their primaries.

Her political activities in the peace movement led to a short novel, *The Eye of the Heron*, and to *The Word for World Is Forest*, and then to *The Left Hand of Darkness*, considered by many to be her best work.

Her voice was pleasant and relaxed as we talked about the genesis of her book. "It all started when I began to imagine a society without war, a people that does not think in terms of war. They have murders and forays but never wars. What kind of people would they be? I thought. Obviously, they'd be different from us. But in what way? That's how I came to the idea of an androgynous society. As one character says in the book, war is a displaced male-generalized activity, something that men do and women don't." War, as she defines it in her book, is "a vast Rape."

Still, the question of why a talented and versatile writer like herself has chosen science fiction, a genre considered by the mainstream literary world as marginal, is still there. One reason, as said before, is her need to distance herself and her private life from her subjects. But as with all else in Ursula Le Guin, the reasons for her writing science fiction are complex and many.

At one time she explained that fantasy is the best medium to describe the journey inward to self-knowledge, because for her, the journey to other planets, to outer space, is a metaphor for the journey inward into the unconscious. This inner journey cannot be described in the language of rational everyday life, she said. Fantasy is the natural language for telling "the spiritual journey and the struggle of good and evil in the soul."

Perhaps the first reason for her writing can be traced to her childhood, growing up with parents who both were writers, scholars, and excellent storytellers. Born in Berkeley, California, on October 21, 1929, Ursula K. Le Guin was the youngest child of Theodora and Alfred Kroeber. Her mother, after earning her master's degree in clinical psychology, married, and three years later, with two babies, was widowed. Later she married Alfred Kroeber and had another son and her youngest and only daughter, Ursula. When her own children were having their children, Theodora, now in her fifties, began to write, making a name for herself with the biography of the sole survivor of an Indian tribe wiped out by North Americans, *Ishi in Two Worlds* (1961).

Ursula's father, Alfred Kroeber, was an anthropologist who spoke several languages and was renowned for his work on the California Indians. Even before she could read, Ursula would listen to her father tell Indian legends and myths.

This home was an excellent greenhouse for nurturing a writer, and Ursula, from an early age, enjoyed the best training in psychology, anthropology, sociology, and writing. "I had an emotionally and psychologically and intellectually very rich and very serene childhood," she told me. "I loved where we lived. I had a large, warm family. It was a place where a small girl could grow and flourish like a flower in the garden."

As a child Ursula read everything she could get her hands on: myths, legends, fairy tales. Once, when she was about twelve, she picked up a book in the family's large library, and while reading it, she was struck by the realization that people were still making up stories and myths! It was a decisive moment. She had discovered her native country and her inner lands.

In fact, she had completed her first short story three years earlier, when she was only nine. It was about a man persecuted by elves. A year later she wrote her first science-fiction story about time travel. She submitted it for publication but the story was rejected, and she did not try to publish her work again until the age of nineteen.

Instead, she plunged into reading, and there is no better apprenticeship for a writer than reading. She read mostly fiction, poetry, and science fiction, some of it trash, "because we liked trash." In her teens she stopped reading science fiction and did not read it for fifteen years, because it was too much about "hardware and soldiers"; instead, she turned to the classics.

She graduated from Radcliffe College with a major in French in 1951 and earned her master's degree in French and Italian from Columbia University in 1952. A year later she began to study for her Ph.D. and won a Fulbright grant to study in France.

Crossing the Atlantic on the *Queen Mary*, she met her future husband, Charles Le Guin, a professor of French history. Their marriage in Paris signaled the end of her doctoral studies and the beginning of a long and happy family life which later included two daughters and a son. In 1959 Charles was assigned to teach history at Portland State University, and the family has lived in Portland, Oregon, ever since.

Giving up her work on the doctorate allowed Le Guin more time to write. She kept writing and watching her drawers fill up with manuscripts and rejection slips. In ten years she had written, aside from poetry, five novels, some about a fantasy country in Central Europe named Orsinia, but none was accepted for publication. It became for her a matter of "publish or perish." Her fantasies did not fit any existing category, and if she wanted to publish she would have to find an acceptable form. She began to write science fiction.

Le Guin admits that her "first efforts to write science fiction were motivated by a pretty distinct wish to get published." Not having much hard-core scientific knowledge she wrote "fairy tales decked out in space suits." It paid: she got them published. She was thirty-two when she managed to sell her first story, "April in Paris," to *Fantastic* magazine (1962). Her first science-fiction novel to be published was *Rocannon's World* (1966). This signaled the beginning of a brilliant career that has produced science-fiction stories and novels, children's and young adults' books, essays and poetry. "I have cut across so many boundaries that the critics don't know what to do with me," she laughs over the phone. "I write in so many categories."

Two more science-fiction novels, *Planet of Exile* (1966) and *City of Illusions* (1967), followed almost immediately, but her real success came with the publication of *A Wizard of Earthsea* (1968) which won the prestigious Globe-Hornbook Award for Excellence. With the award came national recognition. Then, *The Left Hand of Darkness* (1969) won both the Hugo and Nebula Awards, and when her novel *The Dispossessed* (1974) appeared and also won the Hugo and Nebula, Le Guin became the first science-fiction writer to have won both awards twice.

It would take too long to list all her books and stories and all the awards and prizes she has won. Just reaching her sixties, Le Guin no doubt will continue to add considerably to both lists.

Many feminists have complained that Ursula Le Guin's characters are predominantly male, and even her Gethenians, the people on planet Winter, who are both men and women in one, appear to be basically male. However, her own life can serve as a model of the successful, modern, sophisticated, and liberated woman who has managed a brilliant career, successful marriage, and motherhood, without sacrificing any of them.

"When the kids were babies I wrote at night, from nine to eleven or as long as I could stay awake. Then, as they began school, I had the whole schoolday to work; I felt as if I grew wings. Now, I try to work in the morning, from about seven to two."

She could manage her writing because of the steady support of her husband. Theirs was a partnership with "mutual aid as its daily basis." They divided the work conventionally: she, the house, the kids, the cooking, the novels; he, the teaching, the bills, the car, the garden. When she needed help, he gave it "without making it into a big favor"; when she wanted to complete a story, he would take the kids. "He never begrudged me the time I spent writing, or the blessing of my work." It is difficult for one person to do two full-time jobs but two people can do three full-time jobs, she said. "That's why I'm so strong on partnership. It can be a great thing."

No wonder that love, bonding, and intimate relationship take such a significant place in all her work! This is the one idea that overrides everything else in *The Left Hand of Darkness*. Moreover, in this book she carries the idea even further and maintains that true love between individuals must precede, and is the only basis for, national, international, or universal relations.

"Does your happy and fulfilled life refute the notion that a writer has to suffer in order to write?" I asked her. This made her burst out in peals of laughter. "I think that this notion seems to suit men wonderfully well. They love to smite their brow with their hand and say, 'Oh, how I suffer,' while some woman is actually doing all the work. I'm quite leery of this idea. I think writing is quite hard enough work without complaining about all the rest. I get impatient with Conrad or Flaubert who, while complaining, were actually being looked after very nicely. They were not really handling the complicated part of life that any woman has to handle if she has responsibilities for the household or of getting the meals. You know, as I watch women writers, I see them cope with it all along with their art, and we are talking here about real work, not psychological suffering."

Le Guin seems to have been blessed with a happy family life as a child and as an adult. Yet in her novels and essays she refers again and again to pain and suffering as a necessary price for happiness. In *The Left Hand of Darkness*, the moment Ai gains profound love he also loses it. Where had her experience of sorrow come from? I wondered.

There was silence at the other end of the line, and I wondered whether she was thinking the question over or looking for ways to avoid touching upon her private life. "I guess," she finally said, "one carries in oneself a tragic sense of life. If you believe, as I do, that the great tragedies, such as Sophocles' or Shakespeare's, were the truest things ever written, then you know that what is within our grasp is essentially tragic."

In *The Left Hand of Darkness* she wrote that the only certainty a person has is his mortality, the knowledge that he is going to die.

"Yes. No matter how lucky one can be, there is considerable suffering involved in being alive, in being human."

"There is a strong sense of inescapable tragedy in your book," I said.

"I agree. I realize that underneath everything I write there is this sense of the tragic. This is the way I'm made, how I see life. It doesn't mean I don't appreciate life. I see much of my writing, but mainly my poetry, as celebration and I like writing which is celebration."

We resumed talking about the genesis of the book. "A book like that," she said, "doesn't have any single beginning. As I mentioned before, first I had the idea of creating a society without war. This led me to the androgynous society. Then I had the characters. And as the characters began to interact I began to see the plot. I saw two people dragging a sledge across the ice."

"My favorite part in the book," I commented.

"Mine, too," she said enthusiastically. "I had to do a great deal of work before I began writing. I had to figure out how an androgynous society actually works. Also, I had to do a good deal of reading about living in a very cold climate."

"I never quite understood," I admitted, "how the bitter cold climate on Winter, which features so prominently in the book, is connected with the idea of androgyny?"

"I have no idea," came her clear answer. "One of those underground connections, I guess. I can probably explain it less well than a critic. I don't think it is particularly linked to the sexual issue. The link in my mind is to loneliness, Ai's loneliness for being one of his kind on the planet, and to Estraven's, because he has isolated himself. This is a story of extremely lonely people coming together, and the cold accentuates, and reflects their loneliness. Before I began writing I read *Winter in Finland*, which was very helpful. I wanted to know what one does when it's 30 below zero for a month!

"Also, I read what I could concerning the special sexuality of the people on the planet. I checked out human sexual physiology, but to tell you the truth, I didn't have the courage till after the book was printed, to take it to a doctor and ask: Is this plausible? It was our pediatrician. He read it and he gave it back to me, saying it's plausible but it's disgusting!" (She laughed merrily). "I thought it was charming. 'Yes, it did work,' he said, 'you did it pretty convincingly.'

"I also had to write the history of both countries on the planet Winter. It's not in the book, but it underlines it. How did the two countries get to where they are now? Why are they as they are?"

"In your article 'Is Gender Necessary?' you write that *The Left Hand of Darkness* is not about gender but about betrayal and fidelity—"

"Have you seen the revised article?" she interrupted excitedly. "This is very important for me. I have a new book that just came out, *Dancing at the Edge of the World*, and in that you'll find a revised version. Nothing has been changed in the text, but notes and comments have been added, where I disagree violently with some of the things I myself have said there. I have become a much stronger feminist and my thinking is considerably clearer since I wrote the book, which was itself part of my becoming a feminist."

Several essays in *Dancing at the Edge of the World* present strong and clear feminist statements. In "Woman / Wilderness" Le Guin criticizes civilization for leaving out the experience of women as women, an experience unshared with men. "The misogyny that shapes every aspect of our civilization," she wrote, excluded "the being of women." Another essay, "Prospects for Women in Writing" ends with a strong proclamation and a feminist commitment: "To keep women's words, women's works, alive and powerful—that's what I see as our job as writers and readers for the next fifteen years, and the next fifty."

A major flaw in *The Left Hand of Darkness*, as Le Guin herself came to admit and as many of her critics expressed, is, as she says, "that the Gethenians seem like men, instead of men-women." This flaw is mainly the result of her use of the masculine pronoun "he." While Le Guin is very imaginative in her use of language—in inventing names and places and landscapes that do not exist—in this novel she has used a quite traditional grammatical structure which, in English, is strictly divided along masculine-feminine lines. Reluctant to invent a new pronoun to herald the new age of human beings, equal in life and in language (it would drive the reader mad, she claimed), she preferred to use the masculine pronoun, which, in many ways, negated the main idea in the book.

It is strange, even inexplicable, that even at times when she could have used the neuter "people" or "human being" or "person" or "child" or "youth," she stubbornly has used explicitly male words such as "man" and "son." Even the woman investigator in *The Left Hand of Darkness* admits that "the very use of the pronoun in my thoughts leads me continually to forget that the Karhider I am with is not a man, but a manwoman." And if the woman reporter who meets the Karhiders face to face prefers to call them "he" and not "she," one may conclude that, as Le Guin presents them, they do resemble men. This greatly diminishes the overall impact of the original idea of a sexless society.

It is interesting to note that the Gethenians, who can be both mother and father, feel closer to the children "of their flesh," those to whom they actually gave birth. Estraven writes to his son of the flesh but does not mention the other two children he has fathered. Likewise, King Argaven of Karhide, although he fathered seven children, is especially fervent about giving birth to a child of his flesh even at great risk to himself because of his age. Is Le Guin saying that the mother-child relationship is stronger than the father-child's?

Le Guin's recently revised article, "Is Gender Necessary? Redux" is her clear recognition of her flawed treatment of gender in *The Left Hand of Darkness*. She tells me, "I wrote the original article in reaction against the kind of criticism that was bothering me very much because I was about to begin to agree with it; so I was quite defensive, and then my defenses broke down and I said, No, they are right. Estraven appears to be a man, I shouldn't have used the male pronoun. And then I revised the article."

"Have you ever considered revising *The Left Hand of Darkness*?" I asked her.

"I think that this would be almost impertinent. You have to let the whole work stand. You made a mistake, it's your mistake, then you go on and do better. I've had two opportunities to work on that. One is the short story directly related to *The Left Hand of Darkness*. I wrote it first then revised it for later publication."

The story she is talking about is "Winter's King," written about a year before *The Left Hand of Darkness*, and it concentrates on King Argavan of Karhide on Planet Gethen. In her first version of the story there is no mention of the ambisexual society. This idea came later and was incorporated in *The Left Hand of Darkness*. However, in response to the strong criticism of the use of male pronoun in the book, Le Guin revised "Winter's King," using the feminine pronoun for all Gethenians, while keeping the masculine titles such as King and Lord, to remind the reader of the ambiguity.

"The second opportunity I had was in the writing of the screenplay for *The Left Hand of Darkness*," she explained. "I've made up a pronoun. I referred to Gethenians not pregnant or in kemmer by the invented pronoun 'a' (pronounced "uh") in the nominative case, 'a's' in the possessive case. I thought, 'Since it was to be used only for dialogues, you can do it without driving people mad.' You see, this is the main trouble with made-up pronouns, to read a whole novel with something in place of he or she is just not possible. Actually, "they" used to be the English genderless pronoun until the seventeenth or eighteenth century, when the grammarians declared the 'he' was the generic, but it's quite arbitrary. In colloquial English we all still say, 'Anybody missing a notebook, will they stand up?' We say it all the time. But I couldn't refer to Estraven throughout the book as they. I did try to put in a made-up pronoun, but it leapt out of every sentence."

"Still, there are many times in the book that you wrote man or son, when you could easily have said people or children."

"Yes, over and over. There are many places I'd like to revise in that sense. I masculinized the book most unnecessarily. I agree with you. It gives me consider-

able pain now to see how easily I could have degendered it. But I feel a moral com-
punction about revising an old book."

"In this particular case, revision might well be a creative adventure," I suggested.

"It would be fun to try, I admit. The trouble is that the book has been in print
ever since it was published; there has never been a time when it dropped out of
print, when I could have done something about it."

"The name Ai, for the Envoy from Earth, carries triple meanings. But what
about all the other invented names in the book?"

"No, they don't carry any meaning. They were picked purely for sound. Like a
musical phrase."

"Except Argaven, maybe. I found him to be very aggravating."

She burst out laughing. "Oh, I never thought of it," she said in her sing-song
voice. "In 'Estraven' people heard 'estrogen,' which embarrasses me. Isn't that awful? Estraven is from Estre. So I thought, Estre-van, coming from Estre, what a
pretty name, I liked the sound of it. It's purely aesthetic, my name making-up."

"Do you play music?"

"Well, not much, I played the recorder. But I've a musical daughter."

"I was surprised to find so few reviews of *The Left Hand of Darkness*, a book
which had won two major science-fiction awards, in the mainstream press. Does
the press ignore science fiction now as much as it used to?"

"Very nearly. The newspapers, if they review science fiction at all, tend to put it
in a little corner called sci-fi, you know. Since 1969, when the book appeared, the
academics are paying much more attention to science fiction. And we do get articles, some highly intelligent, some very academic, but they too appear only in
very specialized publications. But just ordinary newspapers, no; science fiction is
still ghettoized pretty consistently.

"What has also changed is that since the early '70s, when the whole English
curriculum was opening up, many science-fiction courses are taught in schools.
High school teachers have discovered that science fiction is a wonderful way to
get high school kids to read and talk about what they have read. The Russians discovered it long before we did; they have been using science fiction as a teaching
device for decades."

"Does it bother you," I asked her, "that you are categorized as a science-fiction
writer and thus excluded from what is generally considered 'literature'?"

"This is a very complicated issue," she said. "I object very strongly to the genrefication of literature. There is an assumption that everything called genre is secondary. This is simply untrue. Are writers such as Marquez, Borges, or Calvino automatically second-rate because they aren't writing realistic literature or mainstream fiction?

"On the other hand, there is marketing. In order to get the books to the interested public, libraries, and bookstores, publishers need categories. And there is another aspect. As a writer of a despised genre, you have a kind of freedom. You are not nagged by the academics and critics, you can do whatever you please. In some ways I do feel trapped when I'm called a science-fiction writer, and in other ways I feel delighted. On the whole, I think that boundary lines are changing, although conservative people don't want to admit it."

"Any advice for a young science-fiction writer?"

"Read, and read the best. One doesn't have to have scientific knowledge. My science background is pretty minimal, but I was brought up to have a healthy respect for science, for I was a daughter of a scientist. If I need to know anything for my story, I go to the library and read about it. I think that most science-fiction writers work this way.

"Science fiction begins at the moment where science ends, and then you can go on and build on what is known. Therefore, science fiction is getting more and more difficult to write because science develops so fast that the science-fiction writer has difficulty coping with it. This is one reason why there is less and less technological science fiction written because technology has overtaken it. It's different if you use social science, as I do, because social science is very slow moving and the writer is much freer."

Is Le Guin romantic? No doubt. If a political mission depends on a love relationship between two individuals, as is the case in *The Left Hand of Darkness,* Le Guin is certainly a romantic. We all know that this is not the way politics is done; that in reality human relationships are sacrificed for political goals. But as Le Guin writes in her introduction to the book, she deals with "what if," not with "what is." We are surrounded by "as is"; we need to speculate on alternatives that are rewarding and stimulating, even if they remain in the domain of "thought-experiment."

I Am a Woman Writer, I Am a
Western Writer: An Interview with
Ursula Le Guin

William Walsh/1993

From *Kenyon Review* 17 (Summer/Fall 1995). Reprinted by permission of William Walsh.

Ursula Le Guin is America's preeminent writer of science fiction. However, one should not be confused and call her only a science fiction writer, because—as she will tell you—since the publication of her first novel, *Rocannon's World* (Ace Books, 1966), she has published more than fifteen novels, four collections of poetry, five short story collections, seven books for children, two books of criticism, screenplays, edited anthologies, and she has made a half dozen recordings. She has published more than sixty short stories in the *New Yorker, Tri-Quarterly, Kenyon Review, Omni, Redbook, Playboy,* and *Playgirl.* Her most recent books are *Going Out with Peacocks,* a book of poems from HarperCollins, *Wonderful Alexander and the Catwings,* a book for children from Orchard Press, and *A Fisherman of the Inland Sea,* a book of science fiction short stories from HarperPrism.

In 1972 Le Guin won the National Book Award for *The Farthest Shore.* In addition to being a five-time winner of the Hugo Award and a four-time Nebula Award winner, her other honors include a Newbery Silver Medal Award, a Pushcart Prize, the Prix Lectures-Jeunesse, the Gandalf Award for fantasy writing, and the Boston Globe-Hornbook Award. She holds a B.A. from Radcliffe College (1951) and an M.A. from Columbia (1952), and has taught at, among others, Mercer University, University of Idaho, Kenyon College, Portland State University, Tulane University, and Bennington College.

Born in 1929, in Berkeley, California, she spent most of her life on the West Coast, and currently lives in Portland, Oregon, with her husband, Charles A. Le Guin, a historian. Her father was anthropologist Alfred Kroeber, and her mother, Theodora Kroeber, published *Ishi,* a national best-seller.

This interview was conducted in Macon, Georgia, on 30 March 1993. It was a sunny and breezy morning as we sat outside in her mother's backyard in the shade—talking and drinking coffee.

WW: During the introduction of your reading last week, you mentioned the labels placed on writers by critics as well as the deficiency of the canon in regard to women. I would like to address both of these issues. First, I have read endlessly where you are considered a science fiction writer, and often that's the only category. I never thought of you in that single category because I first came to your essays. Do you find the categories limiting and how do you deal with this?

UL: Right from the start I've always written other material. I started out publishing poetry long before I published prose. I've never been known as a poet, and I'm always having to tell people I have four volumes of poetry, two of them hardback. So, OK, I'm mainly a prose writer—that's fine. The first two stories I published were within a couple of months, one was science fiction and one was realism. One was in a science fiction magazine and the other was in a university quarterly. One, according to the wisdom of the time, was respectable and the other was not respectable. But it's not the respectable genre that I get categorized in. There is something very strange about the whole process. I've always written realistic fiction, science fiction, fantasy, and books for kids, but the category that sticks is science fiction. I do write science fiction. Some of my books and stories are pure science fiction—I love the stuff. It's one of the things I do. There is something funny about this categorization—you get typecast like some actors. Poor Leonard Nimoy—nobody believes he has round ears. I began to see it as something not in relation to myself but this whole modernist, mid-twentieth-century idea of a canon in English literature, which, in fiction, is strictly realism, and everything else is subliterary, nonliterary. Maybe that was true in 1925, but it's just not true now. There is no way you can say that realism is the only literature going. I mean, most of our best novelists are not even writing realism anymore—writers like Toni Morrison, Gloria Naylor, Leslie Silko. They are using realistic techniques to tell stories that are not realistic.

WW: The fact is that it's very easy to categorize writers into genres and subgenres. . . .

UL: It's a neat way of sweeping things under the carpet, particularly for the academics and the more narrow-minded reviewers. Book reviewers are terrible about this. Take my book *Always Coming Home,* or Karen Fowler's *Sara Canary,* which is a knockout book—if they can perceive those books as science fiction they'll sweep them under the science fiction rug and then they don't have to deal with them. Several reviewers have done that. *Sara Canary* is a good case in point because some people think it's science fiction and some people don't. There's a character who you can see as an alien if you want, but she may not be an alien at all, just a woman. It's a kind of litmus paper novel.

I don't know why there is so much arrogance toward science fiction. People have come up to me and said, "You write sci-fi. My children read that." What am I supposed to say, "Isn't that wonderful! Of course, you're a grown-up and you don't read it." (laughing) There is equal or more arrogance toward writing for children. Often people say when they find that I write children's books, "I've thought of doing that" as if I'd go up to a dancer and say that I thought about ballet in my spare time. It's incredibly arrogant. Children's literature is as tight a discipline as writing poetry.

Another thing about science fiction and fantasy, you can't use the same critical apparatus to read it if you are seriously reviewing a book or teaching a book. For this you need some different techniques for understanding. In other words, you have to learn how to read a science fiction book.

WW: What would these techniques be?
UL: Some of the key suppositions are different. In realism and science fiction, the writer has a contract with the reader that the writer will live in the reader's world—even in science fiction, which may be the future or a plausible future. In science fiction, as in realism, nothing happens that couldn't happen or shouldn't happen. Whereas in fantasy, the contract is just the opposite. The reader agrees to enter the writer's world and follow its laws. That's a major step a lot of people will not take. They don't want to enter a world they don't share with everybody else. A fantasy world exists only in the book. Some people love that. Most children love it. They love to get into different worlds. It seems that a lot of people lose that capacity somewhere in their teens and then they are scared of it.

WW: I would agree that this is true in literature, but deviates in film. People seem more accepting of film and of entering a fantasy world or a science fiction world because they love to be taken away.
UL: . . . Although we don't have many good fantasy films. It's more often science fiction, which pretends to be our world extrapolated forward.

WW: *Star Wars* is really cowboys in space.
UL: Yes, and a lot of fantasy is cowboys in fairyland, too. I watched *The Thief of Baghdad* the other night, which is probably the greatest fantasy film ever made. It's beautiful, and I noticed how much people have been drawing from it ever since—even Disney. But most of our fantasy is animated, which makes it very

safe because it isn't real people. There is a real fear of fantasy in America. Reading science fiction seriously is complicated, because like any literature the people who read it begin to share a language. And by now, science fiction has been written seriously for thirty or forty years. The writers mostly don't explain very much, and if you are not used to reading this stuff you may feel "what is going on?—I don't understand." A lot of the signals are in shorthand. You have to learn to pick up as you do with any literature. You certainly do in poetry. Perhaps, people growing up reading only realism may be unwilling to learn another dialect of the language.

WW: When you are writing, either science fiction or realism, is there a different mindset you have to place yourself in so you can pull from a different world. With science fiction you have to expand the outer limits of what you perceive to be reality, as opposed to realism.

UL: I don't see that opposition. Science fiction and realism are versions of the same literary trends—they both depend, in a sense, on science to tell us what is real. Before about 1700 all literature was basically fantastic. We had a religious consensus. The higher reality was a religious reality, the earth was basically a lower reality. There wasn't any science to tell you that this was possible or this was not possible. Sometimes it's difficult to tell fiction from natural history between the Middle Ages and the 1500s. Invention and reality are pretty much mixed together. As we began to move into the age of science, industry, and technology, we had a touchstone—yeah, this is possible—science says we *can* fly to the moon. Science also says that we can't fly to the moon on wings, flapping our wings and breathing, because there is nothing to breathe between the earth and the moon. That kind of voyage becomes strictly fantastic. You get a clearer line between realism and science fiction on one hand and fantasy on the other. However, since I write all of them, to me it's just a different mood—do I want to enter the commonly-agreed-to-be world or do I want to say, "Reader, come over here across the wall and I will make you a world that never could be. We both know it never could be, but we can enjoy it for itself."

Science fiction is always a metaphor. We are really talking about right here, right now. We call it the future because in what we call the future we are very free to move around and invent.

WW: Last night I was thinking about a writer who published a book in 1960 about flying to the moon. That would have been considered science fiction. But that same book published July 30, 1969, would not have been science fiction. I was toying with the idea of science catching up to the imagination.

UL: There is a statute of limitations about fiction. Like Jules Verne inventing the submarine before anybody really invented it, and he's very cagey about what it is, but he also invented something like atomic power to fuel the submarine. He was doing this in the 1880s. People love to talk about science fiction as prediction. But actually its record of prediction is dismal. It's like one story from the 1930s and early '40s predicted anything like the atom bomb, the major event of the mid-twentieth century. The writers had no clue anything like this was in the works. The future and space travel are just metaphors. They are very useful and beautiful metaphors for talking about us now, but they are not predictions.

WW: I would never have thought of science fiction as prediction. . . .
UL: A lot of people want to. They read it like astrology.

WW: In your writing has anything come true that you invented or imagined without prior knowledge that this "thing" was a possibility, something that has later come true?
UL: No, because I don't write high-tech science fiction. My technology tends to be complex and largely invisible. There's a kind of wiring diagram science fiction that goes into great detail about the technology of future spaceships and wars; it bores me to tears.

   In my book, *The Lathe of Heaven,* something happens but it's never quite clear what happens, in April 1998. It looks like we sort of blow up the world, but you can't be sure, because the book is full of dreams and visions, and you are never sure which is which. I wrote that book in the '70s when 1998 was a nice long way away. As it comes closer I start thinking: I hope we get through April 1998. (laughing) After 1998 my book will be a little bit different. Like Orwell's *1984;* since we got through 1984 you have to read the book a little bit differently. It's more of a period piece than it was. But at least nobody can seriously believe that I am predicting, which I never was. I was telling a story.

WW: I remember as 1984 started becoming more of a reality, everyone who had read *1984* almost feared the entire forthcoming year—the closer the world came to 1984, the more we feared what was supposed to be. I think everyone else was worried, too, that Orwell would be right because there were television shows, and newspaper and magazine articles appearing everywhere on the predicted doom of our individual freedom.
UL: In a way it did happen. Orwell's original title was *1948.* The publishers said he couldn't call it that, because that was this year. Orwell said that's the point. He

was talking about what was really going on, now, 1948. This is what I mean when I say the future is a metaphor.

WW: That's like Heller's *Catch-22*. Arbitrarily it was changed, I believe, originally from *Catch 19,* because another writer published a book with "19" in the title, and now the term "catch-22" has become a cliché in the American dogma ever since.

UL: That's a good story, but *1984* is kind of a pity. I can see why the publisher did it, but Orwell was right. He was writing about 1948 and all that it included.

WW: It's interesting to observe how people believe Orwell was predicting the world's future when in fact he was describing the present, and, by an editor's decision, changed how we saw ourselves. I wanted to follow up my first question with the second part, which has to do with the literary canon, and for the most part, the exclusion of women writers.

UL: There again things are changing. There has been a steady campaign mounted in the last ten to fifteen years by feminist critics, both male and female, against that exclusion. It's beginning to be the old guard that says the only women writers are Austen, Brontë, Woolf, and maybe Plath. And Dickinson, of course. The only good women writers are dead virgins. (laughing) Not only dead, unmarried, but preferably childless. In other words, as much like men as possible. I don't know why this is going on. I really don't. It just seems so damn silly to me to leave out half our writers. Nearly half of our fiction has been written by women. Often while they were alive these women were beloved and popular, respected, but as soon as they died the lid went on. There's been this whole process in the last fifteen years of rediscovering women writers who were either undervalued or just plain forgotten. A great case in point, Margaret Oliphant, a Victorian writer, who I think is better than Trollope, more varied, more interesting—a fascinating writer that no one has ever heard of. She was a better writer than Trollope, and she knew it. She said very bitterly, "I was paid for my best book what Trollope got for his pot boilers." And he ground out potboilers by the score. There has been a misogyny and a stupidity at work, which we are coming out of. And yet, when you look at the grants, prizes, and awards, it is still clearly male dominated. Just start counting the Nobels. A woman gets the Nobel once every thirty years. The prizes do not reflect the reality of who is writing.

WW: That's true, but it is changing. There's Alice Walker, Toni Morrison, Mary Oliver. . . .

UL: Sure, you can name them, but now start naming the men. If my figures are right, publishing both poetry and fiction is about fifty-fifty men and women, but prizes, grants, and awards are nowhere near fifty-fifty. I don't want a quota system, God knows. This is art we're talking about. But I really do believe that right now most of our best writing is being done by women. Anybody who is honest about fiction in America in the last ten years, and maybe poetry, must say look at these women writers!

It's explainable partly because of the feminist movement. We're learning how to write as women. A lot of us feel that we've found our voices. In poetry, I read men poets complaining about how narrow and tight the poetic canon is, but they're not reading the women poets. There's a big change going on and we are in the middle of this big change. I may be fighting a battle that has essentially been won, but most feminists learned to be cautious about that, because every time you think you have won the battle you suddenly find yourself right back where you were a generation ago and all the doors are closed again.

WW: Nadine Gordimer won the Nobel Prize in 1991.
UL: Before that it was Pearl Buck.

WW: . . . In 1938.
UL: The Nobel is such a weird prize anyway.

WW: It's interesting to see who has won the Nobel Prize at certain times. Isn't it a coincidence that Saul Bellow won it in 1976, an American winning during our bicentennial. Then, of course, Robert Penn Warren not winning, and he is perhaps our most distinguished writer.
UL: Year after year, I and thousands of members of PEN [an international association that promotes cooperation among writers in the interests of international goodwill and freedom of expression] voted for Jorge Luis Borges, who was the obvious international candidate for the Nobel. They would not consider him. They didn't like his politics. I was shocked that Italo Calvino never got it. It seems they never give it to the really risky writers. Bellow is a safe writer.

WW: I wasn't dismissing Bellow, and I do like some of his work, especially *Herzog.* . . .
UL: I am dismissing him just a little bit, because he is a really safe writer, sticking with mainstream male writing, what people are supposed to write about, what's accepted as the subject of writing. He hasn't taken any risks as far as I can see. He's safe as houses.

WW: What types of changes would you like to see made with the canon?
UL: We are in what we must call post-modernism. I hate the word. It's a stupid word. Maybe we can get a better name for what everybody is doing. People are writing differently and the genres are all merging. Magical realism is certainly one of the early signs of this, coming up from South America. We're mixing fantastic and realistic techniques to make a superreal picture of what's going on in the world. The old lines, walls, and pigeonholes just don't fit anymore. I don't know how criticism should be redone, but it should start by carefully reading and observing what is going on, instead of saying it's what everybody used to do and so they should be doing the same thing.

Reviewers tend to have trouble with a writer like Toni Morrison, getting a handle on her, because she is doing something truly new. This is always difficult. Virginia Woolf . . . it's taken us fifty or sixty years to figure out what she was doing in her novels. We are just beginning to get some good Virginia Woolf criticism, because she was way ahead of her time. Everyone said James Joyce is it. OK, he was it for then, but to me Virginia Woolf is still it, while Joyce is an interesting phenomenon historically. Woolf is still a writer who took risks that we don't even know how to explain. It's a matter of rereading, learning to read, and seeing what is there, instead of what "ought to be there."

WW: When I was an undergrad I had a very good teacher who approached literature as one entity, and within this entity there were subentities. We discussed literature as a whole; however, he always set portions aside and told us that we probably would always see groups of writers, so here are the categories you're going to find and probably never escape: Jewish writers, women writers, southern writers, etc. It was a very thorough understanding of the literary scene, and we spent about half the time on women writers without really discussing them simply as women writers.
UL: This was when?

WW: Early '80s.
UL: In 1975 you would have spent a quarter of that much time. And in 1965 you would have read Dickinson.

WW: We studied O'Connor, Walker, Oates, Welty, McCullers, Bishop, Plath, and Rich. Others who slip my mind momentarily.
UL: There's women's literature, but there isn't men's literature. Modernism is male, white, urban, because anything that isn't urban is called "regional," and

northern because it isn't "southern," and eastern because it isn't "western." There is a norm that is not honestly declared to be a norm.

WW: So if you want to be a writer with longevity you'd better be a white male living in New York City?
UL: I think that's changing. The fact is in the 1980s most of the great American novels were written by women. But ten years ago the literary establishment was fighting it. Some are still fighting it.

WW: I don't know who or what controls these things, this governing device, but is it a fear that those who govern the canon won't be taken seriously if someone else is taken more seriously than themselves?
UL: I suppose. Privilege always defends itself. You can see it as a gender thing; male dominance is deeply entrenched. But then you get other prejudices like the old *New Yorker* when they wouldn't publish anything that was identifiable as science fiction. The old *New Yorker* had a policy: No science fiction in this magazine. Why? What were they defending themselves against? It's an arbitrary hierarchy of privilege and excellence. If you stick to it long enough you convince people.
I think the movement is away from that. Of course, the movement begins not with the critics and reviewers, but with the writers. The writers are doing something else. They have been for years.

WW: If you had your voice in the matter, instead of being defined by critics as a science fiction writer, how would you like to be defined?
UL: Novelist, short story writer, and poet, because I do write in different forms. Then if they want to say realism, science fiction, fantasy, children's literature, that's fine—so long as the terms are used descriptively and not just judgmentally. Yes, I write science fiction. No, I'm not only "a science fiction writer." Don't box me in! However, I will get provocative and say I am "a western writer" because we need to redefine that category. Then they say, so you write westerns? and I say no. I am a western writer. I was born in the West and lived most of my life here. I write as a westerner. And I will say yes, I am a woman writer. I finally learned how to say that when I was in my fifties. I am a woman writer, not an imitation man.

WW: What do you mean by "imitation man"?
UL: The canon was so male dominated and male writing was considered the only kind of writing, and women were only "good writers" as long as they imitated men. We all learned to do it except a few mavericks like Virginia Woolf, who never wrote like a man.

WW: Do you mean using a certain male writer or male-authored novel as a criterion or guide to what should be written?

UL: What interests men is what will interest the novel reader. That was the assumption. Thus, men are at the center of the book. This is something we have not really changed. If men are at the center of the book it's considered to be of general interest to the reader. If women are at the center of the book, it is considered to be of interest to women. *Searoad*—the book you have with you—I had to fight my own publisher from saying it was a book about women for women, and only women could possibly be interested in it. I said, "My God, my sales are generally pretty good. Shall we not try to cut them in half by saying stay away from this book, boys, you'll hate it?" In *Searoad* there are women who don't seem able to keep men in their lives or don't have very good luck with men, women who live alone. I think that's what some of the reviewers and my editor homed in on, and why they said this is all about women. So what? There aren't any women in *Moby Dick*, but that doesn't keep women from reading it. Even if a book is mostly about women, like *The Color Purple*, which is very woman-centered, men read it. I know some men have trouble politically with the book, but aesthetically there's no barrier. There's a false rule. If it's about men everybody wants it; if it's about women it's only for women.

WW: This supersedes literature. Take the movie *Thelma and Louise*, for instance. Before I saw the movie almost every male friend of mine said it's a movie for women, and then women said *City Slickers* is a male movie. So it may not be only in literature but may encompass human nature in a social context.

UL: Of course, *Thelma and Louise* had a threat element in it to some men. It was pretty blunt. (laughing) If you were in the theater, as I was the first time I saw *Thelma and Louise,* when all the women burst into a cheer when the women blew up the truck—if I'd been a man I would have thought: Hey, I didn't know they were that mad.

It was very impressive. I think a lot of women who saw that movie didn't know they were that mad until they saw it. That's why it's an important movie.

WW: What are you working on now?

UL: I'm waiting to see. I spent a lot of last year working on the *Norton Book of Science Fiction,* which if you know Norton Books, was an enormous amount of reading. I had a ball, but I didn't get much writing done. I never know what comes next. I've been writing some short stories.

WW: You didn't write much as a result of all the reading you did last year, and as most of us know that's a very thin line to balance on. How do you normally balance the writing life against everything else, and what types of things pull you away from the work?

UL: Correspondence. Answering letters. It seems to be the thing I cannot control. Although I have a very good friend who works as my secretary. She's incredibly helpful—she'll say, "Don't answer that letter; answer this one," and helps me work out an answer. I get an awful lot of mail because of the types of things I write. There's a very lively and intense readership of science fiction, fans, and they write the authors. A lot of fiction writers get no response, a couple of criticisms and a few notices in *Poets & Writers* and that's it. It's nice to get a response. Then I write children's books, and kids write spontaneously. Those letters are ones you want to answer. But teachers increasingly make kids write authors— every kid has to pick an author and write the author and ask them really stupid questions, which you can tell the teacher told them to write. Or huge questions, like where do you get your ideas from. I mean, come on! (laughing) And then there's a moral dilemma—this is a child writing to you; you feel that you should answer this child. I feel that rather strongly as a woman, as a writer. But it can take half a week to answer letters. I wish teachers would realize that this is *not* putting a child in touch with a writer. It's just wasting the writer's time and the child's time. I think it's treating both of them with disrespect. If a child wants to write an author, fine. The kids writing me on their own usually tell me what I did wrong. (laughing) Or they suggest what the next book ought to be. They are great at that.

WW: Have you ever used their suggestions?

UL: (laughing) No. They're usually kind of wild. It's what a kid would write, and they're usually funny.

Then, of course, there's business correspondence, where I have to say no I can't keynote your meeting. This eats up my time, and distresses me a lot. I don't know why I can't get it under control. I guess some writers just end up not answering letters, but that seems very arrogant to me. The real problem is lack of energy. When I was in my thirties I had three kids I was bringing up. I did not have any help except from my husband who was an enormous help. But I could write novels and bring up kids. I had energy. Like you, I didn't sleep much. But when you get in your sixties you don't have that much energy, and it gets more difficult.

I'm slower as a writer. I don't know that I'm better, but my writing is more complex than it used to be. The last sixty pages of *Searoad* took me two years, and I was appalled at how slow it was going. What's wrong with me, I thought. Well, it just took that long. You have to let everything run its own course.

WW: Are you selfish with your time?

UL: All artists have to be a little rigid and say no I'm not going to answer the telephone, or no, I can't do something. I'm not very methodical. I used to be very contemptuous and disdainful of people who went to writer's retreats. There I was with my family and housework and other stuff, and I used to think why do you have to go off to some farm and be protected? Now I understand. Now I do need genuine solitude to write. It's the energy thing. I can't put the walls up anymore. Sometimes I even need to be away from my husband. We have a beach house and a town house. Sometimes we split up and he writes here and I write there. He says he doesn't need it, but he knows I do. That's a big change. I find it a little humiliating, like I ought to be able to write anywhere. But I really can't.

WW: As we sit here in Macon, you're three thousand miles from your home, do you find it difficult to write here?

UL: In a brief visit to a place like this, I write poetry, because it comes when it will and if you are open to it, it'll come. I'm writing reviews right now while I'm here. I would hate to start a short story here knowing how broken up my time is going to be. A short story is very intense and once I start I pretty much have to finish it in one deep breath. Even though it might be four or five days I want those four or five days.

WW: How do you view your readership?

UL: I have a very loyal readership. People look for my books. So I learned from that how reciprocal an art writing is. When I started, it seemed very lonely, because you are writing in a void—you don't know who your readers are. I still don't know who my readers are mostly, but I have a sense of them being there. I do hear from them. I do know they are there. They buy the books. I have a much stronger sense now that it is the reader who completes the book for me. It's slightly mystical. I tell the story as well as I can and I do it as an end in itself. When I'm working on a story I don't think of myself or the reader. If I do, it's fatal. I'm simply making something, and I make it as well as I can. But when it's published you're sending it out into this void, hopeful it's full of readers. And the way they read it is what makes it a story. They finish it. If it's not read, it doesn't really exist. It's wood pulp with black marks on it. The reader does work with the writer. You can't help but get mystical about it, because it's such a strange process.

Where you feel it is in performance, and this is one reason why the older I get the fonder I am of performance art, either reading a story or an actual performance piece of poetry, poetry and music, poetry and dance, various things I've been involved in. It is a mystical experience when a performance piece and an audience work together on stage. It's this incredible energy where you give it to them and they give it to you. That's so addictive, as anybody who's into performance knows. What happens when you publish a book is the same thing, but it's continuous, and so mysterious because the audience is out there somewhere but you don't know them. And yet, it does happen. I think what I'm trying to say is that I hope this happens whenever I publish something. I hope the same energy begins to flow through my work to the reader and back to me, both empowering each other.

WW: Your feminist views are forthright. . . .
UL: Yes, I am a feminist.

WW: I've noticed that television and radio interviewers and newspaper writers act, when they hear someone is a feminist or when they mention it in an article, as though it were a profession one chose opposed to what one ought to be doing regardless. The media seems amazed or surprised by this. I've told my classes before that I'm a feminist, and everyone, male and female alike, breaks out laughing. I ask them what would they want me to be? Like being a humanist, it's something each one of us should naturally be doing, taking up a cause for oneself as well as for others. It just seems to me that the media is always in shock over feminism and has to ask a woman what drew her to be a feminist.
UL: Yes, I know. (laughing) It's like what drew me into breathing.

WW: I bring this up because I'm interested in your position on the feminist movement over the years, where it stands today, and where you would like to see it progressing.
UL: It'll take a few hours. (laughing) Briefly, I was slow and kind of stupid in some ways. This present wave of feminism started in the mid-'60s. It was partly fueled by the misogyny of the New Left. There's no doubt about that. Women found themselves pushed aside. The men were going to end the war and run everything. A lot of anger came out of that. I was slow to get in, but there began to be questions: What are men? What are women? Are there essential differences?

This obviously led me to write the first book of mine that really hit, had success, and has been in print ever since, *The Left Hand of Darkness,* which is about people who can be either male or female for a few days a month. By the end of the book, most of the characters are both mothers and fathers. The book was a thought experiment. What if ? What if there is no difference between men and women? Let's remove all possible biological and psychological differences and see what we've got. What we got was a novel I certainly enjoyed. But I didn't realize at the time that there was anything very radical about it. It was really the first book of its kind (except a science fiction book by Ted Sturgeon called *Venus Plus X,* which I didn't know when I wrote mine).

WW: In your writing, and this may pertain more to the science fiction, of all the things or ideas that you have thought of or worlds you have invented, when you wake up tomorrow what one thing would you like to see in place that we don't have today?
UL: This is looking at the utopian element in my writing?

WW: Yes, because this establishes a multitude of dilemmas. We have the idea that we would like to cure world hunger but that doesn't take into account that we will have to cure world thirst also. If there is no disease, then no one dies and it creates a new set of problems, and then there is some other aspect that is troublesome.
UL: That's the plot of *The Lathe of Heaven,* where the doctor keeps asking the guy who can dream true to cure this and cure that, and so he does and it always makes something worse, then he has to work on that one.

WW: Exactly. If you bring one utopian aspect to the world tomorrow, what would it be?
UL: I can't pick one because I don't think that way. It's all network. You know the butterfly theory—if you kill a butterfly in North Carolina, it may result in a typhoon in China. Small causes have very large results. To answer your question I can only talk about my book that is a pure utopia, my utopia, my dream world: *Always Coming Home,* where I took my Napa Valley of north California and moved it into an imaginary time, the "future." I lessened the world population radically and let these people in the Valley develop a local culture, which isn't male or female dominated, and is pretty much consensual. They do a lot of singing and dancing and thinking. I created a "dream world" that I tried ground-

ing absolutely and solidly in a real place, the Napa Valley, which I know stone by stone. Marianne Moore said real toads in imaginary gardens is what poetry is about. Well, what I did was create imaginary toads in a real garden. I tried working out in that book the world that I think I would like best to live in. Although this one will do.

Coming Back from the Silence
Jonathan White/1994

Jonathan White: What attracted you to science fiction?
Ursula Le Guin: I didn't exactly choose science fiction. I went where I got published, which took a long time because my work is so odd. For the last fifty or sixty years, literature has been categorized as "realism," and if you weren't writing realism, you weren't respectable. I had to ignore that and say to myself that I could do things in science fiction that I could never do in realism. I tend to be prickly about this subject because I get tired of being put down as a science-fiction writer. The fact is, in the postmodern era, all the barriers are breaking down pretty fast.

Science fiction is a child of realism, not of fantasy. A realistic story deals with something that might have happened but didn't, right? Many science-fiction stories are about worlds that don't exist, but could exist in the future. Both realism and science fiction deal with stories that might be true. Fantasy, on the other hand, tells a story that couldn't possibly be true. With fantasy, we simply agree to lift the ban on the imagination and follow the story, no matter how implausible it may be.

JW: Didn't you say once that fantasy may not be actual, but it's true?
UL: Wouldn't you say any attempt to tell a story is an attempt to tell the truth? It's the technique you use in the telling that is either more or less plausible. Sometimes the most direct way to tell the truth is to tell a totally implausible story, like a myth. That way you avoid the muddle of pretending the story ever happened, or ever will happen.

Who knows how stories really work? We're so used to stories with all the trappings of being real that we've lost our ability to read anything else. When you read a native American story, you have to relearn how to read. There's nothing in

92

them to draw you in. There's no sweetening of the pill. Maybe there's a coyote, but there's no description. We're used to a lot of fleshing out, and we're used to being courted and drawn into the story.

JW: Nora Dauenhaeur, a Tlingit woman and coauthor of *Haa Shuka, Our Ancestors,* reminded me last summer that Native American stories are usually told to an audience that already knows them. In fact, they've heard the stories over and over again, through many winters. As a result, the storyteller often uses shorthand—a single word or phrase—to remind the audience of a larger event with many details. She pointed out that we are telling stories like this all the time, particularly among friends and family with whom we share a history. We may say, "Remember that time we were caught in a dust storm outside of Phoenix?" And that's the story, all of it.

UL: Yes, exactly. You don't describe the sky or the clouds or what you were wearing. There isn't any of the scene-setting in Native American stories. It bothers me when I read gussied-up Native American stories. They're no longer sacred. When we embellish a Native American story, it turns into just another story. Our culture doesn't think storytelling is sacred; we don't set aside a time of year for it. We don't hold anything sacred except for what organized religion declares to be so. Artists pursue a sacred call, although some would buck and rear at having their work labeled like this. Artists are lucky to have a form in which to express themselves; there is a sacredness about that, and a terrific sense of responsibility. We've got to do it right. Why do we have to do it right? Because that's the whole point: either it's all right or it's all wrong.

JW: We tend to have a linear, cause-and-effect way of looking at the world. I wonder if one of the things that attracts us to stories is their ability to change our way of seeing?

UL: The daily routine of most adults is so heavy and artificial that we are closed off to much of the world. We have to do this in order to get our work done. I think one purpose of art is to get us out of those routines. When we hear music or poetry or stories, the world opens up again. We're drawn in—or out—and the windows of our perception are cleansed, as William Blake said. The same thing can happen when we're around young children or adults who have unlearned those habits of shutting the world out.

The tribal storyteller is not just providing spiritual access but also moral guidance. I think much of American writing today is an exploration of ethical problems. I'm thinking particularly of novels by black women such as Paule Marshall,

Alice Walker, Gloria Naylor, and Toni Morrison. The stories these women write are gaining literary praise, but they're also doing something terribly important for their people, who are not just black Americans but all Americans. In a sense, these women are fulfilling the ancient role of tribal storytellers, because they're trying to lead us into different spiritual and moral realms. They're intensely serious about this, and that's why they're so beloved as novelists.

JW: Stories can also help us remember who we are. In *The Book of Laughter and Forgetting*, Milan Kundera says, "What is the self but the sum of everything we remember?"

UL: Yes. To remember, if my Latin is correct, actually means to put the parts together. So that implies there are ways of losing parts. Kundera talks about this aspect of storytelling, too. In fact, he says that history, which is another kind of story, is often deliberately falsified in order to make a people forget who they are or who they were. He calls that "the method of organizing forgetting."

History is one way of telling stories, just like myth, fiction, or oral storytelling. But over the last hundred years, history has preempted the other forms of storytelling because of its claims to absolute, objective truth. Trying to be scientists, historians stood outside of history and told the story of how it was. All that has changed radically over the last twenty years. Historians now laugh at the pretense of objective truth. They agree that every age has its own history, and if there is any objective truth, we can't reach it with words. History is not a science, it's an art.

There are still people who insist on teaching history as a science, but that's not how most historians work anymore. My husband, Charles, who is a historian, says, "I don't know the difference between story and history. I think it may not be a difference in kind, but a difference in their attempts to be truthful."

The history of the last hundred years still has a tremendous intellectual bias toward the white European point of view. Defined by historians as the written record, it conveniently illegitimizes all oral traditions and most indigenous people right from the start. In fact, in its view, everybody but white Europeans is "primitive." If you don't have a written language, you aren't part of history.

JW: Are the current changes in how we look at history also changing the way we look at indigenous cultures?

UL: Absolutely. It's a de-centering process. We've been pretending that Europe was the center of the world for too long. With the help of anthropologists, and now historians, we are finding that there is no center, or that there are many centers.

Nobody has "the answer." It's amazing how much resistance there is to this. Every-body wants to be "the people," everybody wants to be "the center." And everybody is the center, if only they'd realize it and not sneer at all the other centers.

JW: Because history, as it has been practiced, concerns itself only with the writ-ten record, language acquires a loaded role in terms of our perception of reality. Like history, language can become a tool of forgetting, a tool of estrangement. As a writer, how do you work against that?

UL: This is a tricky area. As a writer, you want the language to be genuinely sig-nificant and mean exactly what it says. That's why the language of politicians, which is empty of everything but rather brutal signals, is something a writer has to get as far away from as possible. If you believe that words are acts, as I do, then one must hold writers responsible for what their words do.

One of the strangest things about our culture is our ability to describe the de-struction of the world in exquisite, even beautiful, detail. The whole science of ecology, for instance, describes exactly what we're doing wrong and what the global effects are. The odd twist is that we become so enamored of our language and its ability to describe the world that we create a false and irresponsible sepa-ration. We use language as a device for distancing. Somebody who is genuinely living in their ecosystem wouldn't have a word for it. They'd just call it the world.

We can't restructure our society without restructuring the English language. One reflects the other. A lot of people are getting tired of the huge pool of meta-phors that have to do with war and conflict. The "war against drugs" is an obvious example of this. So is the proliferation of battle metaphors, such as being a war-rior, fighting, defeating, and so on. In response, I could say that once you become conscious of these battle metaphors, you can start "fighting" against them. That's one option. Another is to realize that conflict is not the only human response to a situation and to begin to find other metaphors, such as resisting, outwitting, skip-ping, or subverting. This kind of consciousness can open the door to all sorts of new behavior.

I am struck by how much we talk about rebirthing but never about rebearing. The word itself is unfamiliar to most people. Yet both women and men are ca-pable of rebearing, women literally and men metaphorically. A door opens just by changing the name. We don't have to be reborn; we can rebear. This is part of the writer's job, either to rebear the metaphors or refuse to use them. Gary Snyder's lifelong metaphor is watershed. How fruitful that is! Another of his is compost-ing, which is a lovely word that describes the practice of creating.

JW: The use of language to name the world seems to have two sides. On one hand, things are given names as an expression of intimacy and respect; and on the other hand they are given names to create distance and separation. In your story, "She Unnames Them," for example, barriers are broken down as the names for animals are taken away.

UL: "She Unnames Them" is really an Adam and Eve story that I subverted. Eve takes all the names back because they were either wrong from the start or they went wrong. As she does this, the barriers between herself and the world are dismantled. At the end of the story, she has no words left. She's so close to the animals that she feels vulnerable and afraid, yet full of new desire to touch, smell, and eat.

Why do I feel like the way we give names is wrong? I don't want to flog that little story to death, because it was meant partly as a joke, but we do use names to cut ourselves off. Talking about a dog is different from talking about Rover. In the language of war, we don't talk about killing or even casualties anymore. We use strange euphemisms instead, like "body count" and "friendly fire." The language of pretended objectivity is often used this way, too. We manipulate names as categories of reality, and the names then become screens between ourselves and the world. The names become a tool of division rather than of community.

My father worked with the Yurok Indians of California, among other tribes. If you read his Yurok myths, you learn that every rock and every tree had its name. It was a small world they lived in, not a planetary one. They were in intense community with it, and their naming was a way of respecting their independence. But anything is reversible, and naming can become the destruction of community, where we hide from the real world by using more and more words. I know people who refuse to learn the names of trees. They have a concept of "tree," but the names simply get between them and the real tree.

I grew up in the Napa Valley without learning the English names for many of the plants and animals. When I started writing *Always Coming Home*, which takes place there, I had a wonderful time learning the flora and fauna of the area. For a while, I knew the name of every wildflower. But what you learn late doesn't stick. Now when I come across a flower whose name I've forgotten, I say, "How do you do, little yellow flower, whatever your name is." I used to crave to know the names, and I enjoyed learning them. It's funny, by naming a thing, do we think we get control over it? I think we do. That's how magic works. If you know the name of a thing, then you know its essence. At some level, I think we all must believe that.

We're naming creatures, but we need to respect that some things are beyond names. Like the mysterious essence of an animal in the wild. If our names make them appear tame or petlike, as in Walt Disney's world, then it's degrading. Some of the California Indians knew that when you name an animal, such as a deer, you are addressing its metaphysical nature. They called that universal quality "Deerness" or "The Deer." It's a profoundly mysterious and important matter, and very hard to put into words, but I feel I know what they're talking about. When these Indians hunted, they asked Deerness to help them. The deer that comes to the hunter is related physically to all other beings, but it is also an embodiment of Deerness. It's the gift of Deerness. This way of looking at the world can apply to every living being. When we name something we are naming its essence, and therefore its sacredness.

JW: In *Buffalo Gals*, you say that all creatures talk to one another, whether we are able to hear or not. But this conversation—this community—is not a simple harmony. "The peaceable kingdom, where lion and lamb lie down, is an endearing vision not of this world": What do you mean by that?
UL: The vision of the "peaceable kingdom" denies wilderness. In the Christian tradition, the denial of violence, of the fact that we eat each other in order to live, removes you from this world. Heaven is supernal bliss where there is no violence, no eating, no sex. When lions and lambs lie down in the wilderness, the lamb ends up inside the lion. That's how it is. You can deny that in order to gain another world. But if the only world you want is this one—and this one seems quite satisfactory to me—then the myth of the "peaceable kingdom" is only a charming painting.

JW: You continue in *Buffalo Gals*: "Some rash poets get caught in the traps set for animals and, unable to endure the cruelty, maim themselves to escape." You give the example of Robinson Jeffers. Was Jeffers maimed because he took too personally his disappointment in the dark side of nature?
UL: Jeffers was a very strange man and poet, with an enormous component of cruelty and violence in his work. He had incredible sympathy with animals. He could give you an animal in a word or two like very few poets can. I think he honestly felt them, even though he often perceives them through violence. I can't explain Jeffers, he has always awed and annoyed me. I'm grateful to him as one of my predecessors writing about California. Even as a teenager, I knew he had California right.

The poem that most reveals Jeffers's self-hatred is the one about the cavemen who torment a mammoth to death. They trap it and roast it alive. He's full of this kind of disgust for humanity. Yet he soars out into a great vision; never a happy vision, but a great vision. He's a difficult case when you're talking about animals.

JW: The trap of shamefulness seems like an easy one to fall into. If we want to be alert, we have to take all this in—the violence, the killing, the cruelty—
UL: Yes. But since we're capable of compassion, we know it hurts. This causes all sorts of difficulties. My aunt was a biologist, and I watched her drop an artichoke into a pot of boiling water and say, "I wonder if it can feel that?" She was a very hardheaded biologist. Humans have to think about these things, whether we like it or not. It's the nature of our humanity to feel uncomfortable and full of guilt and shame and confusion. But we still participate, because we have to eat. Much of what animals do naturally we have to do consciously. That's our gift and our curse. All we can do is be conscientious about it—do it rightly, not wrongly.

JW: In *Always Coming Home*, hunting for food and skins was primarily done by children and adolescents. Under the supervision of adults, young girls and boys were allowed to hunt rabbit, possum, squirrel and other small game, and deer. Why was hunting considered inappropriate for adults?
UL: You're supposed to outgrow it. The same thing is true of war. In one chapter, I describe a small war with the Pig People. It's modeled on the warfare of the Northern California Indians, which was usually just a matter of standing on a hill and shouting insults. Sometimes people got mad enough to hurt each other, and occasionally someone was killed. Mostly it was the young boys who engaged in war, not the whole tribe. What comes up in the chapter on the Pig war is the report that there were adults involved in the war. That's a shameful thing in the Kesh society. Both hunting and war are looked upon as occupations for adolescents—adolescents who are already a little out of control and needing to prove themselves. You can continue to hunt into adulthood if you're really good at it, of course, but I was implying that it's something most people outgrow.

People should be able to figure out their place in the life-death cycle without killing animals. The trouble is that it relates to what Hemingway said: "You can't be a man until you've killed another one." I say bullshit! Why don't you try it without a gun? Maybe there's a gender difference there. Maybe a woman can do it and a man can't. I hate to say that, but you wonder. It isn't built into women to be hunters in our culture. Even a fisherwoman is unusual.

Having a close relationship with an animal, particularly one that lives a short life, can be an intense, constant reminder of mortality. Cats only live ten years, so most of us see a lot of cats die in our lifetime. Going through the death of a pet, particularly for children, can put us through the same emotional process that hunting does. We don't have to kill an animal to get there. It's a very interesting subject, and I hope the difference is cultural and not inherent to gender.

JW: Another aspect of hunting is that it teaches us where our food comes from.
UL: That's a different subject. That's not a spiritual process but a matter of facing the facts. What are you willing to do for your food? Most of us would kill an animal to eat it, if we had to. I could, and would, if I were hungry or defending myself. I'm not saying I would enjoy it, but for those two reasons I would kill an animal. I have Buddhist friends who don't even swat flies. I can't go that far. If something is biting me, I squash it. A pest is a pest.

JW: It's clear from your work that language and writing have become sharp tools for reestablishing human society's (and humanity's) place in the larger household. Much of that effort to envision anew, at least in the last thirty years, has been inspired by feminist principles. You say your goal is always to subvert, to create metaphors for the future "where any assumption can be tested and any rule rewritten. Including the rules of who's on top, and what gender means, and who gets to be free." How were you introduced to the feminist movement? What role has it played in your writing?
UL: My introduction was slow and late. All my early fiction tends to be rather male-centered. A couple of the Earthsea books have no women in them at all or only marginal woman figures. That's how hero stories worked; they were about men. With the exception of just a few feminists like Joanna Russ, science fiction was pretty much male-dominated up to the 1960s. Women who wrote in that field often used pen names.

None of this bothered me. It was my tradition, and I worked in it happily. But I began coming up against certain discomforts. My first feminist text was *The Left Hand of Darkness*, which I started writing in 1967. It was an early experiment in deconstructing gender. Everybody was asking, "What is it to be a man? What is it to be a woman?" It's a hard question, so in *The Left Hand of Darkness* I eliminated gender to find out what would be left. Science fiction is a wonderful opportunity to play this kind of game.

As a thought experiment, *The Left Hand of Darkness* was messy. I recently wrote the screenplay version, where I was able to make some of the changes I wish I could make to the novel. They're details, but important ones, such as seeing the main character, Genly, with children or doing things we think of as womanly. All you ever see him doing are manly things, like being a politician or hauling a sledge. The two societies in the book are somewhat like a feudal monarchy and Russian communism, which tend to be slightly paranoid. I don't know why I thought androgynous people would be paranoid. With twenty years of feminism under my belt, I can now imagine an androgynous society as being much different—and far more interesting—than our gendered society. For instance, I wouldn't lock the people from the planet Gethen, where the story takes place, into heterosexuality. The insistence that sexual partners must be of the opposite sex is naive. It never occurred to me to explore their homosexual practices, and I regret the implication that sexuality has to be heterosexuality.

I gradually realized that my own fiction was telling me that I could no longer ignore the feminine. While I was writing *The Eye of the Heron* in 1977, the hero insisted on destroying himself before the middle of the book. "Hey," I said, "you can't do that, you're the hero. Where's my book?" I stopped writing. The book had a woman in it, but I didn't know how to write about women. I blundered around awhile and then found some guidance in feminist theory. I got excited when I discovered feminist literary criticism was something I could read and actually enjoy. I read *The Norton Book of Literature by Women* from cover to cover. It was a bible for me. It taught me that I didn't have to write like an honorary man anymore, that I could write like a woman and feel liberated in doing so.

Part of the women's experience is shared with men and part of it isn't. Experiences that are only women's, like childbirth, have been described a thousand times, mostly in novels by men. These descriptions have nothing to do with the actual experience. Generally, I don't think men in our culture want to hear from women about childbirth because men want to have their way. So, women's stories have been cast in the form of men's stories. A women's story has a different shape, different words, different rhythm. Theirs is the silent crescent of experience that we are just beginning to find words for.

The incredible upsurge of woman writers and poets in the 1980s is a sign that women are finding their voices. They're beginning to talk about their experiences without using a male vocabulary or meeting male expectations. It's sticky, because the language is so male-centered that it excludes much of the feminine experience. Sex, for instance, is always described from a male point of view, as penetration, insemination, and so on. A lot of women still deny that their experience is different than a man's. They do this because it's scary to realize you don't have the words to describe your own experience. The few words we do have we get from our mothers and the women who taught us when we were young. Virginia Woolf says, "We think back through our mothers."

One of the functions of art is to give people the words to know their own experience. There are always areas of vast silence in any culture, and part of an artist's job is to go into those areas and come back from the silence with something to say. It's one reason why when we read poetry, we often say, "Yeah, that's it. That's how I feel." Storytelling is a tool for knowing who we are and what we want, too. If we never find our experience described in poetry or stories, we assume that our experience is insignificant.

JW: The natural landscape is another of those vast silent areas you speak of. As a writer, have certain landscapes had a particularly strong influence on you?
UL: Mostly I don't know where my writing comes from. Experiences are composted, and then something different and unexpected grows out of them. In 1969, my husband and I spent a couple nights in French Glen, the mountainous area of southeastern Oregon. It was my first sight of that sagebrush high-desert terrain, and it got into me so instantly and authoritatively that a book grew out of it—*The Tombs of Atuan.* The book isn't about the desert but about a community surrounded by a terrain similar to what you find in southeastern Oregon. The desert is a buried metaphor in the book. I have no idea of the reason for the emotional economy of it, but I know the book came to me as I was driving back from French Glen.

The central landscape of my life is the Napa Valley in Northern California. I grew up there and I consider it my home. I've often thought, "How can I get this beautiful valley into a book?" That was the main impulse of *Always Coming Home.* I wanted to write about people living in the Napa Valley who used it a little more wisely than we do now. When I was a child, it was the most beautiful and diversified agriculture you ever saw. There were vines and orchards and truck gardens. It was the way a cultivated valley ought to be. But there was too much money in vines, so they pulled up the orchards and truck gardens. The only thing growing there now is money.

JW: What role has your interest in indigenous people played in your work?
UL: I wasn't aware that it played any role at first. Although my father was an anthropologist and an archaeologist, my entire formal training in this area amounts to one physical anthropology class. Obviously I have some temperamental affinity with my father, but I often say that he studied real cultures and I make them up.

He had an eye for exact concrete detail, and an interest in it. He also had a respect for tools and the way things work. I got a lot of that from him.

When I started thinking about *Always Coming Home* I took a lot of time to discover what the book was going to be. Once I realized I wanted it to grow out of the Napa Valley, I looked around for a literary precedent. I couldn't find anything except a couple of swashbuckling romantic novels about Italian wine-growing families. The only literature of that earth was Native American oral literature. The people of the valley itself, the Wappo, are gone. Even the name they used for themselves is gone. There are people with a little Wappo blood, but there is no language, no tradition, and there are no stories left. So I read other Northern Californian myths and legends and songs. There's a good deal of information available there. My father collected much of it himself. I read widely from traditions all over the United States. My problem was to find a way to use the literature without stealing or exploiting it, because we've done enough of that to Native American writing. I certainly didn't want to put a bunch of made up Indians into a Napa Valley of the future. That was not what I was trying to do. What I got from reading California oral literature was a sense of a distant and different quality of life. You can't hear the voices but you can pick up the feeling.

JW: In *Always Coming Home*, the historical period, which followed the Neolithic era for some thousands of years, is referred to by the Kesh as the time when people lived "outside the world." What do you mean by that?

UL: I was playing with the idea of our present growth technology from the Industrial Revolution on through the present—the last two hundred years. We don't know when this period will end, but it will. We tend to think of our present historic era as representing the highest evolution of human society. We're convinced that our exploitive, fast-growing technology is the only possible reality. In *Always Coming Home*, I put people who believe this into one little capsule where the Kesh could look at them as weird aberrations. It was the most disrespectful thing I could do, like wrapping a turd in cellophane. That's sort of a Coyote metaphor.

JW: Speaking of Coyote, she wanders in and out of much of your recent work. How did you meet up with her?

UL: She trotted through a project of mine in 1982. It was an essay on utopia called "A Non-Euclidean View of California as a Cold Place to Be," and when the tracks of utopia and Coyote crossed, I thought, "Yes, now I'm getting somewhere!" The idea of utopia has been stuck in a blueprint phase for too long now. Most of the writing you see is similar to Callenbach's *Ecotopia*, which is another "wouldn't the future be great if we did this or that?" Or, in science fiction, it's been dystopia: utopia gone sour. These blueprints aren't working anymore.

Coyote is an anarchist. She can confuse all civilized ideas simply by trotting through. And she always fools the pompous. Just when your ideas begin to get all nicely arranged and squared off, she messes them up. Things are never going to be neat, that's one thing you can count on.

Coyote walks through all our minds. Obviously, we need a trickster, a creator who made the world all wrong. We need the idea of a God who makes mistakes, who gets into trouble, and who is identified with a scruffy little animal.

Conversation with Ursula K. Le Guin

Victor Reinking and David Willingham/1994

From *Para-Doxa: Studies in World Literary Genres* 1.1 (1995). Reprinted by permission of David Willingham.

The Le Guin home sits on a hillside overlooking the Willamette River in Portland, Oregon. We arrived at the appointed hour, bristling with tape recorders, brandishing sheaves of prepared questions. Ms. Le Guin recoiled at the door, wondering whether we were FBI agents or encyclopedia salesmen. After introductions, she ushered us in to a simply furnished but elegant living room, prepared a pot of peppermint tea, and responded graciously and generously to our questions for the next two and one half hours. What follows is an abridged version of that conversation.

P•D: What were you doing when you went to Paris in 1953?
UKLG: I was a graduate student on a Fulbright scholarship, going to Aix-en-Provence to look for a thesis subject, but Aix was not a good place to find one. Charles and I had met on the ship going to France—he was on a Fulbright, too, going to Paris to work on his thesis. When we decided to get married I moved back up to Paris. But it was very difficult to get married in France. The *fonctionnaires* were extremely obstructive. There were endless trips to people behind *guichets*. We had been through about six weeks of this and we finally had got it right. We took our papers to the most obstructive lady at the most important point and she read them over and her face got longer and longer, and she got very quiet, and then there was this pause and we could see something change, and then she looked up with a dreadful little smile and said, "You've not spelled your name correctly." In Georgia they spell it without a space between the "Le" and the "Guin." She said, "Mais non non non, ce n'est pas français." We had to get every single mention of the name initialed and stamped and sealed, and it took another week. But finally it worked. We got married under the Napoleonic code, by golly, right in Paris, at the *mairie du sixième,* by a nice little round mayor with a bright

colored sash across his chest. We picked the free day of the week, Thursday I think it was. The other days of the week you had to pay something, maybe twenty-five francs, so we were married at a bargain price. And then we went to the pretty little non-denominational American Church on the Left Bank.

P•D: Is "Le Guin" a Breton name?

UKLG: Yes. In Brittany it's usually "Le Guen," the name of the nobleman who stood up and suggested that the nobles abrogate their rights in the Revolution. "Le Guen de Kérengal" was his name. We figure we probably belonged to him. It's hard to get a Breton dictionary, but it's our guess that it's probably the same as "Gwyn" in Welsh. "Blond," "fair," "white," something like that.

P•D: Do you go back to France often?

UKLG: No, we trucked off to England for Charles's sabbaticals. We had three school-aged kids (Elisabeth, Caroline, Theodore). To pick up three American kids and put them into French schools is a really big thing for them. To take three American kids and put them into an *English* school is something of a culture shock but, after an initial period of adjustment, they loved it. They had to learn the language when they were in working-class schools—Cockney—but they learned it very quickly . . . , and then we just fell in love with England. Both times we lived in London, Charles was doing work at the museum.

P•D: What kind of history does he do?

UKLG: He was a French Revolutionary historian when he started out, but he's branched out, and now teaches the history of Canada, and biography, and other things.

P•D: Did you abandon your search for a dissertation topic when you started becoming a fiction writer?

UKLG: Well no, I'd started becoming a fiction writer at about age twelve. I gradually abandoned the idea of doing a thesis after our year in France. Charles went back to finish his thesis at Emory and I got a job as secretary of the Physics Department. And I realized, kind of painfully, and much against my father's will, that I didn't need a doctorate any more. I had married one. We didn't need two in the family. I had been getting my doctorate in order to support my habit— writing. My father had been strong on this. He said, "You know, if you want to be a free writer, you've got to be financially independent." He was sad that I had got that far and then stopped. He was doing exactly what he wanted to do most of his life. He was a pretty happy man.

P•D: He was getting paid for what he wanted to do.

UKLG: Exactly. And he knew that I couldn't ever get a situation quite like that. But teaching, he's right, is a good source of income for a writer.

P•D: Did your mother also have university posts when she was doing her research?

UKLG: She met my father when she went back to college. She had an early marriage; her husband died. Then she went to UC to get a degree in psychiatric social work—they called it "applied psychology" then, I think—and she had to do an anthro course. That's when she met my father. So she got a masters, but she didn't start writing until all us kids were gone.

P•D: What about your children? How has your career affected them?

UKLG: Every one of them is a *good* writer, but none of them is a "writer" by trade. The middle one, Caroline, teaches writing to freshman at Blue Mountain Community College. She teaches kids how to get words onto paper. Which I think is a neat career.

P•D: My daughter (VR) is a big fan of yours. She's fifteen, and she wanted me to ask what influence your children have had on your writing? She says people always ask writers about their parents, but never about how their children figure in it. She says you must have read to them, and in the process of reading, some ideas must have come to you.

UKLG: Yes, of course. One of my stories came directly from what Caroline said when she was about three. She came up to me with this small matchbox and said, "Guess what's in the box?" and I guessed three or four things and finally said "What?" and she said, "Darkness." And I thought, "Wow!" and wrote a story called "The Darkness Box." So sometimes it's quite direct. Tell your daughter I tried to talk about it a little bit in an essay called "The Fisherwoman's Daughter" in *Dancing at the Edge of the World,* about how we can either have books or babies, and then I try to talk a little bit about this very strong feeling that having children enormously enriched my existence, and therefore my writing, and that it would have been a much thinner, poorer thing without. There's a lot of mythology on the whole subject.

P•D: Did you ever read portions of your writing to your children as you were writing?

UKLG: No.

P•D: Not even after they were published?

UKLG: No, not even after they were published. We tried once, and I was so embarrassed reading it to them that I stopped. I think they were grateful. I know that a lot of writers read to their kids, and do it perfectly spontaneously, but to me the idea of "Mommy wrote it, do you like it, dear?" is awful. How can you lay that on a kid? But we read everything else. I was glad to have a third child so I could read all of *The Lord of the Rings* all over again! We took that with us when we traveled to England. We'd live in Middle Earth every night. It was very reassuring to all of us. We read aloud pretty late. I think I was reading something by Jane Austen to the girls once, and I said, "You know, you ought to be reading this," and they said, "Yeah, I suppose we should." So we stopped. But it's a lovely easy relationship. For one thing, you don't have to talk too much to each other. And who doesn't like great stories? Charles and I read to each other every night before dinner. We're working our way with great joy through Patrick O'Brian's sea stories. I think he's a storyteller on the order of Kipling. Marvelous stuff. They're just a delight.

P•D: You noted in one of your letters to us that you didn't like the term "paraliterature" because it implies the existence of a "city" and a "ghetto," and that there was no need for it because "literature" is "literature." But it brings up the notion of the "canon." Harold Bloom, in his latest book *The Western Canon,* puts *you* in his canon. But a lot of critics put science fiction in a literary "ghetto" and reserve the mainstream for "realistic" fiction—what should be taught, what should be prioritized, etc.

UKLG: I did French literature in college, in graduate school. Talk about a canon! We don't know what a canon is compared to the French. The canon of French literature was absolute. And it had been refined to the point where you really only had to have a couple of textbooks to learn everything you needed to know to get through college in French lit. I don't know whether they've dismantled their canon or not.

P•D: With literature PhD reading lists, for example, you tend to get the same books over and over, and this is perpetuated in the books teachers assign to their students. My own (VR) was a case in point. There was not a single woman writer on it. Not even Simone de Beauvoir made it on the reading list of a late 1980s PhD in French literature! Bloom disavows the idea of the canon as an artificially contrived list, and writes instead of a kind of cultural memory . . .

UKLG: Well, but I think you've got to be careful there. What happens to all that fine talk about "this really is better" is that it gets turned into a list, and a canon gets perpetuated, and it gets taught by male professors, and damage is done. I don't think you can separate those two things, the silly, bigoted side of the canon from the side which is a genuine effort to help people find what's really the best, or to keep them from wasting their time on too much trivial literature. I have to position myself as against the canon, because it has been so misused. I don't see how I could defend it at this point, speaking as a feminist, and as a writer in despised genres—several of them—including children's literature.

I'm not sure, either, that I want the canon merely to be enlarged, with a bulge here and there for me or for somebody else. It has to be rethought. It's so complicated. There's the idea of a tradition, and writing in the tradition, and of course that's exactly what a genre is, isn't it, par excellence? When I'm writing in science fiction, or some other genre, I'm happily aware of the fact that I'm engaged in some sort of joint enterprise.[1] Hasn't there been a sort of tendency to say that this is not what goes on when you're writing realism? The author as Tragic Hero (male). Everybody is on his own in realism, and we have the, what's it called—fear of influence . . .

P•D: Bloom uses the expression "anxiety of influence." He has a book by that title, and brings it up again in *The Western Canon:* "We're always reacting because we're anxious about this or that influence."
UKLG: Well, his "we" strikes me a bit like The Lone Ranger and Tonto. Some of "we" aren't anxious. Some of "we" are women, who have found out with cries of joy that we have female ancestors and female influences, which was what we've been wanting all along. There was an anxiety—it was in *not* having our ancestors and our influences, not having our tribe around us, as it were. And that was restored to us in the '70s and '80s. So it's a very complicated subject.

P•D: Bloom's perspective seems to be that the judgments of a group of informed and responsible individuals tend to produce a cultural standard that we absorb by reading and by osmosis. His idea seems to be that there is a kind of "Ur" esthetic, and that somehow the canon creates itself . . .
UKLG: Oh, what a lovely thought. Would that it were so! And to some it is. There *is* excellence, but there is also this impulse to codify. In fact, the idea of excellence becomes imposed from without, on every generation—a "frame"—and the trouble with the idea of making a list or a code or a canon is that it tends to get

rigid very quickly and become institutionalized. Then the door is shut, not only to letting in people who were omitted, but to easing out people who were included. There are overrated writers, and they go on being overrated for decades because there's a canon, because they're on the list. I would offer James Joyce as an example of an extremely interesting but enormously overrated writer who really had very little influence on anybody because nobody can write like Joyce. Who would want to? Whereas Virginia Woolf, his exact contemporary of course, has been enormously influential, and underrated because she's not in the canon. She's in some people's canon, but she's not in *the* canon.

The whole thing jells too fast, and it isn't drafty enough. There aren't enough doors open for writers to be included and excluded as tastes change. I read so differently now than I read twenty years ago, largely because of feminist theory and criticism, but also simply because times have changed.

P·D: But don't you think we have to have some kind of list because there's a limited number of books our students can read. How do you choose them?
UKLG: I have to keep coming back to the fact that what is called "literature," what is called excellent in literature is realism. I think it's a very curious historical phenomenon; we suddenly decided that realism was literature and literature was realism. How it has impoverished the teaching and reading of literature is shocking. If you go back far enough, there is no realism. And you don't have to go back all that far. Realism is a very recent invention. Realism is a little older than science fiction, but not that much. It's much, much younger than fantasy, which I think is probably the original form of fiction. 1830 is about when the novel really got going. Increasingly from then on, literature becomes realism, to the point that you get big problems, like the exclusion of Tolkien, which I think is really insane. He is a major English writer, whether you like him or not. He is excluded not for lack of excellence but through pure genre prejudice—"He's for children," or "He's for people who read fantasy." But he's *not*. He's a major English author. You do have to have a canon of excellence, for teaching, for criticism, but it's got to be more flexible than it's been, that's really all I'm saying.

In a genre like fantasy I'm appalled when I see every three-volume schlock fantasy compared to Tolkien. A lot of readers don't know the original. They need to be taught to see why Tolkien is really a much better writer and will last them the rest of their lives, whereas so-and-so who imitates him won't last the month. I'm not saying there isn't excellence, and that we don't need to teach it.

P•D: It comes down to what has been called the politics of exclusion, and a lot of that does seem to be because of genre . . .
UKLG: Yes.

P•D: That's where the term "paraliterature" . . .
UKLG: Chip Delany is right: it exists. What I'm saying is that I don't want to *perpetuate* this division. So I would always put it in quotes, or do something to show that I'm rejecting a word that I have to use.

P•D: On the other hand, there are dime novels. Maybe that's the real paraliterature . . .
UKLG: That's sub-literature, and a good deal of it is realism. I have to admit I have another reason to resist the word "literature." I have become very interested in "oral literature." We have Native American literature, which is not lettered. Although I access it through print, it is an oral art form. And, of course, we have enormously devalued the oral side of literature in the last century or two and are just getting back to it now. That's another "paraliterature," if you will.

P•D: One of our contributors (Alain-Michel Boyer) sees a link between paraliterature and the oral tradition. He shows how paraliterature displaced the oral tradition in mid-nineteenth-century France when the machinery for mass-producing literature was developed. Just at the time when a strong oral tradition was fading away, here comes what Boyer calls "paraliterature." But even after the proliferation of paraliterature, very often people in the nineteenth century went to a café to listen to somebody reading it out loud. It was written, but it was also spoken at the same time. "Orality" seems to be a key to understanding our roots . . .
UKLG: There are certain writers—Kipling is a very good case in point—he is an embarrassment partly because of his politics, but also partly because his greatest books are for children. *Kim* is a child's book. It is and it isn't. I read it first at ten, and I've read it ever since. But Kipling is not really a novelist, is he? He's a tale-teller, and he doesn't fit in the canon any more than Tolkien does, for different reasons. I think you might find other writers like that. Of course, Kipling's subjects are often exotic, they're not the ordinary subjects of literature, he personifies ships, his tales partake of fantasy and science fiction and all kinds of things. He didn't write within the realist canon. His stuff was odd. There are writers whom we don't think of as "paraliterary" writers, but who have suffered nearly as much from ignorance or neglect or our inability to know how to criticize them, which I think is one of the main problems . . .

P•D: Yes, the two schools of criticism—realist and "paraliterary"—simply don't meet because they don't know each other's vocabulary. Most of whom we would call "paraliterary critics" in France certainly *do* read the canon, but the reverse just isn't true, the realist critics don't care about it . . .

UKLG: They're ignorant. They don't know about it. Sometimes I've met an honest professor or critic who says "I don't know how to read science fiction," and that's the truth, he doesn't, because he hasn't learned. He learned only half his craft. There is, or ought to be, a great deal of overlap, surely, in all this. Reading a good story is *reading a good story,* wherever it comes from. But there are certain technical things you need to know about realism and about science fiction and about fantasy; they're different, they create different expectations.

P•D: With a novel like *The Dispossessed,* it's hard to imagine anyone, even if they've never read science fiction, having any difficulty reading it because the tale itself takes you into it. Sure there are some strange things going on, but they're very "reader friendly." Some science fiction, such as cyberpunk, Gibson, for example, can give a newcomer some difficulty. Chip Delany says that science fiction is as much a way of "reading" as it is a way of writing, and you have to learn that. What is it that we have to learn?

UKLG: That's true for realism, too. You have to learn how to read Jane Austen.[2] We have to learn how to read realistic fiction. A lot of people never do. Some of them, our fantasy readers, don't know how to read Thackeray, or any novels. They don't know what to expect, they don't know what the rewards are supposed to be.

P•D: But in our educational system, if we're taught any kind of reading, it's realistic.

UKLG: Except that the high schools have discovered it's much easier to use fantasy and science fiction. The Russians apparently did it right from the start, they taught science fiction in the school, used it as a teaching device.

P•D: A lot of writers, you included, have managed to bring the excitement of the storyteller's voice into the narrative, and it seems very central to what you do, this notion of the storyteller. It's as though the storyteller has a critical role in the community itself, that the community can't survive without its stories. Is it because the storyteller provides the "memory"?

UKLG: I would say very roughly that the storyteller makes sense for us partly the way we make sense of our own lives, by making them into a story. I think that storytellers make "sense" for the community of what's happening, and so they also do ethical interpretation and judgment. May I cite my brother's book? Karl Kroeber, *Rereading and Retelling*. His field is the Victorian novel, but he works with Native American literatures, too. And he's thought a great deal about what the storyteller's function is, and why they seem to be essential to any vital society. And if your storyteller's Virginia Woolf, you've hit a pretty high-level society.

P•D: To carry on with the idea of the storyteller, in reading the *Earthsea* trilogy, we were struck by the notion that some people—in this case, the "mages"—do have access to the "true" words, the underlying vocabulary or the understanding that somehow surpasses or is beyond the understanding of ordinary mortals . . .
UKLG: . . . *yes,* there's a metaphor going on there . . .

P•D: . . . and in *Dancing at the Edge of the World,* there is an essay about your thoughts on the whole notion of translating, about translation, about how words pass through you, that you're in touch with something, the taleteller is in touch with something . . .
UKLG: It's curious how many writers seem to feel that way. Many of us have absolutely no religious apparatus to make sense of it, but we have this mystical complacent sense of being a channel; we're channeling, like Boopsie in Garry Trudeau. I'm not talking about channeling for existing "other" worlds, but for a story that begins to tell itself . . .

P•D: Do you wonder where it comes from sometimes?
UKLG: You sure do! And I think that's the source of that question that all writers hate: "Where do you get your ideas?" You have a feeling that your job is simply to clear the channel, to listen.

P•D: Then you're translating from something that is available to people who will discipline themselves to listen?
UKLG: The strongest sense I ever had of translation was when I was writing *Always Coming Home,* because when I wrote it I was pretending to translate, but then, of course, I finally had to invent the language.

P•D: There's a wonderful line at the beginning where you say: "the difficulty of translation from a language that doesn't exist is considerable. . . ."
UKLG: ". . . but there is no need to exaggerate it." Yes there is the sense of reaching out to something that doesn't exist and yet is translatable. It is very strange indeed. I know other writers who've had exactly the same experience, simply that a story "arrives" and your job is to shut up and listen and get it down and just try to keep out of its way. That's a very hard thing to tell a young writer.

P•D: On another aspect of "translation," a lot of your works have been translated into many languages. They must pose some unusual problems for translators because the words you create must have different resonances in different languages. What happens when you learn that "kemmer," for example, means "eat pig swill" or something equally off the mark?

UKLG: In fact "kemmer" does mean something in German, I forget what. The only two languages that I can read my translations in are French and Italian. I get along in Spanish by guesswork. I'm always disappointed that they don't, for instance, change a name or a made-up word so that it sounds good in their language. Too many translators, particularly of science fiction novels, are hacks. I've had a couple of excellent translators. I have a marvelous translator for Danish. I can't read the results, but I know he's good, because from him I get pages and pages of questions: "Is this a joke?" "If so, what am I supposed to do in Danish?" He's lovely. But I get almost none of that from anybody else, so I feel that I am probably getting pretty ordinary, adequate translations most of the time.

P•D: Do most of the translators contact you?

UKLG: Every now and then, yes. I've had a couple very good French translations. The woman who did *Always Coming Home*. She and I corresponded at length.

P•D: But basically you just let them go and hope the translator will be competent enough and caring enough?

UKLG: Basically I'm not included in the process. The publishers have kept me out of it.

P•D: How strange! It seems that the first person you'd go to would be the author for any problems you were having . . .

UKLG: . . . and one would think that the translator would want to ignore what the publisher said. I always invite them when I sign a contract or something, to please consult with me with any questions. But it's very frustrating. I've got a mutual translation manuscript out now, with an Argentinean friend, Diana Bellessi. I don't speak Spanish, but I can do her poems with her sitting on me, saying "no, that does not mean 'sit,' it means 'hear.'" It's lovely to work with the person you're translating.

P•D: Do foreign publishers send you clippings?

UKLG: No, never. Those sales are always made through a secondary agent—usually a rather large firm that carries a lot of authors—and no clipping service gets through. So to find out the quality of a translation, you rely on someone who writes you: "That was a terrible translation of such and such!"—and hearsay, of course, and whether the publisher comes back for the next book. I know that in Japan, for instance, from the start I've just sold right along.

P•D: But there's no way for you to track what critics in Japan, for instance, are writing about your works?
UKLG: Not that I know of.

P•D: There have been hundreds of articles written about you, dissertations, etc. . . .
UKLG: They don't send them to me. Still! Even after I put out that plea. Every now and then I get something saying: "I read your essay, and so here is what I wrote. You may not like it."

P•D: Would you really want to get all of it?
UKLG: No. It's really a matter of courtesy. If an artist is alive and you're writing something about him or her, it just seems a very strange discourtesy not to let them know. And all the artist has to say is: "I got your dissertation and I look forward to reading you with great pleasure. Thank you very much." That's all you can do. Unless you do read some and get interested, and then you get into a dialogue with the person. This has happened a couple of times. Usually when somebody told me something that I didn't know about my work. That's how I met Brian Attebery. He did a thesis partly on me. It was a good thesis. I wrote back and I said, "Hey, I like this, I don't like that. . . ." That's how we got into a dialogue and a friendship.

There's a presumption in academe that an artist is "material" rather than a person. It's an objectification of a living being. That's always wrong. Whether it's a scientist vivisecting a cat or a scholar vivisecting a piece by a living author, there ought to be some recognition of the fact that there is a living being out there. It's really a courtesy matter. Also sometimes I think people speculate vainly about questions that I could've answered very briefly. And that seems silly. I'm not dead yet.

There are plenty of writers who would say, "Ursula's crazy. I don't want to read all that stuff." And I actually am very cautious about reading it, because it can confuse one's mind enormously. If you're working at the time, and somebody's telling you *how* you work or *why* you work, it interferes with the process.

P•D: When you say it's disturbing to you, is it because there's some insight into your work that short circuits some part of your process?
UKLG: If they're far off the track, if they're negative, the disturbance can simply be bad vibes, negative energy. Something you've put your heart into, here's some-

body sniping at it; that is very destructive to any artist, or scholar, anybody doing creative work. You have to persuade yourself that people are going to like what you do, or else it's very hard to do. This is why there are so many unfinished theses, right? And the other thing is, when the centipede starts thinking about how its legs move . . . You can't think about it, you've got to be Zen, you've got to just do it.

P•D: Maybe another reason why scholars and academics don't contact you, is that they're afraid to . . .
UKLG: Some of them actually *are* afraid to. And I understand it. I feel that myself towards people I respect . . .

P•D: But if you're writing a significant piece, sending it in the mail isn't going to be too difficult a fear to overcome, except that maybe the answer will come back that this is a piece of nonsense.
UKLG: Yes, the fear of rejection by somebody you respect is very painful. And some writers can be incredibly cruel even to student pieces. I've heard stories about it.

P•D: There's a sort of related question having to do with "fame" in Chip Delany's book. He quotes Rilke, "Fame is the sum of misunderstandings current about you."
UKLG: Oh, I love it. The thing about Chip is he can remember things like that. He has the most fantastic memory. I adore that quote, and I'll forget it before tonight.

P•D: There was a story Doris Lessing told about sending off a new novel under a pseudonym to see what the reaction would be, to get an honest answer back, to see if the publisher would respond to the novel and not to her as Doris Lessing. The response came back: "It's a promising first novel but you'll have to work it over quite a bit."
UKLG: Well, she got it published. And she got reviews that were somewhat patronizing. That was a very gutsy, feisty thing to do.

P•D: I guess the general idea is how does fame affect a writer . . .
UKLG: The downside is interference with one's time. The endless letters asking if you'll keynote, or will you introduce this book, or will you blurb that book. An enormous number of requests and invasions of different kinds. That was why I was so prickly with you people to start with [ed note: referring to an exchange of

letters related to UKLG's agreeing to be on the *Para·doxa* Board of Editors]. I get a lot of approaches, and most of them I just have to say "no" to. The upside is that you *know* you're being read.

There are more fan letters written within science fiction—not as many as there used to be because so many of those people are now communicating electronically—and if you write for children or for teenagers, they write to you. You get this feedback, which is rare for many authors. I know a lot of novelists who have never heard from a reader unless they do a signing. They know they have readers but they never meet them. And there are so many novels that sell a few thousand copies, and that's it. I don't know that I'm "famous," the word doesn't quite seem to fit, but my books seem to stay in print and I have a lot of readers, and that is incredibly supportive. It makes me feel that it's worthwhile for me to try something else. It gives me self-confidence.

And so when I'm whining about the other side of it I have to say, "Hey, come on, do you want it all to dry up?" Sometimes I get cross. Sometimes it seems like they keep talking about the same few stories. Of course they always talk about the older books. Sometimes I feel sorry for myself. A book like *Searoad*, which I think is one of the best things I've done, which I know is one of the best things I've done, got very little attention. People didn't know what to do with it. It didn't fit any particular category. Even within realism it's an uncomfortable book. That's my fault, you know, but to an extent all artists think "Why do they keep talking about *that?* What I'm interested in is *this.*"

I've been very, very lucky. I've had almost no pressure from my publishers to do anything. I've been incredibly fortunate, for instance, in having Buz Wyeth as my editor at Harper for many years now. What I do, Buz will take. And he's never said, "Do *another* this or that."

P·D: What happened to *Searoad?*
UKLG: They didn't publicize it much. The hardcover got remaindered. The paperback is still selling in two editions. A book like that you probably would have to push, and get some big names saying that this is the greatest thing since white bread. And they didn't. They can't do it to every book.

P·D: *Searoad* was very engaging. It may have been surprising for readers who had thought of you as a traveler to strange shores and exotic lands.
UKLG: Oregon is a pretty exotic place to a lot of Easterners. . . . I've always written realism as well as non-realism. But if you write sf you tend to get type-cast.

P•D: *Searoad* was a very interesting way of creating something like a novel that was not a novel, where the chapters are different stories, but stories with more than a passing connection. The last story particularly, the one where the Hernes matriarchy establishes something like an archeological record of the place, certainly an anthropological record, through layers of accumulated experience, and contacts, and houses that rise and fall over the course of time. How did you arrive at that unpredictable sequence or chronology of the stories in 'Hernes'?

UKLG: The voices came seemingly arbitrarily in time. They were related by place, but they were free in time. I wish I could tell you why it was written that way. It is almost entirely in the order that it was written. It took two years to write and it's only sixty pages long. That doesn't mean I was at my desk every morning of the two years, but I was working on it in my head all the time. I had to wait for the voices to come. A voice would come and I would write down what it said, as it were, channeling again. If I tried to push it or force it or demand something to write, it would be wrong, and I'd have to throw it out. I had to sit and listen. And I kept it almost entirely in the order in which it was written. When it was performed last year here (in Portland) as a staged reading, the woman who prepared it for the stage had to cut it a lot, and she ended up putting it into chronological order, because as a read-aloud piece it was confusing. That was very interesting. It changed the import of things. I don't know why it hangs together the way it does, but I know it does. For the staged reading the chronological order was right, but I would never want to see it printed in that form. It's not like *Always Coming Home*, which I genuinely meant for people to read in any order they felt like, to bounce around in it. What I wanted in 'Hernes' was a kind of layering.

P•D: There are a number of men in *Searoad* . . .
UKLG: But it's a woman-centered book . . .

P•D: It is a woman-centered book, where the men are in the background . . .
UKLG: . . . they're marginal. They're like women in most canonical novels.

P•D: Well, yes, and yet it felt like you still had a very sympathetic feeling for these people, these men.
UKLG: Well, sure. I don't eat men. I just don't feel they must be always at the center, at center-stage. Some of the criticism that has annoyed me, that hurt me, has been related to *Searoad*. Some critic said that "all the men in the book are either weak or wicked," which totally floored me. Kim Stanley Robinson is on me

about what he calls "the absence of the good young man." Well, there aren't any "good young women" in *Moby Dick,* but it's still a good book.

P•D: There's certainly no absence of male protagonists in your work overall.
UKLG: In *Fisherman of the Inland Sea* I'm back to a mixed cast. But there was a time when I had to do, in a sense, some affirmative action. And this book (*Searoad*) was an example of it. But I suppose if I have a favorite character in it it's probably Bill, the middle-aged guy who's not too quick.

P•D: The potter?
UKLG: Yes. I just love him.

P•D: That's an extraordinary scene where he's visited by the woman . . . The visit occurs in two stories, two chapters, . .
UKLG: Yes. You get two sides of it. *The New Yorker* rejected that story because my editor at *The New Yorker* couldn't figure it out. Bill has this ethical problem about asking full price for flawed pots. The editor said, "Of course he shouldn't be getting a full price for flawed pots. What's the problem?"

P•D: That *was* the problem.
UKLG: I was kind of amazed. Editors can be very strange.

P•D: The town itself (in *Searoad*) is somehow our guide through the story, the buildings going up and falling down were, in a way, the map, a guide through their lives that makes them cohere in a way . . .
UKLG: "Place" is obviously enormously important in all my work. Look how many maps there are in my books. Often a map is one of the first things I do.

P•D: There's a kind of verbal map in one of the stories in *Fisherman of the Inland Sea* that you said gave you trouble, "The Rock That Changed Things." In a way the rock mosaic resonates with all the strong images of "place" and maps in your work, "place" that will survive the esthetic, the wisdom, the library that's maintained and preserved by the elite in the castle.
UKLG: Yes, well, of course the professors preserve their knowledge in their layout of the rocks. It was all very much about academe, that story.

P•D: Why did you say that the story gave you so much trouble?
UKLG: Well the satire is a bit heavy-handed. I'm not very fond of allegory, and that story is verging on allegory. I'm not particularly fond of a story that has

a meaning; I'd much rather have *thirty* meanings. "The Rock That Changed Things" resisted me to the point to where I couldn't make it any better, to where I gave up on it. With a certain sense of defeat. Generally I stop writing something when I'm pretty satisfied with it. (Then I come back to it after six months and think, "Oh my God, that isn't what I meant at all!") But "The Rock That Changed Things" is a specific case of being defeated by a story. All stories resist in one way or another. "Hernes" was incredibly resistive, I mean those people wouldn't talk to me for months on end. But "The Rock That Changed Things" defeated me. I didn't get it right. I don't know why. I don't know where. If I knew what the trouble was, I would have fixed it.

P•D: Do you wish you could rewrite any of your fiction in a way that you rewrote the essay "Is Gender Necessary?" as "Is Gender Necessary? Redux," where you have in brackets or italics: If I were doing it today this is how I'd do it, but I'm not going to change it; however, please, if you're going to quote me, quote the brackets if there are any.

UKLG: That technique is thanks to feminist criticism and theory. You owe it to your readers to leave a record if you've changed your mind. That's good feminist practice. Of course a person can change his or her mind, but don't pretend that you always thought the way you do now. That's the trouble with being a writer (dancers are so lucky!): People come at you with something you said in 1960 and say, "Why do you believe this?!"

The great problem in *The Left Hand of Darkness* is the pronoun problem. I've been enormously tempted to do something about it, but I think that would be profoundly dishonest. The book is the book. It was written twenty-five years ago. It has its own integrity. So, to me, the only honest thing to do is to write a screenplay of it and get around the problem in a different way, take the story and do it in a different form all together. But not rewrite it.

P•D: Is that something you're working on?
UKLG: Yes, I've done a screenplay with Paul Preuss. I won't say more about it now because it is actually in people's hands. I think the best thing for writers to do with the movies is to keep their trap shut. Woody Allen said, "Take the money and run," and he's right.

P•D: There is one essay where you talk about making a film, in Texas, of *The Lathe of Heaven.*

UKLG: Thanks to David Loxton of WNET, I had a lovely movie-making experience. Most authors come out of it scarred, battered and swearing.

P•D: You also said some place that you had a filmscript that you were working on, but that you weren't willing to change it, to accommodate the Hollywood machinery.

UKLG: That's what came out as *King Dog: A Screenplay*. Capra Press did a series of books that when you get to the end you have to turn the book upside down and start at the other side like the old Ace-Doubles. There's a screenplay by Raymond Carver and his wife on the other side of *King Dog*. It was a piece that came to me first as a kind of epic poem. It was dreadful as an epic poem, ghastly. So I looked at it and said "the good thing about this is the dialogue. It's a screenplay." So I turned it into one, but it wasn't salable, so I reformatted it as a reading screenplay. A few people have found it and liked it. I'm very fond of it. You're always fond of your babies that nobody knows about.

P•D: You have reviewed some of the science fiction written by Doris Lessing . . .
UKLG: They kept asking me to review it . . .

P•D: How does it happen that such an accomplished writer, when she switches genres, suddenly becomes so clumsy. Is it that she didn't learn the rules of the game?
UKLG: That may just be it. As a science fiction writer, she's a young writer. Yes, those are surprisingly clunky books. Also science fiction often encourages people to preach; it's so easy; I've done some of it myself. But I'm very aware of the pitfalls. Look at somebody like Heinlein: many of his late books are just tirades. Some science fiction troubles me ethically.

P•D: It comes back to a question of excellence. Bloom seems to be saying over and over again "look, any list will die, all lists are stupid." He says that there is what he calls the "school of resentment," the deconstructionists, etc., who just don't get it. It's as if there is this shining "esthetic quality" that will rise to the top. If it's not there, you can't do anything about it.
UKLG: In a very general sense, I agree. I find incredible beauty in Native American literature now that I have *learned* how to read it, but it took me years to learn how. You have to learn how. The trouble with most of the canon is that they narrow it too much, and you *don't* learn how to read things. It sounds like I'd be interested in what Bloom says. But how can he talk about shining esthetic qualities and then include Philip Roth as a great novelist? If he's there, why and how am I?

There's one thing I wanted to ask you: Are you going to try to handle "Kiddi-lit," children's literature, in *Para·doxa*?

P·D: Yes.

UKLG: It's very strange what we do with children's literature. We idolize a couple of things like *Alice in Wonderland* and treat the rest as if it were dirt. Children's literature is very lively. There have been a number of good—not great but very good—novels written for young adults. Good, solid novels. The whole children's literature field is very interesting. Rather chaotic right now. So it would be fun if you could get an article or two. The trouble is, I would predict you might have trouble here. Kiddilit people talk only to one another. Talk about a ghetto! There are some very good critics; Paul Heins, Eleanor Cameron are true critics of chil-dren's literature, in the old critical tradition of looking for excellence and know-ing how to teach the reader how to find that excellence.

P·D: The *Earthsea* trilogy is classified as "Young Adult" literature, and your Na-tional Book Award (1973) was for Children's Literature. It seems like an odd cate-gory to put it in because it's quite compelling for adults. In fact there's language in it that's not so transparent.

UKLG: Well the fourth book is rather problematic. The first volume is certainly read by nine- and ten-year-olds now. It was published for "eleven up." And that means "up," all the way up. Most modern fantasy is "eleven up." *The Hobbit* is probably eight up; *The Lord of the Rings,* a good eleven-year-old reader will at-tack it and chew his way through. Fantasy is different from realism in its accessi-bility to both children and adults. There are very few definitions of these things, of what constitutes a children's book, or what constitutes a Young Adult book, but the main thing about a Young Adult book probably is that the protagonist is under twenty. The fourth *Earthsea* book, *Tehanu,* has a young child in it, but the child's been abused, and the actual protagonist is an old woman. So it is not a book for nine-year-olds. It's a book for some twelve-year-olds these days, though. Those kids are reading amazingly sophisticated things.

P·D: Were you writing *The Wizard of Earthsea* and *The Left Hand of Darkness* at about the same time?

UKLG: They came together. One I wrote in '67 and the other in '68.

P·D: But you didn't have them going on simultaneously?

UKLG: No. I'm like Gerald Ford, one thing at a time. I know writers who can juggle two or three things at the same time . . .

P•D: That must have been a prolific period in your life . . .

UKLG: Well, I've written an awful lot, but you get on a roll every now and then. I've been on a roll with short stories for about a year.

P•D: There are both creative and academic writers on the Editorial Board of *Para•doxa*. We hope to get people who write about writing to talk to people who write, and vice versa.

UKLG: Academics and authors can be very touchy and quarrelsome. I hope it works! There's so much to be said about this whole thing. We ran away from the question of "excellence," and yet when you talk about the arts you *have* to talk about excellence. I hope *Para•doxa* will make the more rigid teachers of literature realize that they *must* learn how to read non-realist fiction and recognize its excellences. I hope we can drag the English departments into the postmodern age of fiction, even if they kick and scream at us all the way.

Notes

1. Ed note: UKLG had more to say about this "joint experience" in her introduction to the *Norton Book of Science Fiction: North American Science Fiction 1960–1990.* Ursula K. Le Guin and Brian Attebery, eds. New York: W.W. Norton, 1993):

   Science fiction is a "genre," we are told, briskly. But the validity of the concept of genre [. . .] is problematical.

   The definition of a genre is often an act of offense, or of retaliation. The professors and critics who for most of the century have controlled the modernist literary canon define and dismiss science fiction—frequently in absolute ignorance of its texts—as "genre fiction," that is, not "literature," in order to restrict "literature" to the privileged mode, realism. In defiant and often ignorant resentment of "the highbrow establishment," some practitioners of science fiction define it defensively as "popular entertainment," not "literature." Some chic critics go slumming trendily with them. None of this posturing advances understanding.

   Genre is a useful concept only when used not evaluatively but descriptively. Authors and readers of any genre form a community, with certain shared interests and expectations. Modern poetry is a good example of genre as community. So is science fiction.

   Professor Thomas Roberts, author of *The Aesthetics of Junk Fiction,* (1968), makes this parallel, pointing out (in an interview by Marcia Biederman: "Genre Writing" in *Poets and Writers* [January–February 1992]), that people who read poetry "follow *poetry* rather than poems"—that is, they read the genre, not only certain authors, because the *body of work* is at least as important as the individual writers. Excellence within a genre is seen not as a miraculous anomaly of "genius," but as a high point in a tradition. The artist is not expected to reinvent the wheel—only to use it well.

Genre writers and readers share a common stock of concepts, icons, images, manners, patterns, precisely as the musicians and audiences of Haydn's and Mozart's time shared a *materia musica* which the composer was expected, not to shatter or transcend, but to use and make variations on. "The pattern," says Roberts, "has to be fixed, partly because that's enjoyable in itself, partly because that makes it possible to be surprised and delighted by a diversion from the pattern." Transcendence, as in the case of Mozart, may of course occur; it's wonderful, but it really isn't the point. We have let the modern fixation on the Hero-Genius, that phallological fellow who towers in tremendously visible solitude from Byron on, obscure our view of how literature actually works. It works through accreting a tradition. A genre is a faunal tradition.

All right. I say that science fiction is a literary tradition, a genre of fiction, like realism.

2. (Ed note: UKLG provided a paraphrase here of what she had written on the subject in her introduction to *Fisherman of the Inland Sea*.) One has to learn to read Jane Austen, just as much as one has to learn how to read Tolkien or Philip K. Dick. The appreciation of realism is no more or less complex than the appreciation of imaginative fiction. It's worth considering, also, that Jane Austen's England is in many ways more remote from us than most invented science-fictional worlds are. And it's worth remembering that *none of those worlds exists*. They are all word-constructs, inventions, fictions. Realism pretends not to be fiction: but it is. That's its saving grace.

Entretien avec Ursula K. Le Guin

Hélène Escudié/2002

From *Anthologie périodique de "Fantasy and Science Fiction"* #3, Printemps (2006). Published for the first time in English by permission of Hélène Escudié.

HE: Could you define the evolution that took place in the way people, men and women, behave toward each other, and changed their behavior since the sixties. What impact did it have on your writings?

UKLG: Since the sixties, there certainly was a great change. My early writings, particularly the fantasies, the Earthsea books, were written in a tradition, a literary tradition, which was almost womanless. It was about male heroes, doing male things. Actually, in my generation, most novels were very male-centered, and there was no question, and that was proper, and inevitable, and I didn't question it. So my heroes, my central figures, my viewpoint characters were generally men, and women were important but secondary. About 1970, *The Tombs of Atuan* was the first book I wrote, I think, the first real full scale, large size novel with a woman at the center. But of course it becomes a pair. It becomes a man and a woman when Ged comes into the book, although we are always in Tenar's mind, she is the viewpoint character always, that's very important who is seeing the world. Ged is very important because they have to act together to make anything happen.

And then, as feminist theory began to finally get into my head, and as I began to read what the feminists told me to read, which was my female ancestors in writing—I had always read George Eliot, Willa Cather, and so on, certain writers, and of course Virginia Woolf. I had read Virginia Woolf for years, but as I began to understand what she was trying to say, I was reeducated, it really was true. And I think, I'm so grateful to Woolf and all the rest of them because I think I would not have been able to go on writing, that this pretending to be a man all the time, it was beginning not to work. I'm not a man, but I didn't know what was wrong. I didn't know what this sort of discomfort and feeling of frustration was, and I had to learn how to write as a woman, and there's no doubt about that, and I had to fight a lot of my own training and prejudices.

And the first book where I met that . . . it's kind of interesting because it's a little book called *The Eye of the Heron*—and I thought it was a story about a young man, and the young man insisted upon getting killed. And I said, "Please, don't do that, you're my hero, don't, please Lev, don't die." "Stop," he says, "I'm off, good bye!" And it became a story about a young woman because she had to take over. It exhibits what was going on in my soul when I wrote it, that I had to *not* be Lev, but I had to be her, Luz. And after that, then I began to sort of comfortably be a woman, and my writing changed a good deal, I can see it in certain details that I write. I began adopting more different points of view, like choral voices, and things like that. Anyway, I was, as I said, reeducated, I was a new writer. So it's a tremendous change for me and it earned me the disapproval of quite a few male critics. "Oh, what has she done, what has she done, she's become a preachy feminist!" So, too bad.

HE: So it was through feminist writings, Virginia Woolf and others, that you were reeducated, not through everyday life, and what was happening.
UKLG: Not very much was happening. I mean there have been certain political changes due to feminism, but not very much. We have not been very successful politically. Some things are better, but they are always under threat. We are always fighting for them, fighting to keep what small gain we made for equality of gender. But intellectually, the advance was very large and we seem to be keeping it; we seem not to be losing it the way it was lost really almost from the First World War through the Second World War. There was a great setback, wasn't there? Yet that is Virginia Woolf's period. There were some women that were holding to their earlier feminism. It is a complicated history, isn't it?

HE: And it is very disparate in the different countries.
UKLG: Yes, yes.

HE: There were so many things happening, only the result is not what we would like it to be.
UKLG: The sixties, the seventies were an exciting time, I'm so grateful to have lived that, it was so exciting. To me it's so horrid now, to see . . . to lose so much of what we thought we had earned.

HE: Do you think we are losing things?
UKLG: Well, I'm quite worried about my country. Yes, we are going through a very reactionary phase.

HE: In France it's the same.
UKLG: I'm afraid, yes. Eternal vigilance is the price of liberty.

HE: Coming back to Lev, the first time I read your book, I was so shocked to see the hero killed that later I was under the impression that he had died in the second chapter. I reread it this spring and I realized he had died in the middle of the book.
UKLG: Right in the middle, yes.

HE: And I felt the same as you did, when you wrote it.
UKLG: I think that kind of thing, yes, comes through the book. It means that the book, in some ways, is not aesthetically perhaps, as perfect as it might be. But that's all right, you know.

HE: Well, it's striking.
UKLG: It's effective, yes.

HE: Isabelle Stengers, a philosopher of sciences, has called your science fiction "experimental." In fact, like in science, you seem to experiment with a notion, explore the "what ifs" of an idea.
UKLG: Isn't that a typical tactic of science fiction? I think a lot of science fiction does exactly that, "what if" and then you propose a social change, or a physiological change, or a physical change in the world and then pursue it, like a thought experiment, pursue the consequences.

HE: Yes, but you do that in all your work, I think. In fantasy it is the same. It's more general than only in science fiction.
UKLG: Fantasy changes the world deliberately, allowing impossible things which science fiction at least pretends not to allow. Yes, I say "what if magic worked, and then . . . ," and "what if there were dragons . . . ," yes. Then you just follow out, you just follow the fictional enterprise like any novelist, it seems to me, and the more detailed and accurate you are, the better the book will be. And of course, the tricky thing about imaginative fiction, both science fiction and fantasy, is the coherence of the imagination, because you are making a whole world out of words only. It's all made to hold together. Tolkien is very clear about that in some of his essays. He's the best theorist of fantasy I know, actually, Tolkien himself. The European fantasy theorists, Todorov, and those people, they are terrible, terrible. The works they are talking about always seem so insignificant to me. That's not what I mean by fantasy.

HE: You seem to be writing at the same period s.f. books along with fantasy books and history books like those from Orsinia.
UKLG: Pseudo history, of course.

HE: How do you manage to work on such different topics?

UKLG: And also some realist literature like *Searoad*. Well, I go from one to the other. I don't write books simultaneously. I write one book at a time. I'm not one of those writers that can do several things. But I never know what is going to happen next, I make no plans, I wait for a book to come to me or for myself to approach this and find out what it is. And then I write. There is no logic, no planning, no, none.

HE: You said in the interview following the film *The Lathe of Heaven* that characters spoke to you, and that you listened.

UKLG: That's often the way it seems to be, yes, and that is true. It's just the same whether it's fantasy, or science fiction or a realistic novel. I have to hear the voices. I have to know their names and I have to hear their voices; and then, then they tell me the story, as it were.

HE: I noticed that you stopped using telepathy. Could you say why you dropped it?

UKLG: I didn't believe in it. It is a lovely notion but it would make human relationships so different that I realized that I could not imagine . . . My imagination would not tell me how people would act if they could truly read each other's mind. So I just took it out. I just quietly dropped it.

HE: To my mind, it was something that had to do with communication, a different way of communicating.

UKLG: Right. And of course there seem to be sometimes communications that we don't, we can't explain, you know, absolutely. But calling them telepathy gives them a scientific sounding name which is kind of misleading, I think.

HE: There are recurrent themes in your work. For example, I noted that rain is omnipresent in your novels and short stories.

UKLG: Is it? I did not know that.

HE: Yes. Very rarely does the reader find your protagonists in a position where they can die of thirst in a desert. Has rain a special meaning in your work?

UKLG: I don't know. Well, I've lived here a long time, and this is a very rainy climate, but I'm a Californian, from Berkeley, you know, where it rains half the year, pleasantly, not cold, and then half the year, it's absolutely dry. It never rains in the summer in California, so rain is welcome when it comes. And I think particularly as one gets older, one tends to revert to one's original climate, and I miss the sunshine more than I used to. I long for the kind of summer we are having actually, very nice summer, but sometimes the summers are rainy. Sometimes even in July, it goes on raining and raining, I could die . . .

HE: You didn't notice that.

UKLG: No, I never noticed. I noticed the trees, and there are lots of animals, but I didn't notice rain, and I have no explanation.

HE: We often also find winter and harsh weather, like in *The Left Hand of Darkness*. It reminded me of *Orlando*, when the protagonist falls in love with Sasha. The Thames is frozen, and they ice-skate on it. Is there a connection with this novel?

UKLG: That's a wonderful scene, yes. I first read that . . . my mother loved Virginia Woolf, and she gave me *Orlando* when I was fifteen or sixteen. And I read it then, not understanding it very well, but just loving some of those wonderful scenes. But also, how old was I when I got permanently fascinated with the early Antarctic explorers, Scott particularly, and all those ones, those early British ones who wrote about it, and some of the others too. They were such good writers, marvelous writers, Scott himself and Shackleton. It wasn't so easy to find those books then, now they are sort of fashionable—but I would hunt for years to get one of those volumes.

So I had an irrational fascination with the idea of those men tracking across the snow, perhaps because I never saw snow till I was seventeen years old, living in California. We did not go up in the mountains. We lived in a completely snowless world. And so it was very exotic and wonderful too. And then I went to the East coast for college and it snowed very heavily. Boston was over your head that winter. I thought that was wonderful, I thought it was just enchanting, you know. And I still love it—I think people who grow up with a lot of snow often kind of hate it, you know, it's a lot of trouble, but it was exciting to me.

Concerning *The Left Hand of Darkness*, there is no particular reason why they live on a snowy planet. It's just because I wanted to write about one and I had all this information from Scott and Shackleton about how to cross ice, and about how to drag a sledge. So it was fun to use all this. It's merely aesthetic, purely aesthetic appreciation.

HE: I was wondering if it had something to do with love, because of the scene in *Orlando*, if it was a symbol.

UKLG: Well, of course, love in winter, there is the image of being isolated in the cold, in the little center of warmth, like the tent in *The Left Hand of Darkness*. It's a very powerful image to all of us, I think, yes. It's different from love in summer.

HE: Yes, and I was wondering if there was a symbolic link with fire?

UKLG: Well, the hearth, yes. The hearth is a pretty powerful symbol to me. I grew up always in a house with a fireplace, in summer outside, an outside fireplace, and we sat there and told stories. And in winter, the house in Berkeley that I grew up in had a fireplace just like this and that is where we always sat, and so the family affection, shelter, everything that the hearth means in all the European languages, it echoes in me very deep and very simple.

HE: Coming back to Scott, I remember the short story called "Sur" where ladies cross the Antarctic. It was very funny, I loved it.

UKLG: I like that story too. That story was like a gift. There, there was one of these voices. She just began to tell me the story and I said, "Oh, this is wonderful! Tell me more!"

HE: In the story we never know who finances the expedition, who is at the center, the "benefactor" in fact.

UKLG: These are wealthy South American women, and of course I presume they are spending their husband's money, so that's why we never know.

HE: Very often in your novels and short stories, red is the dominant color for plants. Does this color have a special meaning?

UKLG: No, I think that is, particularly in science fiction, that is simply . . .

HE : A device to destabilize the reader?

UKLG: A device, yes, exactly, exactly, yes.

HE: Because it's the complementary color of green?

UKLG: Yes, but actually, you know, I have read speculations about chlorophyll, which is our green color. It just about as easily could be red. It's almost like a matter of chance that we ended up in a green world, so I thought, "Oh that's nice, I can use that in science fiction." So that's all; otherwise it's not significant.

HE: I was wondering if it could represent the Natives of America, so close to nature and being part of it.

UKLG: I don't think so. No, I don't think that there was any such symbolism in my mind. It was just, as you say, a way of destabilizing the expectations, I think.

HE: The critics/scholars have also listed a series of images like dragons and more generally winged animals. What do they represent? Has flight a special meaning for you?

UKLG: A fairly conventional one, I may say, the idea of flying in the body, rather than in a big tin can, you know, being a sort of dream of freedom, and my drag-

ons are certainly—the dragons of *Earthsea,* whatever they are—they certainly
are partly wildness and freedom. They are the animal in its complete freedom.
Otherwise—I'm trying to think—there're the cats, the *Catwings* books, that was
simply a kind of childish . . . I drew a picture of a cat with wings, and I thought
"Oh, what fun! Why shouldn't a cat have wings?" and then, "What would happen
if they did?" and so there goes the book.

HE: You have mice also . . .

UKLG: That was because of the artist who illustrated that book. That book
was written for that artist, he was very envious of the artist who did the *Cat-wings* books. He said, "I could have done those. Write me a book with mice with
wings," and I said, "Of course, of course." So I wrote that little book, and he had
lots of fun with the mice. But it was a sort of collaborative joke, almost. And re-cently, there's a story that is not even printed—it'll be out in my next book—about
people with wings.

HE: There are people with wings in *Planet of Exile . . .*

UKLG: Oh yes, there are these really dreadful sort of . . .

HE: Like angels . . .

UKLG: But they are really more like bees, they are mindless, they are brain-less . . .

HE: But they are beautiful.

UKLG: Yes, they are beautiful like angels but they are absolutely brainless and
they act by instinct only, like bees. There are hives . . . Yes, they are quite horrid.
And . . . oh yes, there were the winged cats in that book too, they ride big winged
cats, don't they? Yes, that's right, I've forgotten them, that's so long ago. So the
winged cat idea was already there.

HE: Yes, since the start you have winged animals.

UKLG: Now more recently they have become little cats, instead of really big cats.
I had forgotten about them, yes, and there are some winged people in a recent
story, where again it's kind of . . . it's good and it's not good to have wings. Yes, the
significance there is not entirely freedom; it's much more, well, a mixed blessing,
as we say.

HE: In the last book of *Earthsea,* and in *Tales from Earthsea,* the two girls become
dragons.

UKLG: They are dragons and women, yes.

HE: So the dragon seems to be more feminine, now.

UKLG: Why only women became dragons? As the *Earthsea* books go on, the dragons become ungendered. I think in the early books, I may call the dragon "he." The dragon Yevaud seems to be male but he is bringing up the baby dragons. The mother dragon apparently laid the eggs, and the father dragon hatches them, so at that time, there is sexuality among the dragons in the books. As the books go on, and as the whole idea of the dragons gets more and more complicated in my mind, they become ungendered. And so evidently either a man or a woman can also be a dragon, but in the books, don't ask me why, it's all women. Maybe because women need to be dragons more than men do, in my world. You know, I think that might be the reason. But in all justice, I should have had a man who was a dragon. But . . . I really can't answer that question, as if it were a factual matter. Is it only women who are also dragons? I don't think so, but in my examples, all three of them are women.

HE: And you said a while ago that they represent "wildness and freedom," so these women could represent wildness and freedom in your mind . . .

UKLG: Or they represent the wildness and the freedom that women don't have, because they are not allowed to be dragons, as it were. At one point, in one of the books, Ged is perceived by a wizard as a dragon—that's in *The Farthest Shore*. And somebody, I can't even think who it is, somebody calls Ged by the name of the Maker, Segoy. So Ged is also more than just a man apparently, but don't ask me to explain it, because I don't understand. These are things . . . Sometimes people say things, in the books, and I say "OK," that means something. I don't know what it means, but I know it's right, and I leave it. And sometimes later on, I find out what it means; sometimes I don't. I have to trust the story to tell itself, and sometimes I do not understand what it is saying.

HE: Light and dark seem to recur and do not have the same value in the stories.

UKLG: Yes, right. Yes, the single valuation of light/good, dark/bad . . . It goes very deep in humankind. We do turn towards the light but—you know—it isn't any good without darkness. Yes, so I do find, over and over, in different ways, in different books, we're trying to revalue the darkness from which everything grows. But it can't do it without the light. This is Taoism again, the yang and then the yin, you know. They are the light and the dark, but if I understand Taoism correctly, they are not the good and the bad, or the good and the evil at all. One is nothing without the other and it is their interaction and their constant becoming one another that is the universal process, the cosmic process. And yes, definitely that runs as a theme through a lot of the stories.

HE: Maimed or abandoned children can be found in several of your books. Could you say that they represent a sort of scapegoat, being the most unarmed creatures?
UKLG: I think that's right. The most defenseless kind of human being is a child, particularly a girl child, yes, and so they are the abomination of cruelty. It was surprising to me to realize that that was a theme, as it were, because my childhood having been a very serene and secure one. Where does that come from, you know? Maybe just living in the world, yes . . .

HE: Dream is also a very important theme, and you treat it from different points of view. For example, we see effective dreaming in *The Lathe of Heaven,* and also dream waking, like in *The Word for World Is Forest.* There are also other dreams in *The Farthest Shore,* which are more like our ordinary dreams. You also wrote about dreams in *Dancing at the Edge of the World.* You seem to explore the different possibilities dreams can offer men.
UKLG: Well, it is one of the major human activities, isn't it? We all do it every night. You know, my father was a Freudian analyst, as well as an anthropologist. He became a lay analyst. Freud said that dreaming is extremely important, and I probably absorbed that. Then I read Jung, and Jung has rather specific theories about dreams. Some of them made sense to me; some of them didn't. But so I got a little acquainted with the psychology, and then of course there was all the scientific research on sleep and dreaming that was done mostly in the 1960s, and still going on. And I was fascinated with that. The scientists that were writing it mostly wrote very well, but actually they didn't get very far. There has been no breakthrough since the seventies in sleep and dream research, or not much. But it seemed like they were going to be able to explain what dreaming is and what it does. And that's the period when I picked up the idea for *The Lathe of Heaven,* which is simply "what if dreams came true," and take it literally, take a metaphor. I had all that research to use, and so all I had to do was invent my sleeping machine. It is just one of those science fiction inventions which looks plausible and is absolutely nonsense. But that's part of the fun of science fiction; you agree to believe.

HE: Talking about dream waking, like in *The Word for World Is Forest,* while I was reading this book, I was very much interested in Australia, and more particularly in the aborigines, and I think they do something like that, don't they?
UKLG: They certainly seem to use dreams.

HE: I don't know exactly what they do.

UKLG: I don't either, because I haven't read that much on them. My father studied a people in southern California, the Mojave Indians, who dreamed long journeys, and made sagas, long narratives, including every stopping place and practically every step they took through the desert—a mixture of dream and reality. He translated one of those epics. They are quite dull to us, because we don't live in the desert where every little rock is important, but I was fascinated by that idea of both making a trip and dreaming the trip at the same time. And then there were those people that . . . what are they called, it's a tribe in the Philippine Islands—the research on them has mostly been severely questioned, and some of it disproved, but it looked as if these people used dreams quite consciously to guide their waking life, the way the people do in *The Word for World Is Forest*. And that was the model, that book by an anthropologist who has been at least half-discredited. He either made it up or he was gullible. It's as if he wanted to believe something that really wasn't quite the way he wanted it to be, but anyway, it was very exciting when it was first published, and it seemed to be good scientific evidence for people actually using dreams as a community enterprise. And apparently the Senoy people do encourage children to tell their dreams. They tell each other dreams and if it's an important dream they discuss it. Freud would have loved it, doing Freudian work as a community project. And so I thought that was endearing, and interesting, and so I played with it in that book. Unfortunately, I'm afraid, it was almost as much fiction as my book. I think what particularly interests me with the Senoy and the little I've heard about the aborigines is the community aspect, the fact of talking about it openly, and everybody saying "what is that about, what does that signify," instead of the Freudian sense of the dream as intensely personal and exclusively personal. This is a very different approach.

HE: And it goes back to your community concept.

UKLG: Yes.

HE: I would like to talk about translation: a thought experiment is difficult to translate. For example, in "Schrödinger's Cat," you write at the beginning, "I don't know what I grieve for, my husband, my wife, my children." How can you translate this short story? In French, you have to put the past participle in the feminine or the masculine form, so this story seems to be untranslatable.

UKLG: Yes, that's right. I didn't realize that. I love translating, it is an enormous pleasure to me, but there are times when you just want to scream, because there is no way to say it, or else it gets conky.

Essentially, it is a thankless job, translation. It's very badly paid, and you don't get much credit for it. Of course, most of my work that has been translated into French has been by commercial translators who work for a publishing company, and just sort of translate automatically, and they are OK, but they are not distinguished translations. My Danish translator, I don't know Danish, but he's wonderful. He writes me long lists of "What does this mean?" or "Is that a joke?" and I know that I have good translations in Danish, because of the correspondence with the translator. I'm told that my German translations are abominable; my Spanish ones seem pretty good. Translation is not highly respected work. So like many translators I do it for love. I've been working on Gabriela Mistral, the Chilean poet.[1]

HE: And you translated the *Tao Te Chin*.

UKLG: I don't really call it a translation because I don't know Chinese. It is a version built up from all the other English versions, and a couple of French ones, and the Chinese word for word translation, and a lot of help from my collaborator who does know Chinese, ancient Chinese. It was a lot of fun, oh yes, it was wonderful to work out my own reading of the infinitely re-readable book. I'm looking now for something to translate. I translated Mistral because I discovered that she really has not been brought into English very much, Neruda over and over and over, but not Mistral. I fell in love with her. You have to fall in love, I think, to do a long translation. Yes, and then it's fun. When I was thirty or so, I loved Supervielle, and I did some stories of his and I tried to interest an American publisher. No, no. He wasn't fashionable.

HE: Some of the critics said that you are a "mythopoeic writer"; others said that on the contrary, you destroy myths, or you distort them. More generally, they say that you seem to have borrowed from Norse, Celtic, Teutonic myths. From my point of view, you also borrowed from ancient Indian myths.

UKLG: My father's work with myths and legends was with the Yurok and Karuk and Mojave Indians of California, very different people; their myths are very different. I was not influenced by those directly because I read them late in life. They are totally different from our literary tradition and it would be very hard to work them in stories. My mother wrote a little book called "The Inland Whale"—that's hard to get hold of, but it has been reprinted, by Indiana, I think—where she re-

---

1. Ursula K. Le Guin, *Selected Poems of Gabriela Mistral,* Albuquerque: University of New Mexico Press, 2003.

tells six or seven Californian myths. She was writing that when I was already a grown woman and had become a writer myself. Those stories certainly had some influence on me. In general, I would say, my influences do not come from Native American stories, because the culture, the society is so different, it doesn't come over easily into the European tradition of writing. Not until I wrote *Always Coming Home* could I begin to play with the way the Native Americans looked at the world. I didn't read my father's work until I was quite a grown woman, and already had found my own way as a writer, so I don't think his writings really influenced me very much. It was his personality.

HE: Maybe the stories he told you . . .
UKLG: And the stories, yes. It came from the stories, yes, he did tell us some Indian stories when we were little, mostly quite terrifying ghost stories, the head that rolls after people, oh, terrible, wonderful thrill, you know, for children . . . But the whole question of myth is confusing to me. I interpret the word as an anthropologist does, meaning a story that people tell, as a community, which in a sense defines and asserts that community, whether as a people or as a spiritual group. So do we write myth at all? Or is the word really misapplied to novels and the kind of stories we tell? I really don't know, to me it's a puzzle, and so when I'm asked if I write myths I say, "Well, no, because I can't speak for my people, I don't have a tribe," you know, and people say: "Science fiction is the mythology of modern times," and I say: "Mmm . . . ," maybe, you know, maybe, partly, but there are many other mythologies going. And certainly, whoever said I was out to destroy myths, I don't know quite what they meant. I wonder what they had in mind.

HE: Maybe your way of subverting things . . .
UKLG: Well, that's the feminist trick of taking a folk tale, or a fairy tale, and retelling it from another point of view, but that's not mythology. That's folk tale, fairy tale, that's the gendering of society. Again I'm not sure that the word myth is very helpful. You retell a story from a different point of view and then it becomes another story but everybody does that. We don't tell that many new stories. All we do is retell stories differently. I don't think I can be very helpful. If you can follow this up later, if you think about it and find some way . . .

HE: I wasn't sure you have borrowed from Norse, Celtic. As you said, you retell things . . .
UKLG: In a few places, you can definitely tell. For instance, in my first published novel, *Rocannon's World,* I am retelling part of the myth of Odin, and anybody

looking for that kind of one to one correspondence can find a few others. But I don't think it's a very major part of my work.

HE: They wrote about Freya, in "Semley's Necklace."
UKLG: Yes, Freya's necklace is the germ of that story. I grew up with a couple of very good English versions of the Norse mythology, and was very fond of those stories. They're grim and tragic, and full of trolls and giants, and everything a child likes. I always liked them better than the Greeks who were always tricking one another. They are more intellectual, they are really less heroic, they are often rather despicable, and as a child, I preferred the heroic Norse. And after all the Norse gods are all killed. It is a tragic race, and that moved me as a child. And an awful lot of the Greek stories have to do with Zeus either seducing or raping somebody, and I wasn't aware of it as a child but I think I resented that. "So that's him again," you know, "What is he going to do this time?"

HE: Your work has been described as ethical fantasy; my idea is that it reflects more a philosophy of life than an ethic of life.
UKLG: I don't know what an ethic would be. I don't have a clear idea. An ethic should be something one can state, as a proposition as it were, and I can't. But I don't know what the philosophy is either, except for Taoism, the Taoist understanding of how things work. The ethics of Taoism are very subtle, very complex, and rather reticent. There is no talk about good and evil or right and wrong, or very little talk. What would be the most natural way to do something, the easiest way to do something, that's going to be the right way. But in what sense do you take the word "right," which is such a tricky word in English. Does it mean correct, does it mean moral, does it mean just easy, or . . . So again, I'm not very helpful. I was afraid of this philosophy section.

HE: Now let's talk about Sartre.
UKLG: Sartre. Oh, mon Dieu!

HE: You put Sartre on stage in "A Trip to the Head." You speak about him . . .
UKLG: Yes, I insult him slightly.

HE: I was wondering why, why you chose him.
UKLG: Because when I was in college, I was doing French literature. It was my subject, French and Italian, and one of my professors became a friend. He was a young Frenchman, Louis Pamplume, and Louis was . . . I guess he was a sort of

Catholic existentialist. He had me reading quite a few existential philosophers, most of whom I did not understand very clearly, but it was very exciting and I did read some Sartre. I probably was in the generation that would have read Sartre anyway. I saw one of his plays, *Huis Clos,* a good play. He was fashionable, and much talked about in the fifties in America. It was his high days. I realized gradually that I found him in too many ways detestable—the incredible negativity of some of his work . . . Of course he is out to shock and so on, but I was a very serious twenty-year-old, so I went into rebelling against Sartre, and others of that kind, so that's why I think I was making jokes about him, later on.

HE: Animals in your work seem to say something. They seem to be symbols of something. For example, in *The Eye of the Heron,* you have the "wotsit," in *A Wizard of Earthsea,* you have the "otak" . . .
UKLG: Very important connection, yes, yes . . . Animals are very important to me. I really am not happy if I do not have animals with me nearby . . .

HE: I didn't dig enough yet to find the meaning of each of all these animals. I'm sure they convey an important meaning . . .
UKLG: All I can say is that I don't dig very much myself into what I mean but—let's put it this way: in real life, in actual life, people who have no connection to animals at all almost frighten me. How can you live in the world without animals, without watching them and . . . I mean, it is a privilege to have an animal and live with one. We've always had pets, and my daughter is crazy about horses, and all the rest of it. There has always been an animal connection, very strong, to me, and it seems to me so important. It is a connection and if it's broken, something is terribly wrong. I wrote about that in the introduction to the book *Buffalo Gals;* I think I said what the animal means to me. And both of the poems that I quote in there, both the one by Levertov and the one by Rilke also, they can say why I think it's so important and why animals keep creeping into my stories, or the stories are about them.

HE: Some of your short stories are very striking, like "Schrödinger's Cat," for example. You seem to have shifted to another dimension in the collection of stories entitled *Unlocking the Air and Other Stories.*
UKLG: There are a couple of rather short stories in there. They are very allusive, and I simply was not being kind to the reader. There again, I think very likely I could not tell you what they "mean." They were not so much expressing an idea

as a mood. Like a piece of music, I'm using words to try to catch a mood, but no more than that. So that to interpret them intellectually would probably be a mistake.

HE: For example, I remember one: "The Spoons in the Basement" . . .
UKLG: That's a true story. I had that dream. That's one of the few times that I have actually used a real dream. I had that dream exactly as it's told in the story, and it's true about the spoons too. This house presented us with the spoons. So, there, I was simply, as it were, recounting actual experiences without trying to explain them. So it remains as enigmatic as a dream. Yes, and that's probably all I can tell you. If there are other meanings, that's for the critics, not for me.

HE: Concerning children's books, did you test their impact on your own grandchildren?
UKLG: No. I've never read my work to my children or my grandchildren. It seemed unfair, "Do you like it? Dear? You'd better, I'm your grandmother . . ."
I have sometimes given manuscripts to other people to read to their children, where there's no personal weight or tension, and received criticism. And of course when the books are published, I get letters from children, and I get lots of criticism, and it's very interesting. Sometimes it's extremely funny and they are full of ideas for more stories, but sometimes they say quite interesting things about the stories. Children can be very keen critics. But many children's authors do write for certain specific children, and I don't. I just have the story to tell, and I tell it and hope the kids like it, you know.

HE: It seems to me that some of the stories want to teach something, although you said that you did not like to sound "preachy."
UKLG: Art and preaching are two different things and they don't mix. A sermon can be a work of art, but it's hard for a work of art to be a sermon. It is difficult to write for children without some ethical stance and program because an adult relationship to a child is always an implied teaching, isn't it? It's inevitable. That is simply the nature of our relationship. It may be just affirming the fact that there is love in the world or something like that, but it's clear-cut when you write for children. And I don't worry about it when I'm writing for children because I know that all children's books . . . if they don't deliberately teach something, the child will use them to learn something from them. I learnt from everything I read as a child; everything I read now I'm learning from. I may be learning something quite different from what the author intended. And I've been clearly aware all my

life that, as a reader, I could make the book into what I wanted—to some extent. So I am aware, as a writer, that my reader is going to make the book their book, not my book, but the reader's book. So that's right, that's how it should be, but it does mean that if you set out too bluntly to teach a child, I think usually they'll resist it, they'll reject it, or they'll twist it into something you didn't mean at all. It's a very interesting problem. I have often been told by critics that my writing is too didactic, my adult books, that the moral is too clear. And I'm always embarrassed and afraid they're right, because the book as I wrote it was sort of an argument to me, and when it's written, it all becomes clearer. And so it seems perhaps more didactic, and less a sort of on-going argument which usually it was, while I was writing it. I never wrote a book, ever, with the intention of teaching something . . . I have had polemical intentions for instance in *The Word for World Is Forest*, that was written in the middle of the Vietnam war and I was very angry. Some of my stories are openly polemical, but that's a bit different, art and polemics can go together.

HE: And it's funny because, when I first read *The Word for World Is Forest*, as I don't have the same background and I was less touched by the Vietnam war than you were, I didn't feel that the war was very important.
UKLG: It seems to have survived its subject, yes.

HE: For me, it was all the dream waking, and all this philosophy of life that Selver describes that was important.
UKLG: Good. Yes.

HE: It's exactly what you said earlier. You have a reading and you learn something but it can be very different from the intention of the author.
UKLG: Yes, because it's what you put into the book as well as what the book is offering you, so it's a combination, it's a chemistry which is going to be different every time the book is read.

HE: Yes, and when you read it twenty years later . . .
UKLG: It's entirely different.

HE: A spiral structure has often been noted in the analysis of your books. Would you say that is could represent a combination of the upwards line corresponding to the myth of progress, and the circle as seen in the Taoist philosophy?
UKLG: I don't think there is . . . Let me think. The myth of progress is not one that interests me very much. The myth of social progress and evolutionary prog-

ress is one I distrust very deeply. I believe in change. Change does occur and must occur, not "always change for the better." That's the myth of progress. In Taoism, the circle is not a closed circle and it's not static. It's in constant balance and shifting, always shifting. So there are several images at work here. I'm not sure that you can write in a spiral exactly, except that the spiral means that you've got a circular shape. It's not linear; it's not bong, bong, bong, in a straight line . . . My stories seem to go round in a circle. They often end pretty much where they began, but things have changed, so I suppose that makes the spiral. You are in the circle, but you're not exactly at the same place, ever; you can never in fact go back. You cannot. Time does not allow it. We don't go back. So I suppose you could call it a spiral shape.

HE: That would be more a combination of time and space.
UKLG: Yes. Yes. After all, we say that the Earth goes around the Sun in a circle, but it doesn't. It goes around the Sun in a spiral because the Sun is moving, so when everything is moving there actually are no closed circles.

HE: You said, "utopia is process rather than progress."
UKLG: It is the same idea.

HE: More generally, in nearly all your stories, a process is at work. Does it mean that nothing is ever complete, that even after death the process can carry on?
UKLG: Yes. I think so.

HE: So death is not frightening then . . .
UKLG: Death is quite frightening to the personality, since the personality seems to be entirely mortal. But if you can hoist yourself from your personality for a little bit and look at the process as a whole, then it's rather reassuring. It's certainly going to go on, there's no doubt about that.

HE: Concerning your work about Orsinia: this country is fascinating insofar as it reminds the reader of familiar things although it does not exist. How come you did not live there long?
UKLG: The last story about Orsinia is "Unlocking the Air." We are in the city of Krasnoy, and the older couple are the young couple in "A Week in the Country." It's thirty years later; they're the same people, Stephan and Bruna. But since I wrote that story, which of course was a story of when the communist grip loosened from Central Europe, I have not been able to go back and it distresses me. I wonder what's happening in Orsinia and I have no messengers, nobody will

tell me. I keep listening, and I get no news. So I just don't know. I invented the country . . . and I invented it before any of the published stories. I was writing Orsinian stories that never were and never will be published, when I was a very young writer. I don't know quite what was at work but I read a great deal of Russian literature in translation, Tolstoi and Tourgueniev particularly and Tchekhov who had a very deep influence on me. And I was at home in some ways in Europe as I was not in California, or Massachusetts. I had a spiritual home, and I was in love with France, totally, madly in love with France, and French literature. And so I found this sort of halfway, half-imaginary homeland that I could be in. I had a freedom there, which I did not have in trying to write about my own country. It gave me just enough imaginative freedom. It was something I needed very, very much at age nineteen, age twenty, when I was learning to write stories and novels. So I wrote about that country. *Malafrena* was actually the first novel I finished. The version which is printed was rewritten very much fifteen years later, but the first draft of *Malafrena,* I guess I was twenty or twenty-one. And it was a great pleasure to be able to go back and rewrite it and make it into a grown-up novel. Beyond that, that's all I know about why Orsinia exists, and why I cannot go back I don't know.

I was always fascinated with the 1820s, that romantic decade, and the revolution of 1830 which was of course a disaster everywhere, and 1848. I still read with great joy about that period, I don't know why. It's funny how you find a decade, or a period or a place that you just respond to.

HE: It is a long time ago, and it's a very confused period . . .

UKLG: Very confused, yes. Very good writers you had in France particularly, Vigny, people like that, oh! I love Vigny, and they meant a great deal to me, those people. I haven't read them for many, many years. But they also shaped my view of the world.

HE: In the discussion on the DVD *The Lathe of Heaven,* you say that George Orr is a "go-with-the-flow man," and you link his character to the image of the jellyfish. Although he is very passive, he survives in the end. It is also the philosophy of the Hain, who observe without interfering. However, there always seems to be a moment when one has to intervene, and therefore modifies the current situation. Has it to do with the Tao philosophy, and if so, how can one determine when to act?

UKLG: Ah yes, that is the trick. And it certainly is Taoistic, absolutely. And you know, Lao Tse will say to answer the question "how does one determine when to act," well, if you're really living the Tao, if you're on the Way, you just know. You know that this is the moment and you put out your hand and the wheel turns. That image comes up as far back as *The Left Hand of Darkness,* actually. Estraven is a person who instinctively knows the moment to act, and what we call instinct of course with human beings never is instinct. It is intuitional. It is some sort of combination of feeling and mind, yes. But in order to make stories . . . of course, it really would be hard to write a story about a jellyfish because the jellyfish is going to drift and drift and drift forever. So you have to bolt the jellyfish up against something and then the jellyfish has to do something finally. But of course, what George does, as I recall in the book, is to press an off switch. He doesn't turn anything on, he turns something off so it's a negative action, even then, and that's why it was so hard to make a movie out of it, because movies are about positive actions. I thought we did pretty well, by making it look pretty and scary and so on. But actually, it was a hard book to make a film-script of.

HE: It is a hard book. I had to re-read it several times to understand what it meant. It's one of the most difficult.
UKLG: I agree. It really is the first book in which I simply let the story lead me. If George had a dream, I wrote it down and then figured out what the consequences were. So I had to trust the book as I wrote it and that can often lead to a certain amount of obscurity, I think. But so long as the story remains clear, the meaning simply follows.

HE: But it made you think all the time, because each chapter raised questions.
UKLG: Yes, each chapter is a new world you have to figure out each time. And the role of the aliens, the "turtles," you know, I don't quite know what's going on there. I know it's essentially important to the story, but I don't quite understand what it is myself. It's just the way it is.

HE: Could they be another facet of George?
UKLG: Well, when they first appear, it certainly does seem as if they're responding directly to him as if he brought them, but once they're in the world, then, they're in the world. Maybe George did them in a sense, you know, maybe they are an accomplishment of his but once they're here, they're here, and then you never get rid of them again.

HE: Yes and they, too, have a sort of philosophy of life.
UKLG: Very Taoistic, yes, as well as I understand it, yes, their statements are somewhat obscure but they seem to be good Taoist "turtles."

HE: More generally, how do you choose the names of the characters, the towns, the countries? Some of them are very short, like Lev, Ged, A-Io, full of vowels and melodious. Others are very long and sometimes unpleasant to the ear, like Therem Harth rem ir Estraven, Harr-Orry, Erhenrang, Karhide, full of consonants and difficult to pronounce.

UKLG: Well, particularly in a novel, if I have invented a world on which there are different societies or different countries, or as in *The Left Hand of Darkness,* there are two countries there and they have different languages and the languages, all the words that come out of those languages have to be consistent with each other and different from the other one. So in Orgorein, the sounds are somewhat different than in Karhide, and so one of the first things I have to do, somewhere early in the book, is to make a phoneme pool, that is to say the sounds that that language uses, and have that either clear in my head or even write some of it down. So that all the names in Karhidish sound somewhat like each other, are self-consistent, the way French and English are, so that although the reader may not realize it, it isn't arbitrary and random. And even in a short story, when there are names of people and places, they should sound as if they came from the same languages; they should have some phonemic logic to them. And then of course, I may have to develop the language somewhat. There are some words of Karhidish that are very important in the novel, like "kemmer," and so I have to know a little about the language I make up. To me this whole thing is not a superficial aspect. Inventing languages—Tolkien called it "the secret vice"—he has a very funny and very true article about people who invent languages—inventing languages is very closely allied to inventing people, inventing novels, inventing fantasies. I'm word-oriented, word-driven, words are my medium, so for me in the invention of a fantasy, the names are absolutely essential. But it gets very mystical; it's very hard to talk about. If don't know the character's name, I don't know who that character is. Like Ged, until I knew Ged's name, I didn't know who he was at all. I just knew there was going to be a wizard, a boy. I can't tell you very much about the process, again it's like I sit and listen, until I get it right. Sometimes I write down: "Does that look right? No," "does that sound right? No." What can I say about that?

I enjoy it, I enjoy making up words. Of course, in one book, *Always Coming Home,* I did finally have to invent a fair amount of the language, because my composer friend who was writing the songs had to have words for these songs. And the words could not be just arbitrary inventions, they had to say what they meant in English, and so that was months of work. I enjoyed it very much but I had not expected to do it. When I conceived the book, I thought of Kesh as being a nonexistent language from which I was going to translate, which was a lot of fun. But finally, after most of the book had been written, it had to become at least a partly existing language from which I could translate, because I needed the language itself for the songs. So it led me in a little deeper that I had meant to go into language invention. But it is lots of fun, you know. You can decide—you are a sort of God with your language—you can decide that you will signify possession by a prefix. Alright, that's how it is, but then you've got to stick to it. You've got to write your grammar down, and have somewhere you can refer to it or you forget, you know. It's just like learning any language. I forget my languages and have to check back. I've forgotten Latin three times, and I've forgotten Kesh. I love learning languages but I don't retain them very well. You're on to a subject that to me looms very large in my writings, the whole subject of language, and not only my language English, but any language. As we said before, I love translating, I love learning languages, and I also love inventing languages, or bits of languages.

HE: But why are the names so different?

UKLG: Well, partly, to distinguish the languages. When you name a character in a story, aesthetically speaking, the name should be not too formidable looking. The reader should be able to at least figure out how they want to pronounce it. If it's all SQXX, it won't work—and Americans are very timid about language, and very lazy. You know we don't teach foreign languages; we don't learn foreign languages. And I know many people that have told me they can't read Russian novels because the names are so strange. Ay ay! You're missing a lot because you can't bother to pronounce Alexiei, you know. So I have to be a little careful about not being too difficult, but I have become very arrogant about that as I grow older, and sometimes I give my characters enormously long names. The Hainish people have very long names. Then they are cut down, as obviously they would be in ordinary usage. You are not going to call somebody a thirty syllable name, but you have to know it. The whole thing about naming and the individuality of the difference in names of course is connected to the magic in Earthsea, which is naming magic, so it's a big subject.

HE: So, you love creating new languages, like in *The Dispossessed,* "The Author of the Acacia Seeds," *Earthsea, The Left Hand of Darkness,* etc. As you said in some of your works they are only words scattered in the book. In others, like *Always Coming Home,* they are real languages explained and detailed with the origin of the words, and even extracts of literature, like poems, or stories. There are also linguistic analyses. More generally, the problem of communication is presented again and again under different aspects. Is it linked to your activity as a writer, or do you perceive it as being a more general aspect of everyday life?

UKLG: That's interesting. Surely, it's both. A writer communicates in words, through words, using words to communicate things which often cannot be said directly in words, have to be said indirectly. That's why we have poetry and fiction. But then communication as a general human problem . . . what keeps people from understanding one another. They may literally speak different languages or they may share the language but speak it differently and mean different things by different words and so on. Except in very tight small societies such as scarcely exist any more there is always a great danger of misunderstanding people. And then there's the problem of the stranger, which I write about a great deal. It's the person who comes into a world or a society that isn't his own, and has to try to understand and be understood, and language then becomes almost a metaphor for comprehension and communication. And this of course is in *The Left Hand of Darkness*. It's an obvious example that Genly misunderstands the Gethenians, but Estraven also misunderstands Genly because Estraven has no way to understand a one-sexed person and the society. He can't really imagine the society he comes from. Of course it's fun, as a novelist, to play with mutual misunderstanding. It's one of the great subjects of the novel.

HE: And in that respect could the stranger be the metaphor of the writer then?
UKLG: No, I think if I ever had a metaphorical writer in my stories, it's the wizards in Earthsea. People who can make magic are probably equivalent to the artist.

HE: About Earthsea, you said: "Wizardry is artistry: the trilogy is about art, the creative experience, the creative process" (*The Language of the Night*, 53).
UKLG: Yes. That was when I was using the word "creative."

HE: More generally, I feel that in many of your books the reader can find the image of the writer, the creator in front of her white page, and also the thrill this act of creation can bring.
UKLG: Yes, I think that's fair, yes. And I would include the scientist along with the artist, as a creator or discoverer, because creation and discovery are pretty much equivalent in my mind—invention, *invenire*—and a good many of my main characters have been scientists, like Shevek and so on. And there again the feeling that

the process of discovery or working on a science is fairly close to that of the artist, so they all are in somewhat the same position, and the wizard too because the wizard has to follow the laws of that science or that craft.

HE: In *The Lathe of Heaven,* Dr. Haber pronounces a word to put George Orr in a hypnotic trance. This word is ANTWERP. Why did you choose this particular word?

UKLG: I chose it because I know that hypnotists, when they have a keyword like that, try to find a word that is not a common word and does not sound like a common word so that it is not done by mistake. They don't want to put somebody down or bring them out mistakenly. And ANTWERP is definitely an unusual word, and an unusual sound in English, so that it is the only reason why I picked ANTWERP. I was just thinking, "What's a word that we don't usually say" and I thought of a word from Holland because Dutch is just such a formidable language. Nobody in English knows how to pronounce Dutch. I don't know what ANTWERP is in Dutch; I don't know how to pronounce it. Dutch is mysterious. That's why my mind chose it. I very seldom do anagrams or puns or directly concealed meanings. There may be a sound echo in some of the words but I try to avoid those games, those letter games. I really don't like them. I don't like puzzles in rhyme, in fiction.

HE: Although you did one in Omelas.

UKLG: Yes, but that was the sound, you see, because I do read signs backward. I just thought "melas, say melas, that's pretty," omelas, because obviously "o" could fit in, "homme hélas," and so on. It was a pretty word, and then I thought, "Well, where is it?" So the story began to grow. A story can grow from a word, from the sound of the word, a sound in my head, just like a poem. A story can grow out of a meaningless word.

HE: And this one is beautiful.

UKLG: Yes, although it's very much mispronounced. I call it Omelas with the accent on the first syllable, but it has many pronunciations by many readers.

HE: I always wonder how you pronounce the names.

UKLG: Some of them are not self-explanatory. Ged, for instance, it never occurred to me that it could be pronounced differently.

HE: I heard somebody call him Djed.

UKLG: I just assumed that people would do a hard /g/ like "get." But people do call him differently. In fact, there was a recording made in England where they

mispronounced it all the way through. Oï!! They didn't ask me. Mostly I say "pronounce it as it seems right to you" but with that one I say, "Well I hear it as Ged."
Jed in American English, [djed], is Jedediah. It's a biblical name and it's very much
associated with nineteenth-century prospectors and mountain men and rough
people, you know, hairy people who live in Tennessee, and it's all wrong. It's not
my Ged.

HE: I noted that you have recurring phrases like "the Order of Things," with a
capital O and a capital T, like in "Direction of the Road," and *Dancing at the Edge
of the World.*
UKLG: "The Order of Things" rings no particular bell in my mind. Of course it's
a familiar phrase in English.

HE: I was wondering if it had a symbolic meaning.
UKLG: Not one I know. It opens a big set of questions, doesn't it? Is there an
"Order of Things," and then if so can one know it, and so on . . . I would say that
particularly when capitalized that way, it has almost a medieval flavor, that there
is an assumption that there is an order, that it is the right order, that we should
learn that order and obey it and so on, which is not really the way I think. I think,
in "Direction of the Road," the oak tree, who is very conservative—a deeply conservative person—to the oak tree there is an Order of Things, which it is his duty,
as an oak, to uphold because that's what oaks do. Now, a marijuana plant perhaps
does not care about the order of things at all. But the story is about an oak. So
there I would say that there is a little humor in the use of the phrase and it's possible that I may be teasing just a little bit.
    The question of cosmic order is of course . . . you know science is based on
the assumption that there is an "Order of Things." A physical law is a law, and is
not broken and that is both reassuring and magnificent. But it so easily can also
become cramping, describing, canalizing the world into an immutable order in
which nothing ever changes. That's rather frightening.

HE: Another one is "third time is the charm."
UKLG: That's old, old English. I bet it isn't just English, I bet it's European. Yes,
think of the folk tales: the first son of the King goes out, and he's defeated in the
quest, and the second son goes out, and he's defeated in the quest, then the third
son goes out, and although he's the young one and the fool, he's the one who gets
the princess and kills the dragon.
    The structure of story in European folktales is often threes. In the New World

it's fours. They do things four times, and sometimes in the Pacific North West they do things five times, so the stories are rather long stories, but there is a little variation usually each time. You notice it with the Pueblo myths, the fourth try is the charm. It's a saying. You hear gamblers say that, "third time is the charm." It's a proverb.

HE: I never know if these phrases have a deeper meaning.
UKLG: Or if I invented it possibly, or I'm just quoting a proverb. You can take an old saying like that and give it a deeper meaning, yes.

HE: Talking about experiments with points of view, you said that it was a "more cooperative and egalitarian way of storytelling." Could you comment on that?
UKLG: Yes, in *Unlocking the Air* and also in *Searoad*. The last stories in *Searoad* are the voices of the women. They're all relations; they're all members of the same family, of different generations, and the whole story is told in their voices, alternating and jumping around through time, back and forth. I think Virginia Woolf is probably the person whose technical daring and her skill at doing that kind of thing and moving from one head to another head, from one point of view to another, in the years and in the ways, is the most admirable. Nobody has written anything like that that I know. I was fascinated by what she did. She was doing something new in story telling, something new in the novel, by that moving point of view. The nineteenth-century novel does it too, of course, in a very different way.

HE: Faulkner . . .
UKLG: Well, before that—Tolstoi—I always come back to Tolstoi when talking about novels. Tolstoi slips from one mind into another without saying much about it. He is actually marvelous at it. I don't know how he does it. I just re-read *War and Peace,* and I still have no idea. He can go from a man's mind into a mind of a hunting dog, and back, and you don't feel confused; you know who is thinking all along. It's incredibly skillful. In *War and Peace,* we're in Natacha's head, and in Pier's head, and in Andrej's head, and many minor characters, we get into the minds. We have the point of view of dozens of people. There's only one that we're never in his head and that's Dolokhov, the most villainous man in the book, the man who creates destruction wherever he goes. He's psychopathic, and I think Tolstoi felt there was no getting inside that mind, or he did not want to, I don't know.
    Anyway, growing up with writers like that as models, it began to seem arti-

ficial to me to do what most . . . what so many twentieth-century novels do, is stay always in one third person viewpoint, a limited third person, which is very like first person in that you never move out of it. And why not move out? When I move around and get this change of perspective, it's something which only literature can do. A film, a movie has a point of view but not in the same way. The point of view is the camera after all. Storytelling does not privilege one point of view, and I think that is very important. It is very often women who use these changing points of view, and I think it's because we are all, consciously or unconsciously, trying to get away from a one privileged point of view which is the right one, and we're saying, "Well, no, there is no right one." There are many, and you have to put them together to begin to get something that makes more of a community truth. Also it's an entertaining way to tell a story, changing points of view. I use it a great deal when I'm teaching in workshops in writing. I exercise the students' point of view—"now write the story from a certain point of view, now change it and write it from the opposite." If you are watching a person, now you have to be that person, and so on. Many of them have never tried that and sometimes they are frightened, and sometimes they say, "Oh, wow, this is fun." It's interesting.

HE: And in the same way, when you use first person point of view, it's sometimes very destabilizing for the reader. For example, in "The Wife's Story," the female reader imagines she is the wife, and in the end it's not at all what she expected.

UKLG: That, of course, is deliberate trickery. The first time I did that consciously with some moral purpose, was in *A Wizard of Earthsea*, where I think you don't really find for quite a while that everybody in the book except a very few foreigners is brown or black. And so I put the children who are going to read the book into a brown skin, although at that time fantasy was almost exclusively read by white children. After they get used to being Ged, they find out that their skin's brown. I do that trick quite often, in many different books.

HE: In "Mazes," also . . .

UKLG: Yes. First person narration has certain possibilities of making the reader say, "who am I?"

HE: "Engaging readers as collaborators in the creative process" seems to be your aim in the more recent books. It seems to me that you could run the risk to engage in a blind alley. What if they don't want to follow you?

UKLG: Then they won't finish the book, but that's their privilege. I am old enough and secure enough as a writer now that I can take certain risks that I might have been more timid about when I was younger. And I have also gained considerable respect for my readers. I am amazed sometimes where my readers will follow me. It seems to me I'm asking a great deal of them, and that's fine, they'll go right along, you know.

HE: And they want more . . .
UKLG: Yes, It's wonderful.

HE: *Always Coming Home* has been called a multimedia event. Can you describe the making of this work?
UKLG: I'm trying to think back. I wanted to write about some people that lived in a walled city in a valley in the Andes, in South America, like Machu Pichu, something like that. And gradually, as I thought about it, it got closer and closer and closer to home until I realized that what I wanted to write about was literally my home, the property in the Napa valley in California, which is still in my family, where I spent every summer of my childhood and have been almost every year of my life even if only for a brief moment. And this piece of land which is extremely dear to me, I wanted to write a story about people living there who were worthy of living there, who were using that very beautiful country properly instead of what's happened to the Napa valley now. It's agro-business, exploitation of the land to a disgusting degree—the amount of poison being used in those vineyards is appalling. You have to go away sometimes when they're poisoning the vineyards. They didn't need to do this. Anyway . . . It's all gone wrong. What was one of the most beautiful places in the world, it looked like Provence, it did then . . . So I wanted to write about that and it took me a long time to get ready for it because I wanted to know more than I knew. I knew the ground and the plants, and everything physically, in my body, but I didn't know the names of them. I didn't know the geology. I didn't know many of the familiar plants; I didn't really know what they were called, their scientific names or their nicknames. So I studied the Napa valley, through many publications mostly from the University of California. That was fun.

And then we went down and lived there, the longest I've ever lived there, all one spring, in 1982. We went there in the winter when it was very muddy and rainy, and lived through till June, and that's where I wrote the book. It was right there, looking at it and being surrounded by it, and imagining where the little towns were. I didn't have a computer yet, and I kept thinking, "I need a computer for this. This would be so much easier to write on a computer but I don't have time to stop and buy one and learn how to use it," so it was written by hand and with a typewriter. And I drew a lot of pictures to show myself what some of their imagery looked like. And I began to think, "This book has to be illustrated." And then I kept writing poetry, and some of them were obviously songs, and let's see . . . I had made friends with Todd Barton. We did a radio play together; I did the script and he did the music. I liked him. I knew he was an active composer, and I knew that he knew a great deal about different musical styles, because he composes all the music for the Ashland theater festival. He does not only Shakespeare plays but he does the music for everything, African plays and Chinese plays and Brackton, Anouilh, and so on . . . Todd can compose in any style, so I said, "Todd, would you be interested in inventing a music for a non-existent people?" And—"Yes, yes," he said. So then, he and I had to work together. He would send me little tapes with little sketches, compositions on them, and he would say, "Does that sound like the Kesh to you?" and I would say, "Well, no, no, this is too aggressive, or too Chinese," or something. So gradually, and of course because of their numerology, their four, five, nine, that was so important, he could do things with fourths and fifths and ninths, and other things that musicians love to play with. So he had a lot of fun doing that, and he developed instruments on his musical computer. A couple of the instruments in the recording are real but most of them are computer-generated. And I asked Todd if he knew any young artists. I needed an artist who was not going to be too willful, an artist who would listen to what I said. "This is what it looks like," you know. I needed somebody pretty young because most older artists, they know what they want, and it wouldn't go, you know. And he said, "Well, as a matter of fact, yes, I know a girl who was in art in college here and she does archaeological drawings." When archaeologists go out, they take an artist with them because the artist can show much more than the camera can. So that's how we got Peggy, and she was twenty-two. She *was* young. And she loved the idea. We were working together, we became friends rapidly, and they both came down and stayed there so that they could see the landscape there, because Peggy really didn't like to draw anything she could not see. She does not draw out of her imagination. We had to make objects for her to draw . . . That was sort of funny, inventing our own archaeology.

So that's how that collaboration came about. And it seemed to me if I was trying to give this sense that the reader is in this valley, among these people, and can move around in the book freely, he does not have to read the book in order, but move around and find anything that's interesting, almost like walking around in a house, that there ought to be visual and sound input as well as just the words on a page. And where I was incredibly fortunate was that—it was Harper and Row, then, my publisher—that my editor there—this was an expensive and risky thing to do—he convinced his publishing house to do it, and to make the book with the tape in it and all that. That was just good fortune, good luck There's no way that they would do that book now. The company has changed very much. I listened to the tape a couple of weeks ago, because I hadn't heard it for years now. It really is very pretty, it's pretty music.

HE: I was wondering if all this work could be done on CD-ROM, with somebody walking and discovering objects . . .
UKLG: It could. It could be done in hypertext too, if I knew how to do hypertext. For the CD-ROM, a couple of computer people got fascinated with the idea of trying to do the program of this. But again there would be considerable time and expense so it would have to be done for pure love probably, but there would be great fun. It would make a lovely CD-ROM. There is a problem, however, with the visuals. If you noticed, in the book there are no faces.

HE: Yes but if you are the person who walks . . .
UKLG: It would be through your eyes, yes, but the trouble is that still we couldn't meet live people, and there is a certain artificiality there. We could do voices on the tape. But Peggy and I discussed it long and hard and she said, "I don't think I should draw these people because whatever I draw will fix an image of what they look like in the reader's mind and it may not be what they would see." And it's true, I mean we know they're short, and kind of delicately-built people, and that they're brown in color and that's about all.

HE: Yes, but it's the same with a film, with *The Lathe of Heaven,* for example . . .
UKLG: But those people are modern Americans. You see, the Kesh are supposed to be really different. That's 20,000 years in the future. They are a different "race" of people, "race" in quotes always. But I mean they look different from us; they're blended, they're not black, they're not Polynesian, they're not white. Obviously all the people have mixed and produced other variations on the human norm. We realized that it was important not to be too specific about it. That's always the tricky bit when you get into the visuals. So Peggy did only landscape, architecture, and artifacts, and I don't know that people have ever really noticed that. Many people I think don't realize they're not seeing the people.

HE: Yes, that's right. I did not realize that. In fact, it was as if I were an anthropologist, finding objects, poems, and I did not really miss not meeting the people.
UKLG: Yes, and of course there are the stories about the people. In the tape, you hear voices, not only singing voices but speaking voices.

HE: You could do them in a sort of blur from a distance, somebody seeing figures dancing or . . .
UKLG: Yes, Peggy tried some of that. Of course, she draws a very clear, sharp line, and blurring was—Peggy is not good at blurring . . . The nearest we come to a human being is a human footprint. It was funny, you know. All restrictions do lead to invention also.

HE: Was it done in a theater, as a theater play?
UKLG: Several years after it came out, our university here had a wonderful dance troop and a very good teacher and choreographer. Her name was Judy Patton. Judy came to me and said, "I want to do a dance from that book." And I said, "All right." So they were all girls, her class of that year. There were nine young dancers. Some of them were really good; they were all quite a company. She got a couple of older women in. We called it the Blood-lodge dances, because they're women's dances, and the music was just rattles and drum, and a flute just now and then, all improvised. I was one of the musicians. I was a rattler; that was lots of fun. And Judy worked the choreography out with her dancers. Essentially, it was all very communal—dancers are so different from other people. I'm fascinated with them. She would suggest something and they would try it. And then one of them would say, "What if we do this?" and they would try and so on. And so it was very communal, the whole construction of it, but then once they arrived at something that was right, they would learn it, so by the time they rehearsed it, it was a quite structured dance.

The people who saw it liked it very, very much. I have a tape of it somewhere. It is a very poor tape, on video; the lighting is bad. I haven't looked at that for a long time. That's somewhere in the basement; I hide things in the basement. So that was another sort of artistic outgrowth from it, that was a great pleasure. The year after we revived it and took it to a different college, and actually we did rather better, I think, the second time. So we did that twice. I had never collaborated with dancers. I had collaborated in films and plays, with artists and musicians, but never with dancers, who use their body for their art, and it is fascinating, it's very different, and they are very different people, very straightforward.

HE: Do you play music?
UKLG: You know the recorder (flûte douce), the wooden flute, I learned that when I was twelve or thirteen, and I used to be pretty good at it. Because I cannot sing, I cannot carry a tune, I played the recorder. We have a musician daughter so we had music in the house for years. It was amazing and wonderful, totally unexpected, how we had a cellist. What did we do to deserve that? But music has always been important to me.

HE: You said in the interview in the DVD *The Lathe of Heaven* that you were an "ear person."
UKLG: Yes, I think so.

HE: More than an "eye" person?
UKLG: Well, I don't know. It's hard to say, isn't it? My daughter, the cellist, said if she had to choose between going blind and going deaf she would go blind at once rather than lose her hearing. Then I thought, "Oh God, what a choice!" I cannot make that choice so I must be both. Listening is very important to me.

HE: I felt that music was very important to you and I was wondering if it was important both as a theme and as a complement to your writings. Because in some of your writings, you use it as a theme, like in "An die Musik," or in *Very Far away from Anywhere Else,* and as you said before, in *Always Coming Home,* it is a sort of complement to your work.
UKLG: Of course sometimes when you write about artists in another art . . . I don't particularly like fiction about fiction writers. I don't like writing about writers very much. It all seems a little . . . I don't know. I don't want to write about writers, but sometimes I want to write about artists. And because I had a musician in the family, I know more about musicians than I do about painters for instance, and so I'm likely to write about them, and of course Nathalie, in that book, *Very Far away from Anywhere Else,* she is my daughter in some respect. I know what a young musician's life is like because I saw her through high school. And music is also such a universal metaphor. We talk about the music in a painting, we talk about the music of poetry, we use music as the most central art, the essential quality of art sometimes you can refer to almost as music. Why, I don't know, but it seems to be quite universally understood so there it is as a sort of metaphor waiting to be used. And because I do hear writing, I do hear the music of the language. The music of prose or poetry is very important to me and that it should have its own music. It may not be always flowing and sweet and elegant

but it has its own musical quality, and it should have the coherence of a piece of music.

HE: Like the languages you invent . . .

UKLG: Yes, every language has its own music. It may be a rough one but it has its own.

HE: I like very much your humor. It seems that you always have a smile in your eyes and that you're ready to burst out laughing. In your writings, I feel that it is a sort of wink to the reader.

UKLG: Yes. There is some of that, yes. Sometimes I feel that many of my readers never realize that I'm being funny, that I write things that are meant to be read lightly. It's so serious, and they're so serious. Science fiction is a rather serious genre; maybe they don't expect . . . I don't know.

HE: But there are other science fiction writers who are funny: Douglas Adams, Ray Bradbury . . .

UKLG: And Philip K. Dick is very ironic also . . . No, I don't know why . . . maybe the readers are often serious, they're engineers, they're nice people, but they're very serious.

HE: A few years ago I read *In a Different Voice,* and I saw that you mentioned this book in one of your essays. Female voice seems to be an important idea, and I was wondering if it could also be linked with the use of language in general.

UKLG: Certainly with literary language. Virginia Woolf was the first person that I know of that said . . . maybe in 1920, she wrote that women do not have a literary language, that we mostly just used what men invented and it's not entirely suitable for what we have to say. And that is a very complicated and subtle statement. It's hard to be very specific, to give an example of what she means. And yet, as a writer, I say, "Yes exactly, I have to learn what my voice as a woman is, not as a sort of imitation man." And it may involve different use of the language, even syntactically it may be different. The sentences may flow in a different way, and it may involve different uses of point of view—what do we know—and it may involve also a less linear approach to storytelling in a more circular way, perhaps less decisive, and so on, I don't know. The Gilligan article has been much disputed, her scientific facts are a little shaky, but I think she made a very interesting point, and I think it's very useful to girls, when girls realize that they have in a sense had their voices taken from them. That is a depressing statistic. If a woman speaks more than about 30 percent of the time in a mixed group she is perceived as speaking all the time, but men actually talk much more than women in mixed groups. This has been measured, this is scientifically pretty solid stuff, that men talk about 70 percent of the time. If the woman talks anything like half the time, then she's accused of talking all the time. That's very mysterious. It seems to be a matter of control. If men are not controlling the conversation—both leading the subject and providing most of the words—they perceive the women as taking it from them. And the women are so used to having it taken from them that they really don't even notice the fact that this is so. I'm sure it's just the same in France, it is generally accepted that women talk all the time, but then when they start measuring it, it's not true. They don't talk as much as men do, so it's a projection. It is a bit depressing but it's one of the things that's good to know. It lets you think differently about things.

HE: Another recurrent idea is the weaving, linked with the web, the spider. I was wondering if it was the idea of slowly weaving a story.
UKLG: That is certainly part of that metaphor because the actual process of writing—particularly a long fiction, like a novel—it is very slow. And it's like weaving in that one is working on an existing structure, the warp of the book, you know what the book is going to be to some extent, you have a warp. But the weaving, you do it moment by moment by moment, and it goes slowly, and it has to form a pattern of some kind, so the parallel, the simile, is really very close. It's quite a close and interesting simile. It's one of those inexhaustible comparisons you can draw. I never have been a weaver. Charles did a little weaving on a small loom. It's a fascinating craft. The hard part of weaving is setting up the warp. It takes for ever and it has to be absolutely right. Once you have your loom strung with the warp, then the actual weaving is rhythmical and pleasant, but setting up the warp, oh, it takes forever. So I have very deep respect for women weaving down in the Southwest. I know how long it took them to set that loom up.

HE: It does not seem to fit with the attitude described previously of non-acting. When you weave, you act.
UKLG: You mean the Taoism idea of non-action. I think Lao Tse would say of course you have to act in order to be alive. You do things, and all craft, all skill, all art is action, but I think what the difference is with weaving, the very good weaver—the weavers who know their craft so thoroughly that it is part of them— does it without any fuss, without hard work. It is easy. It is not so much in that case action against non-action—that's more with political choices and things like that. It's whether the work is hard or the work is easy. Lao Tse says, "If you're on

the way, if you're following Tao, all work is easy." It becomes part of you, you do it naturally, and then you do it right. Whatever it is it comes right, of course, that's Zen, the whole idea. You make one brush stroke and if it isn't right, it just isn't right, but if it's right, it's perfectly right. It's all mystical, the underlying mysticism, and it's all outlook, but it's also true, you know, when you know your craft perfectly well, when you really know what you're doing, then it's easy, and it's a pleasure.

HE: Yes, and you don't feel you're acting.
UKLG: That's right, . . . you're just being.

HE: Love is often ethereal in your work Also, the characters are often separated. Do you feel that physical love is doomed? In *The Left Hand of Darkness,* Estraven dies; in *The Dispossessed,* the couples are forced to part for years; in *Very Far away from Anywhere Else,* they have to wait because they are too young . . .
UKLG: They are definitely too young. Well . . . Isn't this true of a lot of fiction? I mean, the course of true love never did run smooth, that's Romeo and Juliet, and if the course of true love does run smooth, it's very nice but you don't have a story. Love in novels tends to be frustrated and often the lovers are separated and so on, so that something happens.

HE: So it's only a writer's device, then . . .
UKLG: I'm afraid it's a fairly basic one, but I would say, trying to take your question seriously that of course it's partly a matter of when the books were written, not only in my life, but there has been definitely a change in what is acceptable. It's much easier now to write about sexuality than it was when I started writing. It's easier to write about sexuality without getting all breathing hard and being either very serious or somewhat pornographic. It's easier to treat it as just part of life now than it was when I started writing, particularly perhaps for a woman, I don't know, probably not, but anyway, I find that as I get older, I write more freely and with more pleasure about sexuality. I don't write very much about sex, the act of sex itself, because I don't like to read about it. I have never enjoyed reading about sex. It's like reading about a football game, or a wrestling match. It might be fun to watch or to do but it isn't any fun to read about. If I don't want to read it why should I write it? It's action writing, like all sports writing, and like most battle scenes in novels and so on. It's just not my kind of fiction, not what I want. So mostly there is not very much sex in my books, but often they do revolve around the sexual relationships, it's very central.

HE: Homosexuality is underlined symbolically in the short story "In the Drought" by the image of blood flowing out of the taps instead of water. It reminded me of a short story by Ray Bradbury, called "The Aqueduct," where water is also blood.

UKLG: No, I never saw that story. Had I seen it, I probably couldn't have written "In the Drought," because it would have been too close. That image of blood where it ought to be water . . . That was written during a period here in Portland, when there was a man, a rabble rouser, a politician who tried to change the state constitution to make it more difficult for homosexuals, and it brought out a lot of prejudice and hatred among a lot of people here. I had many homosexual friends, mostly lesbian, and it was frightening, they were frightened, physically frightened. I was so angry that the story just burst out of that. I had to say something.

HE: But why blood then, why this liquid?

UKLG: That kind of metaphor, I don't know. That's a bit like a poem, this is the image that comes to you and you don't question, and you just hope that it carries itself. In the Bradbury story it's more explicit, in mine the symbolism is a little bit opaque.

HE: And you have milk in the end.

UKLG: And there of course, in English at least, is the echo that many people would hear of the phrase "the milk of human kindness" which I think comes from the Bible. It's a very familiar phrase in English.

HE: That's the kind of thing I don't know.

UKLG: That's the thing I don't know in French. I might have once way back when I was steeped in French literature, but now in modern literature, I would not catch those echoes. I know that a lot of my work is particularly hard to translate because it is full of those literary echoes, and even if the translator catches them, there's no way to translate them.

HE: Your parents were and still are very prominent people. Can you tell me more about them?

UKLG: My father was a prominent anthropologist, which didn't mean very much to me. It meant he had lots of interesting friends, some of whom were Indians, and they came and stayed with us. There was a lot of conversation, it was a family of intellectual conversations, aesthetic conversations, lots of books, lots of visi-

tors, very exciting, very bourgeois, very safe. My father was an extremely nice
man, he was a steady good nature, kind, funny. He enjoyed his children. My two
older brothers are not his, they are my mother's, but the four of us were very close,
we grew up very close. My mother . . . she was not a prominent person at all while
I was a child. She was just a housewife and mother and a very pretty woman, very
attractive. All men loved my mother, and quite rightly. I mean, she was so nice,
she was very, very nice, she was a terrible flirt too! Both my parents were very
happy about me because they had three sons and they wanted a girl, and I arrived as a girl and they made me very welcome and always there was no difference intellectually between me and my brothers. I wasn't supposed to be stupid
because I was a girl or go to a different kind of college or anything like that. So I
had an incredibly fortunate childhood, as serene and happy probably as a childhood can be. There were no serious illnesses, no great cataclysms, except of course
the Second World War, and a few little things like that. All three of my brothers
fought the war in the service. One of them was on a mine-sweeper in the Pacific,
which was kind of scary. And another thing, it was a very stable childhood. I grew
up in the same two houses, the city house and the country house, till I was seventeen. I had never been anywhere else. That's very unusual for Americans.

HE: I was wondering if having well known parents influenced you in one way or
other.
UKLG: I think only in the sense that reading and writing were absolutely normal
daily activities in the household, so it was very easy to look at myself as "Yes, I'm
going to be a writer." They didn't particularly encourage me, they didn't praise
my little poems and so on. They did but they didn't make a big fuss of that. They
were very wise, I think, in that way. And when it became evident that I was really
absolutely serious about it, that writing was a calling for me, my father talked
with me very seriously, and he said, "You know, you can try to live off your writing, make a living from it, but if you do, you will have to do what the editors
tell you to do, and if you don't want to do that"—because he knew me, he knew
I didn't want to do that—he said, "you have to train yourself and make a living
some other way. And probably, since you have a gift for languages, you might do
something at teaching languages." And I said, "Fine, yes."
   So that's why I studied French and Italian in college, because I enjoyed it
very much, and I thought I would probably take my degree and be a professor of
French, or Romance language, literature. But then you see, I met the professor, I

met Charles, and he was taking his degree in history and really one doctor in a family seemed enough at the time, and we wanted to have a family, so I never did take my degree. I did teach French for a while, but I soon got out of touch with Italian literature and poetry.

HE: What other languages did you learn, apart from French and Italian?
UKLG: French, Italian, and then recently Spanish. About ten years ago, I was looking at one of my own books, I think *A Wizard of Earthsea,* in Spanish, and I thought, "I can read that, this is so like Italian, I can read this book," and I thought, "After all, I know what the book is about." So I read a couple of my own books in Spanish and began to grasp the language that way. And then I bought some grammars and studied the language a little bit and just kept reading. I found I can read Borges. Borges is very accessible to English people. English was his first language, did you know that? His grandmother taught him English before he learnt Spanish, and there is something about his writing that comes over in the English. I can read Borges—well if I can read Borges, I can read anything. It wasn't that easy, but gradually I have learnt to read Spanish pretty well, but I discovered when we went to Chile, that I can't speak. And I don't understand it, I would have to be among Spanish people much, much more, and I haven't done that.

HE: You never learnt German . . .
UKLG: No. My father was bilingual, but he didn't speak German with us. It was always surprising to me to hear him. There were many refugees from Germany, of course, in those years, and he would go off into German with one or other. He said that it embarrassed him to speak German by then, because he felt he had lost some of it, but it didn't sound like it. I also heard him speaking other languages. He knew Yurok, the Northern California Indian language, well enough to talk with Robert Spott who visited us, a Yurok Indian. They would be speaking in Yurok. That was nice to hear. I think hearing foreign languages again is rather an unusual American experience, except in our Hispanic regions—a lot of Americans never hear any language spoken but English. There's nothing on the radio, nothing on television. They are unaware of foreign languages. I was always aware that there were people who spoke other languages, and hearing them.

HE: Maybe that is why you love so much inventing new languages.
UKLG: Yes, a child's ear is caught by anything strange and new, and children who don't hear other languages spoken are being deprived of something.

HE: Would you like to talk about your family, your children, and your grand-children?
UKLG: Well, they are all getting middle-aged now. They are two girls and a boy, and they get on very well with one another. They were very nice children, and I have three granddaughters, one of whom is seventeen now and she is in Toronto with her father, her parents divorced. That's the cellist's daughter. And the other two live in town, and they are very pretty, very nice children.

HE: Do they bring something to you when you work, are they references?
UKLG: I was thinking what it means to a woman writing to have children or not to have children, and it certainly makes life difficult to try to go on writing with small children, babies, and little children in the house, that need constant attention. It is very difficult and there is no solution for you, unless you are enormously wealthy and want to have a nanny or something. My solution was simply—fortunately all my children were sleepy—I could put them to bed early. I was very old-fashioned. Nobody's children go to bed early, they all stay up till midnight, but back then, in the fifties and early sixties, they were in bed by 7.30 or 8 at night. And then they could read or anything, you know. They didn't have to go to sleep at once, but they were locked in, as it were, and then I wrote, so I wrote late. I think lots of young mothers do it that way. There's no use getting up early in the morning, is there, because the children get up too, "Hello, yes, yes, here we are," all bright eyes. But if I hadn't had the children, you know, my life would be impoverished immensely. I would never have engaged in life to the degree that having children . . . and having these hostages to the future and this chance . . . So the whole idea, as you know because you have read my books, "you must either have babies or books," to me that is wrong, totally wrong and even wicked. That's just not true, it's a bad myth.

So I'm very grateful to my children for, just for having come along, and they are very nice people, they are extraordinary, pleasant company. They enlarge life enormously. Each one is a whole new person, they never existed before, they're not like anybody else, not even like their brother and sister. So life is by that much increased and made richer, enlarged, absolutely. It's like friends; a life without friends would be horrible. The degree to which some male writers protect themselves from other people always amazes me. It seems all wrong to me. Yes, you want time to get your work done, and that time is precious and somehow it's very hard to come by, but to achieve it by isolating yourself from commitment to other people—it just does not make sense.

HE: Would you like to talk about something you find important that we did not speak about?

UKLG: I don't think there's anything . . . I can't think of any sort of large subject that you left aside, you were very thorough. I'm sure we could go on and pursue anything that you felt that was sort of just brushed over something lightly and didn't go deep enough but I can't think of anything that I feel you sort of . . . that is . . . I feel as if to a lot of your questions I gave you an answer which you could probably find in my writing, and probably had found in my writing, and that I wish I could enlarge more, but that often when I write about these subjects I say all I have to say. It's still true since I'm repeating it, and I wish that that were not true but it simply is the fact.

The whole subject of hearing . . . It does seem to have come up again and again, as we talked. I talked about listening for a character's voice, and hearing the music of the sentences and so on. This does seem to be central to the way I work, there's something oral about my written fiction, but I don't know quite where I'm getting at, here, because that doesn't mean that I think it ought to be recorded. Recording is fine and I like making recordings and listening to them. But it isn't that. It's just that . . . I suppose maybe what I'm trying to say is that although science fiction is a fiction of ideas and although ideas are very important in my work, they are not the most important things to me. It is rather the music. If you have to separate the music from the intellect, the music is central to me, yes, and the ideas sometimes have to accommodate themselves to the music. Like in that story "In the Drought," in a sense, I can't say why it's blood, except that blood is the symbol of violence and aggression and pain. So they are the obvious connotations, but I can't really tell you why, but I knew it had to be that way, that the music said, "It's a spray of blood," and the intellect said, "O.K. I'll accept that, I won't argue."

A Conversation with Ursula Le Guin

Carl Freedman/2006

The following interview was prepared especially for the present volume and has never been published previously. It was conducted by e-mail during July, August, and early September of 2006. I should like to publicly thank Ursula Le Guin for the remarkable—though, for her, characteristic—generosity with which she devoted her valuable time to this project.—CF

Carl Freedman: I'd like to begin by talking about the relatively unfashionable topic of didacticism in literature. Many people still say that literature with a didactic purpose and a "message" must be, *ipso facto*, bad or mediocre literature: to which my own answer is, well, then so much for Virgil, Dante, Milton, Swift, Blake, George Eliot, Tolstoy, and Brecht, to pick just a few examples. In this spirit I see you as very much a didactic writer. I wonder if you agree and how, in general, you see the relationship between didacticism and art.

Ursula Le Guin: This is tricky territory for me, and comes near a dilemma that I have worried at all my writing life. I tend to think of it more as politics and art, but it comes down to the same thing.

I know what you mean about Virgil et al., and we agree, conversationally. Of course Blake and Brecht are teachers . . . But I assure you that for a novelist to be labeled as a didactic writer is, on almost any level, a kiss of death. The adjective is used so often to imply preachiness, bloodlessness, moralizing, axe-grinding, that even when it is applied with complimentary intentions, almost any serious novelist will wince and try to dodge it. I certainly wince and dodge.

And I reject the description "a didactic writer" because it is reductionist. There is a didactic element in my fiction, absolutely, but there are a good many other elements in my fiction which the label "didactic" eliminates or devalues by ignoring. (It is rather like repeating the semi-truth that Virginia Woolf is an "experimental" novelist, and thus devaluing nine-tenths of her achievement.)

The trouble with using the words didactic or message is that it plays into a very widespread misunderstanding about how art works. Children are taught in school to assume that a story has a "message," and when they write me they ask, often, "How do you figure out how to put the message in the story?" And over and over I answer: I don't! If I wanted to deliver a message why would I write a story?

163

Just to hide the message in, like a gelatin capsule? It is the story itself that means something. Discovering what it means is something that happens to me while I write it and to you while you read it—or possibly (for both of us) much later, thinking about it. And what it means to me may be different from what it means to you; and what it means to anybody may not be twice the same, for rereading can be very different from first reading. But in any case, the story is not, and does not have, a "message." That assumption is a mistake.

The children are always grumpy by now, because it isn't what their teachers told them. One sees why didacticism has a bad name. I am trying to think of a story that might come clearly on as didactic, that seems to have an obvious message, thus justifying your wish to describe me as a didactic writer. How about "In the Drought." It was written under the influence of passionate feeling during a period of intense political activity against homosexuals in my city. Its subject matter is narrow and specific. Its "message" could I suppose be stated as: "homosexuals are being treated unjustly in our society and feel pain from it," and so its didactic purpose would be to encourage sympathy and discourage prejudice in the heterosexual reader. But as a criticism of the story I don't see much use in this interpretation, except for the most naïve readers, unable to read through the symbols. And reducing it to a lesson, a preachment, implies that I assume a right to teach, a right to preach—which I do not. I don't have any answers. But I do have the human right to ask questions. To demand. To feel outrage, to feel pain. To speak of pain and outrage. To bear witness. To have a vision of blood gushing out of a faucet—an image that is not reducible to any simple statement at all.

I read to learn. I have always read to learn. For example, I have learned almost more than I can bear to know from Saramago's *Blindness* and *Seeing*. But for all the intensity of Saramago's moral purpose and the awful clarity of his vision, my whole heart and soul rebel against calling those great novels "didactic." I read to learn, and I write to learn. In the process I share what I am learning with the reader, but I may very well not even know what it is I've learnt; sometimes the readers tell me. This is not false humility, and it is not irresponsibility. I am not a humble writer, and I am a responsible one. I hope the next question won't put me on the defensive like this, repeating arguments I have had to make so often—I hope as we go on we can get our language better in synch.

Carl Freedman: Well, when I described you as a didactic writer, I certainly didn't mean to suggest that you were *nothing but* that. To describe a work of literature as didactic need not, I think, be an attempt to reduce the work to its paraphrasable or propositional content: just as other terms used to describe literary works, such as "allegorical" or "realistic" or "composed in iambic pentameter," are not necessarily meant to *exhaust* the significance of the works described. "In the Drought" is a good example. It's a powerful story; I think there's an unforgettable poetic intensity to the way the whole thing is built on the extended metaphor of red blood flowing from the water tap. Any reading that saw the story as just the equivalent of an op-ed piece about gay rights would be, in my opinion, a very poor—at least a very incomplete—reading. I also think, though, that any reading that failed to engage quite seriously with the hurtfulness of anti-gay bigotry would be at least equally incomplete. It's interesting that the whole matter of homosexuality is never once explicitly raised in the story; but the story's "point" is, I think, made all the more effectively for that.

Ursula Le Guin: Yes. That's the point I was trying to make, I think.

Carl Freedman: Well, then, I'm willing to leave the word "didactic" behind for the time being. Let's consider a different—but perhaps not completely different—category: utopia. In my own reading, there are three works of utopian fiction (and I mean utopia here in the sense of positive utopia; the negative utopia, like George Orwell's *Nineteen Eighty-four*, is a different matter) that seem to me preeminent: Thomas More's *Utopia*, William Morris's *News from Nowhere*, and *The Dispossessed*. Those are three quite different books, though I think they do have important features in common; for one thing, all raise complex and important political issues. But, of the three, only *The Dispossessed* is a true novel, with all the complexities of narrative line and character development that that implies. One reason I admire the book so much is that, of all the works of positive utopian fiction known to me, no other so well combines intellectual and political rigor with narrative excitement and dramatic force. I suspect that this combination is related to the quality you pointed to by famously designating *The Dispossessed* an "ambiguous" utopia. Perhaps we could discuss this ambiguity a bit. What choices—aesthetic, conceptual, or other—were involved in the decision to write an *ambiguous* utopia?

Ursula Le Guin: Well, maybe you have it backwards? The decision to *call* it an ambiguous utopia came *after* the several-years-long process of trying to write it, learning how to write it, and writing it.

At first it was not even clear to me how uncomfortable I was in unambiguous utopias—such as Thomas More's—where right and wrong are clearly laid out and failure to follow the right is not an option.

I had to read every utopian (and dystopian) novel I could find, and every book about anarchism available (not very many, back then, and not easily—fortunately there was a pacifist-anarchist bookdealer in Portland at the time) before I could even begin to see what I was writing about and why I had to write it.

As you can imagine this took some years.

The only thing essential to my thinking that I already had under my belt or in my head was Lao Tzu.

However the core idea and character (a physicist somehow at outs with his society) remained alive in my mind through all this long learning and pondering, and so eventually I was ready to find out what would happen to my physicist if his society was a realized, functioning anarchy, of which he was (or thought he was) a contented, functioning member.

I think it is clear that ambiguity (uncertainty, irony, what have you) was built into the conception from the start, even if it became clear to me only gradually. I was not drawing a blueprint of the Perfect Society. I was writing a novel about how anarchism might work if real people really tried to live it.

The blueprint, or in computer-analogy terms the program, is the antithesis of the idea of anarchism. One could not draw a blueprint, write a program, for an anarchic society. It is a contradiction in terms. Ambiguity is a very moderate term for the many-branched, incalculable quality of the genuinely anarchic.

But since most utopias have been extremely singleminded, programmatic— and also since in the novel the protagonist must choose between the two very different societies presented, each with notable virtues and faults—once it was written, "ambiguous" seemed a modest but pretty fair description of the undertaking as a whole.

Carl Freedman: You say that the blueprint is the antithesis of anarchism. Can't we also say that it's the antithesis of the novel as an aesthetic form? Though I read More's book as somewhat less unambiguous than you do, I think that the superiority of *The Dispossessed* to earlier utopias—not only More's but even Morris's, for which I have a special fondness—is due largely to the way you make use of the full resources of the novel as a genre. For instance, one element of *The Dispossessed* that remains especially vivid in my mind is the convincing, three-dimensional dramatization of the relationship between Shevek and Takver, the committed (one can't say "married") heterosexual couple at the center of the book. The complexities of human desire such as we see here are not, I think, the kind of thing we find in many utopias. Can we say that a utopian novel that is a true novel as well as a true utopia *must* be ambiguous? I'm thinking, in part, of D. H. Lawrence's principle that the novel is the highest form of human expression yet attained precisely because the novel is incapable of the absolute. And I confess—I don't know whether you will take this as a compliment or not—that there are moments in *The Dispossessed* when I am reminded of Lawrence: for instance, a wonderful scene of lovemaking between Shevek and Takver. It almost reads like Lawrence minus the sexism.

Ursula Le Guin: Many goodies in this short paragraph!

I am glad to know that William Morris ranks so high with you. He has a unique place, a unique rank, in my mind. Not so much through his writings as through what he did, what he was, what he built and made and taught. I grew up in a very beautiful house built by Bernard Maybeck, in what is now known as "craftsman" style, more properly Arts and Crafts, an international style in architecture and design which can be traced back, almost entirely, to Morris's (highly practical and highly utopian) workshops. This architecture is the most complete combination of modest livability with pure aesthetic principle that I know of. (Anything I've seen of Frank Lloyd Wright seems to me, in comparison, mostly display and ego). What the effect of growing up in that house was on me, I of course can't specify: but I know it was profound and enduring.

I think what I'm saying is that I grew up in utopia—that I have lived there—in this one respect: the house I lived in. No metaphor. Literally, physically, bodily, the house.

(The book that reflects that influence and understanding far more directly than *Dispossessed* is the utopian novel we aren't discussing, *Always Coming Home*.)

About novels being necessarily ambiguous, yes indeed, except ambiguity implies only a left and a right hand, and novels can be regular octopuses or centipedes, or gardens of forking paths, when it comes to complexities of implication . . .

It is very like Lawrence to believe in a "highest form of human expression." But to place it in the novel, and prize the novel for its incapacity for the absolute, he sounds more like his contemporary E. M. Forster than he usually does.

Lawrence was a powerful early influence on me, Forster a more enduring one. But I do indeed take your comment as a compliment.

Sex is awfully hard to write about, even harder than most physical acts. If your characters are having sex, but you want to keep the scene integral to the novel, without stimulating the reader to extra-fictional desires or activities (pornography), you've got quite a tricky job to do. Hormonal buttons are so easy to press. So the quantity of described sexual activity in my books is very moderate, partly because sex is even harder to describe adequately in fiction than eating, without reducing your novel to a vibrator or a cookbook. But also because I think having sex is a, but not the, central element in most human lives of any length and complexity. And since like most physical acts it's essentially repetitive, other aspects of sexuality are a good deal more interesting to me, as a novelist: such as courtship, the endlessly varied emotions that accompany sexual desire and frustration, the amazing formalities and rituals society imposes on the sex drive, etc.

I fear my anarchists are not as free from sexual inhibitions and confusions as Emma Goldman and others expected. The intersection of personal sexuality and social community seems to always be a dangerous one, with a lot of red lights and sideswipes.

Carl Freedman: Yes, there's been a lot of utopian thought—anarchist, Marxist, and other—that tries to envision a purely "rational" sexuality in which sex would be the entirely straightforward satisfaction of a simple desire. One wonders whether it really ever could be as easy as drinking a glass of water, in Alexandra Kollantai's famous simile that Lenin hated—though, in fairness to Kollantai, she seems to have been more concerned with freedom from venereal disease, unwanted pregnancy, and domestic violence than from emotional complexity.

But, since you mention *Always Coming Home*, by all means let's discuss that a bit. Certainly much less has been written about that text than about *The Dispossessed* or *The Left Hand of Darkness*. One commentator who *has* written about it extensively is the feminist critic Robin Roberts, who gives it a very prominent place in her book *A New Species: Gender and Science in Science Fiction*. Roberts argues that the multivocality and "postmodern" qualities of *Always Coming Home* make it a difficult novel to write about—but also, she maintains, help to make it a profoundly feminist novel. I'd like to hear you comment on that idea, and I'd also like to hear you expand on your fascinating remarks about the connections between *Always Coming Home* and the house in which you grew up. Though I've never thought of the matter in these terms until right now, it makes intuitive sense to me that there is something "architectural," so to speak, about the novel—perhaps because architecture is the art that people live with most, in a completely literal, practical sense. Of course, all this seems directly related to William Morris and your thoughts about him. Morris (who, you know, is said to have been the first Englishman to read the entirety of Marx's *Capital*) died in 1896, and it does seem to me that in so many ways we're still struggling to catch up with him.

Ursula Le Guin: I can comment only on your reference to Robin Roberts's statement that the multivocality of *Always Coming Home* helps make it a feminist novel—with which I'd generally agree. I don't want to get essentialist about it, though; men can multivocalize just fine. Perhaps women writers began using the technique in the later twentieth century as a more or less conscious reaction to the intense privileging of the single voice and single viewpoint that had become so common in fiction, and therefore perhaps associated with male dominance of critical standards. But after decades of rejection of the so-called "omniscient" point of view, it was hard to go back to the changes of POV of the Victorian (and Tolstoyan) novel, the multiple narrators, the shifting inwardnesses, the open or covert comments. Woolf might seem a guide, but I think she in fact shifted voice with the same complete effortlessness as her Victorian predecessors, though with perhaps increased awareness, which puts her beyond our imitation. When I've asked students in a fiction workshop *not* to write in the first or limited third person, some of them are completely stymied: they don't realize there is any other way to tell a story.

I see the "choral" first chapter of Hurston's *Their Eyes Were Watching God* as a great exercise in writing multiply, voicing a community. I was after something of the same sort in *Always Coming Home*, only far more extensive, the fact of community being central to the book. Pandora of course complicates it; the "postmodernism" comes in with her, I suppose.

I don't know how to enlarge on what I said about the house I grew up in being connected to the type of imagining I was doing in *Always Coming Home*, as it's a matter I've just begun thinking about and haven't worked out yet. I don't see the book itself as particularly architectural: it lacks the symmetries and large correspondences that bring the word to my mind (but it is certainly not a mere flaunting flouting of those symmetries, such as Gehry goes in for.) I wrote the book before I had a computer, but was aware even back then that the computer might encourage certain complex movements of narrative—recursions, implications to be followed, forking paths, etc.—that were very much in my head as I wrote the book. I think it's too kinetic to be architectural.

But there's quite a lot of architecture *in* the book. It is pretty specific about the houses and the heyimas, and the layout of the towns. The heyimas are very remotely modeled on Pueblo kivas; the houses are modeled on the central tenets of Arts and Crafts domestic architecture and planning—livability, aesthetic and practical value considered as one thing. Where Morris beats the cerebral utopists all hollow is in the materiality of his imagination. To lead a decent human life in a cramped, featureless, unvaried environment is a tough job; the twenty-story-slab housing development, the hundred-cubicle office, the windows that cannot be opened because the interior "climate" is controlled, the faceless Bauhaus exterior—all utopian in their way, I guess. But not my utopia, or his.

I was amused to find how much I felt at home in Morris's house on the Thames at Kelmscott. Not one thing about it was literally familiar to me, but it was all familiar to me; I remember that house I was in for a single afternoon with vivid affection, while I've forgotten apartments I lived in for years. The title of my book can be read several different ways; one of them of course is simply literal.

Carl Freedman: I like the stress you put on the materiality of Morris's imagination. He has a vague reputation as some sort of dreamy idealist, but materiality—and materialism as a philosophy—seem to me absolutely crucial for him, whether you're looking at him as a utopian thinker, or as a writer of romances, or as a craftsman.

Still on the general topic of utopia, perhaps we could talk about one of your best-known short stories, "The Ones Who Walk Away from Omelas"—which is one of the most memorable thought-experiments that I know in modern literature. The story at first presents Omelas as a marvelous positive utopia—a place of exuberant joy, peace, and beauty, and also of intelligence and complexity; a place of sensual, intellectual, and spiritual fulfillment. Indeed, it sounds, I think, a good deal like a William Morris utopia. But then we learn that all the wonderful things in Omelas somehow depend—absolutely, unconditionally—on the fact that one single child is kept imprisoned and horribly abused. Everyone in Omelas knows this "secret," and of course people feel bad about it, especially after first learning it. But most people decide that the suffering of one child is an acceptable price to pay for the happiness of thousands. There is, however, a minority that refuses the bargain: the ones who walk away. The narrator does not describe where they are going, but the story's final sentence is, "But they seem to know where they are going, the ones who walk away from Omelas."

Now, some readers have interpreted the story as an attack on the very idea of utopia; for them, the story's point is that utopia must always be based on atrocity. I myself, though, have always read the story (which, incidentally, I've found to work very well in teaching) in just the opposite way: namely, as an affirmation of

Oscar Wilde's principle (I'm paraphrasing Wilde here, not quoting) that utopianism is a dynamic, not a static, principle—that what utopia really means is the never-ending search for better utopias. Then again, I was just leafing through the most recent issue of *New Left Review* and came upon an interesting article by the Marxist theorist Susan Willis about the American prison camp at Guantánamo. Willis writes, "Guantánamo is both a shameful secret and a public emblem of power, to which Washington clings with extraordinary tenacity." She discusses "The Ones Who Walk Away from Omelas" at some length, and seems to regard the story as a kind of anticipatory parable of the new "symbolic economy," as she puts it, that Guantánamo represents—a symbolic economy in which the point of torture is not the extraction of pragmatically "useful" information but the production of a "security ideology" that makes Americans feel secure. It should be added that Willis makes clear that at least some of the prisoners at Guantánamo have been swept up by accident or mistaken identity, and are just as innocent as the child in your story.

I'd be interested to hear you comment on any—or all—of these readings of your story, or any other readings that seem to you of interest.

Ursula Le Guin: Wow. What an application of my story! I wonder if you would do me the favor of xeroxing that article and sending it to me? I'd really like to see it, and would be happier talking about it if I'd read the whole thing.

Any particular assertion of what the story "means" will of course receive an indignant or indulgent denial from me. And I have heard lots and lots about what it means, believe me. It's used a great deal in courses in high school and college—philosophy, anthro, psych, lit, sociology, even engineering. Teachers tell me it is useful because it gets students talking. Some of them then write me passionate letters about it. None of them has been quite as contemptuous as a certain famous Marxist critic who dismissed it as merely "nasty," but some of them are enraged by it. It is unfair! they cry—It is unjust! What is wrong with the citizens of Omelas that they don't rush forth and open the door of that broomcloset and set the child free?

So I write back and say yeah, uhhuh, it is unfair, but see, it says in the story that if they set the child free it will wreck everything—everybody else, along with the child, doomed to live thenceforth in misery. That is the contract. Even if they didn't sign it. A lot of kids haven't read parables or folktales, and don't know much about contracts and rules; they don't even know the story of the man and wife who were given three wishes, so I tell it to them. While the man and the wife were talking about what wondrous things to wish for, he got hungry and said,

"I wish I had a nice fried sausage," so of course he got one. At which she shouts, "You idiot, you wasted a wish! I wish that sausage was stuck to the end of your nose!" so of course it is. So of course the last wish has to be to wish it off the end of his nose. This, too, is unfair; and involves rules. Are the rules unjust? Anyhow, I would not deny that utopia may always be based on atrocity—since all privileged human lives are based on injustice, that would seem to indicate a possible rule. But one cannot be sure.

The idea of utopia being the search for utopia seems a promising approach to the somewhat enigmatic ending of the story; but still I am resistant to any certain interpretation, as limiting further speculation/possibility. I think what irritates people about "Omelas," so that they keep thinking about it, is that except for the door shut on the poor child, all the doors of the story remain open. And people do love closure!

Carl Freedman: Yes, they do. And the fact that some people find "Omelas" irritating—or even nasty!—may not be the worst tribute to a thought-experiment. But now I'd like to switch gears and talk about a work of yours that, though quite renowned in some circles—it was short-listed for the Pulitzer Prize—is perhaps not as well known as it ought to be among your readers whose primary interest is in science fiction and utopian fiction. I'm talking, of course, about *Searoad*, a wonderful cycle of related short stories, all predominantly realistic in mode and all set in the seaside town of Klatsand, Oregon. It's not a utopia, but perhaps it could be called a "topia," because the sense of place is very strong and very important for the overall effect of the book. I'd like to ask you about the generic character of *Searoad*. The short-story cycle is one of the major forms of American literature (e.g., Sherwood Anderson's *Winesburg, Ohio*, Hemingway's *In Our Time*, Faulkner's *Go Down, Moses*) and Irish literature (Joyce's *Dubliners*), though curiously rare-to-nonexistent, so far as I know, in English literature (I believe some English critic even invented the idiotic term "fix-up" to describe and denigrate the form). What particular resources have you found the genre to possess, in contrast to the fully unified novel on the one hand and the completely free-standing story on the other?

Ursula Le Guin: Some quick reactions:

I like "topia" very much. A useful word!

And a perfect example of a topia is the (very British) Victorian story cycle *Cranford* by Elizabeth Gaskell, which probably helped Sarah Orne Jewett in Maine write her *Country of the Pointed Firs*. Because these books are important to me, I had in fact thought of the story cycle as probably being predominantly a feminine form. (I know the Anderson and admire it, but am ignorant of the Hemingway and Faulkner.)

A "fix-up," as I have met the term, refers specifically to a book created by sticking together a set of short stories that have something in common but were not originally conceived as connected. The stickum or connective tissue may be developed more or less plausibly—sometimes it is only too evidently Elmer's Glue. But there are some very fine fix-ups. Bradbury's *Martian Chronicles*, despite its incoherencies, is a lovely, enduring book.

A story cycle, or story suite as I have come to call it—after searching for a name, asking around for a name, and finally getting it from Johann Sebastian Bach (the unaccompanied cello suites)—a story suite is not a fix-up. (I am just reading one—Margaret Atwood's latest, *Moral Disorder*. A novel told in stories, definitely.)

My experience is this: As I began to write them, the stories were connected only by place, or by certain characters. But as I went on writing them the stories began consciously to interconnect and inter-implicate, forming by the end something that is unmistakably a whole thing: not exactly a novel, yet achieving very much what the novel achieves, by a slightly different method. (I should guess that this is how *Cranford* and *Country of the Pointed Firs* were written, too.)

This is how *Searoad* came to be, and by the third story at latest I was fully conscious that I was writing not just a story but part of a book.

(*Four Ways to Forgiveness* came to be in much the same way; but that time, this episodic method of composition misled me, so that I published the first four stories as a book before I realized there was a fifth way to forgiveness yet to come. I wish I could join the orphaned final story, "Old Music and the Slave Women," to its siblings.)

Searoad was a response to becoming a part-time citizen of a small Oregon coastal town. Klatsand is a composite/extract of several towns on the north Oregon coast. The book is exploration, satire, and homage. I have always felt that the last story, itself anachronic, episodic, deeply fragmented, and written in several different voices, is one of the most interesting pieces of fiction I've been able to write, and although it has almost nothing to do with my actual life, is as "autobiographical" as I'm likely to be.

Carl Freedman: "Story suite" is a lovely term, I think. Am I right to suspect that the method of composition you've just described with regard to the story suite is somewhat similar to the way that, on a larger scale, the Earthsea sequence came to be? This series is, in any case, one of your major—and certainly one of your most popular—achievements; and it provides an opportunity to discuss the much vexed question of the relation between science fiction and fantasy. Though in general I tend to draw a much sharper distinction between the two forms than many people do, the only point I want to make in this connection right now is just this: Despite the fact that science fiction and fantasy are associated in much discussion and in the commercial geography of nearly all bookstores, it is very rare to find an author who has written a substantial amount of truly first-class work in both genres. You and Delany seem to me the obvious examples; there may well be others, but there surely aren't many. I'd like to hear something about this from the writer's point of view. What are the differences—and the similarities—between the experience of writing science fiction and that of writing fantasy? How, for instance, did constructing the various environments of Earthsea feel, as compared with and contrasted to constructing Winter in *The Left Hand of Darkness*, or Urras and Anarres in *The Disposssessed*? Is inventing a fantasy plot a different sort of labor from inventing a science-fiction plot—or a fantasy character from a science-fiction character?

Ursula Le Guin: This is a tricky one. I know that you distinguish sf and fantasy quite sharply. My take will probably strike you as fatally incoherent. When I look at the literature, at the actual texts, I see a spectrum, heroic fantasy at one end, sf at the other, each with its particular vocabulary, manner, and set of tropes and metaphors—but, more importantly, a vast area of overlap between. And yet when I think about them in the abstract, I see sf as a recent form, a subgroup of realistic fiction—fantasy as a very ancient form and the defining opposite of realism.

These views are contradictory but I cannot solve the puzzle; it's like quantum physics, to do away with the self-contradiction leaves me with only half the picture. But this means that, approaching the difference/sameness from the point of view of writing the stuff, I don't feel that writing sf is in any important way different from writing fantasy, nor from writing realistic fiction, for that matter. You have to construct, sort out, select your fictional world, whether it is a made-up planet, a fantasy kingdom, a utopia, Russia in 1812, or a contemporary town on the Oregon coast. The process is much the same. The degree of invention may vary somewhat, but after all we do not literally invent; we can only recombine. Words fool us wonderfully. Tolkien's sobriety is salutary: ours is a secondary creation. And whatever it's made of, it has to be made with the same care. The made-up planet may be scientifically correct and probable in every aspect and be described with impeccable plausibility—it is nonetheless a complete fantasy, a mental construct without material existence. The fantasy kingdom may be built up out of carefully thought-through historical and sociological facts and concepts that are as plausible and "hard" as the reasoned physical/chemical/astronomical aspects of the made-up sf planet—or it may be a dream-landscape with little reference to daily reality: it is no more and no less a mental construct without material existence, and it requires no less care to make it coherent and convincing. Same with the utopia, Russia in 1812, and the town on the Oregon coast. They all consist entirely of ink marks on woodpulp as interpreted by a reader. Nothing we novelists invent exists, it is all a delusion, it is only words. Possibly fantasy is the most difficult to write, as it relies entirely on its own self-coherence. If you put a word wrong in a fantasy, the whole fabric may collapse. But then, that's true of historical fiction too—one safety match in mediaeval Paris, and you've lost it. (Or you're writing science fiction, in which case you're about to explain the safety match.)

The more I consider it, the more I see fiction writing as a preposterous enterprise.

As for characters: sf conventionally subordinates character to plot or to an intellectual point or pattern; fantasy conventionally tends to display character as role and destiny; one expects fully developed, individualized characters mostly in realistic fiction, in epic, and in drama. But what prevents a fully developed character from occupying a realm where people may not be expecting him? Mr Tagomi in *The Man in the High Castle* [by Philip K. Dick] is a character, a portrait. Is the novel he's in science fiction or fantasy? It is called science fiction, but why? No science is involved in its conception, only history. Its technique is that of realistic fiction; it strives for plausibility; its characters are fully rounded emotionally and ethically. Mr Toad in *The Wind in the Willows* is a character, a portrait, and, like Mr Tagomi, a moral portrait of considerable complexity. But the novel he's in is indubitably fantasy, in which the impossible, even the totally implausible, is described with sober, accurate, realistic detail, so that the reader, while reading, never thinks to question its validity.

That's what fiction does, isn't it? All fiction? It makes a world and makes it seem real. Inner coherence (which can become aesthetic completeness) is the principle secret. It's achieved by imagination, selection, and accurate description—whether any counterpart to it exists in the real world or not really doesn't matter.

What does matter, perhaps, is whether we can find ourselves in the story as we read it, can recognize the emotional and moral weight of human existence. Sf and fantasy are not as relentlessly human-centered as realistic fiction; they both show human beings in relation to the nonhuman, they include the human subject in a larger or stranger universe than the realistic novel does. But the story is still about us. We seem to be all we are ultimately interested in. And so, for writers and readers who see people as individuals rather than as types or groups, character becomes important even in genres where it is usually considered secondary.

Carl Freedman: That sounds to me like an excellent, and thought-provoking, point at which to end. Thank you very much, Ursula Le Guin.

Index